Hello, It's Me

Dispatches from a Pop Culture Junkie

SANTA
MONICA
PRESS

Published by: Santa Monica Press LLC
P.O. Box 1076
Santa Monica, CA 90406-1076
1-800-784-9553
www.santamonicapress.com
books@santamonicapress.com

Printed in the United States

Santa Monica Press books are available at special quantity discounts when purchased in bulk by corporations, organizations, or groups. Please call our Special Sales department at 1-800-784-9553.

ISBN-13 978-1-59580-053-4

Library of Congress Cataloging-in-Publication Data

Epting, Chris, 1961–
 Hello, it's me : dispatches from a pop culture junkie / by Chris Epting ; foreword by Seth Swirsky.
    p. cm.
 ISBN 978-1-59580-053-4
 1. Popular culture—United States—History—20th century—Anecdotes.
 2. Popular culture—United States—History—21st century—Anecdotes.
 3. United States—Civilization—1970—Anecdotes. I. Title.
 E169.12.E68 2010
 973.9–dc22
                                2010002728

Cover and interior design and production by Future Studio

Hello, It's Me

Dispatches from a Pop Culture Junkie

INNOCENCE AND TIME, ONCE
LOST CAN NEVER BE REGAINED

13 23 35 37 45 46

Chris Epting

Foreword by Seth Swirsky

SANTA MONICA PRESS

Contents

Chapter Two: The 1980s

Chapter Three: The 1990s

Chapter Four: The 2000s

Chapter Five: Odds, Ends and Some Articles I've Written

Afterword

And I thank the Lord for the people I have found,
I thank the Lord for the people I have found.
            —Elton John, "Mona Lisas and Mad Hatters"

This book is dedicated to my mom, Sugar, and my wife, Jean. Simply stated, I owe my life to the both of you. For your patience, love and understanding, I thank you. I love you.

To Charlie and Claire—my young man and daddy's little girl—I love you both more than I'll ever be able to fully express, but it won't stop me from trying.

To Margaret—you know what I think (but I'll say it anyway: You're the most remarkable person I know).

To Lee—I hope you know what I think.

And in memory of my grandmother, Margaret Gallo, and my father, Lawrence Epting.

Foreword
by Seth Swirsky

Reading *Hello, It's Me: Dispatches from a Pop Culture Junkie* is like taking a time machine back to the most memorable cultural moments of the last 40 years, with the curious, interested and interesting author Chris Epting as the captain of our ship.

And how lucky we are to have Chris as our own Captain Kirk of pop culture!

Whether he is recalling the way he took his family to visit the house where the Partridge family lived, or watching Mick Jagger dancing alone behind a *Saturday Night Live* stage curtain during a Stevie Ray Vaughan performance, or shooting hoops with Lakers great Elgin Baylor, or witnessing self-help guru Tony Robbins help the Oakland Raiders win a play-off game, or even getting in author Norman Mailer's face after Mailer's bestselling book, *In the Belly of the Beast*, helped free a convicted killer (who then went on to commit another murder!), Chris always seems to be surrounded by fascinating people or in the midst of a once-in-a-lifetime event.

I first corresponded with Chris after having read many of his books over the years, told him what a fan I was and it turned out the sentiment was mutual. See, Chris, a big fan of our national pastime, had read my trilogy of baseball books—*Baseball Letters, Every Pitcher Tells a Story* and *Something to Write Home About*—which consisted of letters to me from major league players. Once we got to talking and finally met (at a baseball game, of course), our bond was sealed.

This book resonated with me particularly because my personal path mirrored Chris's in that I was aware at many moments in my life that I was talking with someone or witnessing something that was to be "noted."

For example, as a songwriter in 1988 (having co-written the Taylor Dayne song "Tell It to My Heart," which was at number 7 on the charts at the time), I remember talking with George Harrison (who concurrently had the number 8 song on the charts with "Got My Mind Set on You") and thinking, "I'm one slot higher than a Beatle! I've made it!"

I recall inwardly laughing when I found myself in Buzz Aldrin's living room in 2003, at eight in the morning, and hearing his wife yell at the second man in history to walk on the moon as he looked skyward through his telescope: "Buzz, it's too early in the morning to see the moon!"

And I still don't know what karma allowed this Long Island boy to have the ball that went through Bill Buckner's legs in Game Six of the 1986 World Series and Reggie Jackson's third home run ball from the World Series game in 1977 in his memorabilia collection.

So, it's easy to see why Chris and I connected: We admire each other's curious natures and share a love of the vast amount of cultural candy we devoured during our upbringings. We also have the mutual goal to capture those interesting moments in life, like fireflies in a jar (with air holes punched out of the lid, of course) through our work. Simply, we both found each other's stories, well . . . fun!

While reading *Hello, It's Me*, you will wonder how Chris met this or that person, where his inspiration came from, who his greatest influences were and how he translated his fantasies into exhilarating action. The catch-all answer is that Chris loves life, wants to seize every day and experience life to its fullest—and then report everything he knows we'll also love right back to us. He documents things sometimes as a fan, sometimes as an astute observer and sometimes a trusted insider—but always with careful, journalistic detail.

As readers, we get pulled in to *Hello, It's Me* for many reasons, but perhaps none more so than the fact that Chris knows how to tell a story. Each episode becomes its own mini pop-operetta, and many of the stories resound not just with a laugh, tear, or smile, but some bit of life lesson as well. In a world that seems increasingly cynical, it's refreshing to discover these interesting, observational pools of experience. It's also clear what Chris's family means to him, and so we get to see how one man's "pop culture journey" has affected his wife and children on their collective journey together, watching them all partake in their own cultural discoveries.

An unexpected bonus in this collection (and one that I was happy to partake in) in the inclusion of "reflections" by various people Chris writes about in many of the stories. To read Chris's recounting of a story, then have a firsthand offering from, say, Mary Carillo, Lou Gramm or John Cheever's widow, Mary Cheever (among others), is a treat that provides many unique perspectives in an already colorful collection.

Well, the time machine's engine is purring, readying itself for takeoff. Time to strap in and let Chris take you through the stories of his life . . . and ours!

Seth Swirsky
Beverly Hills, California

Introduction

Who?

Me.

Chris Epting: age 48 as this book goes to press, a work-at-home, hearth-hugging, doting dad and husband in a traditional, tight-knit, loving, God-fearing, great-discussions-around-the-dinner-table-every-night family and a total product of 1970s culture: *The Partridge Family*, baseball cards, my lime-green Nerf football, *All in the Family*, concert T-shirts, my purple Schwinn Stingray bike with the banana seat, disco, punk, fake IDs, strawberry wine, black light posters . . . innocence that maybe wasn't so innocent. Do you remember?

I'm originally from New York, have lived in California since the late 1980s and currently live in Huntington Beach with my wife and two wonderful kids, and my mom nearby. I graduated from Emerson College in Boston in 1983, and worked as a copywriter and then creative director in the advertising industry for about 20 years. I created many advertising campaigns over the years, had a ball, still do some of that, but embarked on a somewhat different path about 10 years ago: "dream chaser." Though I technically wrote for a living, I remembered that I wanted to be an author as a kid, so I set out to write the books I could never find in stores—books about places where things happened and books about where things used to be, travelogues around the United States that would reveal interesting things about our country. And so that's what I did. Guided by faith, family, self-reliance, compassion, loyalty, work ethic, adventure, ambition, enthusiasm and optimism, I wrote the books I always dreamed about writing. And I'm still doing that. There's more, but that's a brief take on me.

More interesting than me, I think, is who else you'll find in this book: rock stars, an Emmy Award-winning actress, writers, a dinosaur hunter, a famed composer, photographers and a noted broadcaster—people who were there for some of these episodes who graciously offer some perspective and memories to my stories. Since I wanted this book to be essentially less about me and more about those I have encountered, it seemed only right to reach out and ask these people to contribute—so that's what I did, and I'm thrilled with who you'll meet in this book. (Not every story has one of these "codas," but I tried to include as many as possible.)

What

This is collection of stories, essays, previously published articles I'm proud of and meditations on life, all through the eyes of a pop culture junkie: Me. I entered this world wide-eyed and woefully impressionable and I remain that way today, still putty in the hands of the music, movies, books, television (though not so much TV anymore) and other cultural influences that I sometimes become a slave to. Though I can't remember what I had for lunch yesterday, I can recite the dialogue from just about every episode of *The Odd Couple, The Honeymooners, The Brady Bunch* and *I Love Lucy* (and probably 10 additional TV series). The movies I love I know by rote and many songs from 1970s AM radio still make my heart race faster. In short, pop culture (particularly that of my youth) still influences my moods, my wants and my desires—and there's no letting go of it. Coupled with my somewhat over-zealous passion for pop culture, I've had the good fortune to stumble into many situations that have let me experience some of my influences firsthand. I learned early in life to keep my eyes open, because you never know who or what you might miss, and that instinct has, as you'll see in this book, paid off.

This is also a collection that includes a few thoughts and stories on family and friendship, because those are the things that ultimately shape my life, give it value and make all the other stories possible (and these things also affect how I view and filter popular culture).

The Eptings at Fenway Park in 2009. (Boston, Massachusetts.)

Overall, given how road trips and travel writing have become such staples in my existence, I view this book as a sort of "road trip through life," a journey rediscovering those special, tucked away people and places I've met thus far—the personal landmarks that define my life and the lives around me. I've tried to focus on moments that represent some unique, universal truths that hopefully you'll be able to relate to. Some pieces are conventional, beginning-middle-and-end stories; some are merely snapshots of a moment that capture an emotion or era. If the stories seem to err on the side of positive, inspirational and/or redeeming qualities, it's deliberate. I love life; I appreciate having had the benefit of being taught the benefits of hard work by my parents, and I work hard today to make life interesting for myself and my family.

Where

The adventures in this book will take you all over these United States: to a cornfield where Cary Grant was chased by a plane, to abandoned lots where baseball stadiums used to stand, to hotel rooms where rock stars died, to a famed war ship, to where James Dean died, to many places far and wide where things of note took place. We'll go to concerts together, meet celebrities together, go on dinosaur digs and to tennis tournaments, visit

Mayberry, celebrate our families, remember our pets and reminisce about the places that hold all of our best memories. There are locations in this book I sincerely hope you'll want to visit after reading about them.

When

The journey starts in 1972. Originally, the first story was a 1969 recollection about what happened in our house the night of the first moonwalk. I cut it, but if you'd like to read it, send me an e-mail and I'll share it with you. From '72, we then time-travel through the glorious 1970s, '80s and '90s, right up until present day, with the final entry written on October 31, 2009, at a campsite in the California desert.

Why

The idea for this book came to me shortly after being asked by Tom Dooley, editor of the online literary magazine Eclectica, to contribute a few non-fiction short stories. I hadn't spent much time writing those sorts of anecdotal narratives, but the experience was wonderful. Once the three were done, I wanted to do more. I enjoy storytelling and felt like I have a few to tell. Enter Jeffrey Goldman of Santa Monica Press who thought the idea had merit. (Thanks as always, my friend.)

With my amazing wife, Jean.

As to the specific "Why?", there are a few. First, I believe we should all document our lives as we get older and more experienced. We're all historians for our own existence, so why not report on what we've seen and done? Next, I wanted my family to have a record of these things so that they can pass them down to the next generation and hopefully become inspired to document their own lives. Lastly, my hope would be that some of these stories would remind you of things in your own life that you cherish—a first ball game, a first love or beloved dog. Maybe it would trigger the feeling that favorite movie, song or book still brings you—or perhaps the memory of a run-in with a pop culture icon. The small group of readers I shared some of these pieces with felt that way; after sharing a critique, they'd start rekindling old memories, using my stories to help uncork their own tales. That's when I started getting really excited about finishing this book, with the realization that it might actually be cathartic and help you slow down a bit to reflect and unlock all those moments, and maybe even plant the seed that it would be a good idea to write them down and gather up those old photos. Many people I know complain that their life is racing past—a good way to slow it down is to write about it.

I know I get effusive about some of these things but I can't help it. I'm old-fashioned in a traditional, sort of hokey way. I know. I still believe in preserving some innocence, and I know I get overly sentimental about things I care about. That's just me. And I'm happy this way.

I tell my kids, I believe it's good to milk every drop of joy from each day, to be curious, to believe in yourself, to be adventurous, to do what you love, to make a positive difference, to enjoy life and to not take yourself too seriously. To not waste time. To get things done. I want to believe this book is evidence of those traits.

How?

I've already been asked a number of times how I remember many of the older stories with such vivid detail. I believe the two reasons are: first, the writer John Cheever suggested to me when I first met him that I keep a journal and, second, that all of these moments meant something to me and I've simply never forgotten them. (Most of the names are real; I think just two have been slightly altered.) As to how I got all of the other people to contribute pieces, that was just a lot of legwork (and a little hounding).

On the Book's Title

As for the book's title, I'll tell you that "Hello It's Me" is simply my favorite song of the 1970s. When I was 11 or 12, this plaintive Todd Rundgren masterpiece made a huge impact on me—it expressed simple, honest emotions and spoke to the adolescent pain and longing that many of us feel growing up. As you'll read, I've always been a huge fan of Todd Rundgren and though he's done many impressive things as an artist, this song still resonates as a masterpiece to me. It also struck me as a wonderful book title for

Todd Rundgren in 1981. (Philadelphia, Pennsylvania.)

this sort of collection. That said, I hope it spurs more sales of this classic song simply by putting the title out there and making you remember what an emotional, familiar piece it is (that's your cue to download it on iTunes right now).

Chapter One

CHERRY KOOL-AID

Bic Bananas

Woodsy Owl

avocado-colored anything

Mad Libs

platform shoes

Pop Rocks

Binaca

Jonathan Livingston Seagull

string art

GLAM

Screaming Yellow Zonkers

Weebles

SPIN THE BOTTLE

Plymouth Dusters

sand art

black light posters

orange corduroy pants with

bubblegum

Fidgets

COLORFORMS

Mystery Date

Schwinn Sting Rays

FORD LTDS

Evel Knievel

Prell *Wonderama*

mood rings

In Concert

head shops

TUBE TOPS

Spirographs

DayGlo

The 1970s

saying, "Give a hoot, don't pollute."

LED watches

clackers

Saturday morning cartoons

halter tops

ant farms

The Midnight Special

ROCK

Mouse Trap

fake IDs

things that glow in the dark

Ouija boards

STRATEGO

pyramid power

Fernwood 2 Night

brown pockets

Boone's Farm Strawberry Hill Wine

FREEZE TAG

8-TRACKS

Sea Monkey ads

Space Food Sticks

PET ROCKS

toe socks

Zotz

Go Ask Alice

COWL-NECK SWEATERS

And my personal favorites from the era:

TV Shows
The Brady Bunch (1969–1974)
The Partridge Family (1970–1974)
The Odd Couple (1970–1975)
The Mary Tyler Moore Show (1970–1977)
All in the Family (1971–1979)
Columbo (1971–1978, 1989–1990)
The Bob Newhart Show (1972–1978)
Happy Days (1974–1984)
Fernwood 2 Night (1977)
CBS Sunday Morning (1979–present)

Movies
The Godfather (1972)
Mean Streets (1973)
Jaws (1975)
Network (1976)
Rocky (1976)
Annie Hall (1977)
Saturday Night Fever (1977)
Star Wars (1977)
Heaven Can Wait (1978)
The Deer Hunter (1978)

Albums

Exile on Main St. by The Rolling Stones (1972)

Something/Anything? by Todd Rundgren (1972)

The Rise and Fall of Ziggy Stardust and the Spiders from Mars by David Bowie (1972)

Goodbye Yellow Brick Road by Elton John (1973)

New York Dolls by New York Dolls (1973)

The Dark Side of the Moon by Pink Floyd (1973)

Desire by Bob Dylan (1976)

Hasten Down the Wind by Linda Ronstadt (1976)

Ramones by Ramones (1976)

Marquee Moon by Television (1977)

Brandy
(1972)

My twin sister Margaret and I were often at each other's throats growing up, as siblings can be. I think being twins creates even more tension, though, because the timing of your lives is forever intertwined—there's no space between school or friends, so the rivalry burns hotter than under normal circumstances. We shared a record player back then, and we'd frequently go to war over which of our 45s would be in heavier rotation. I'd fight for the Jackson 5's "I'll Be There." She'd rip the needle off to play Diana Ross's "Ain't No Mountain High Enough." I'd trump that with Edward Bear's "Last Song." She'd go to the mat for "Drift Away" by Dobie Gray. (Looking back, maybe I should have let her win a few more rounds.)

But in the summer of 1972, blissful dog days that also featured my lime-colored Nerf football, Margaret and I were brought together by one song that defined a chunk of our adolescence that year. It was the

My "Brandy" single.

piece of black plastic that became our great equalizer, a peace-keeper of such majestic proportions that even today, neither of us can hear it without falling completely under its spell. Inside of the first few seconds of the introduction, we are transported back in time, back to the breakfast room in our house where the small record player sat, back to the time the song first simultaneously seduced us, while creating harmony in our battle of the 45s.

It was "Brandy (You're a Fine Girl)," by Looking Glass.

Remember? It tells the tale of a (presumably beautiful) young woman who tends the bar in a seaside village, listening to weary sailors while dreaming of her distant, seafaring lover. We saw the band on TV just as the song became a hit, a bunch of cool-looking New Jersey guys with long hair who probably resembled many bar bands of the era. But they were different—they had "Brandy"—and I think we went to the record store that day to pick up the single.

This was a classic story song featuring a smart horn section; smooth, earthy vocals from guitarist Elliot Lurie; a killer bridge; and, of course, that intoxicating chorus. To us, it was perfect, a mini-opera evoking love, sadness, loss, mystery—very adult themes woven into a smash AM radio hit that became the soundtrack of that carefree summer.

The song itself has also influenced others besides my sister and me. Remember Barry Manilow's hit, "Mandy"? It was actually called "Brandy" when it was originally recorded by Scott English in the UK. Manilow later changed the title to avoid confusion with the Looking Glass song. Red Hot Chili Peppers covered it and have played it many times live. It was in an episode of *The Simpsons*. And I can only guess how many girls were named "Brandy" back in the early 1970s.

One day in the breakfast room, after watching the automatic arm on the record player double back and play "Brandy" once more, we decided to have a lip-synch contest to see who could deliver a more compelling performance. Who knows, maybe we missed the friction and were simply itching for another fight, but this was an exercise that, if nothing else, would bring us closer to what by now had become our signature song for the summer. We simply could not get enough of it.

In lieu of microphones, we each grabbed a big, fresh lemon that sat in a silver bowl on the table. Using a two-handed approach (later popularized by Patti Smith when she'd appear to choke the microphone with two hands), Margaret nailed the lip synch. She acted out the

Me, around the time of this story (c. 1972).

part, hit every single word perfectly—it was a tour de force performance. For my version, I held the lemon in more of a "lounge" position, not unlike Frank Sinatra or Tony Bennett, and was spotty at best (no doubt intimidated by what she had accomplished, a portend of things to come later in life).

One glaring error I recall was misinterpreting some of the lyrics in the chorus. Instead of, "Brandy, you're a fine girl, what a good wife you would be," I heard (and synched), "what a *good life human being*." So enamored of Brandy had I become that I was now projecting new attributes on her. She was not merely a good potential spouse, she was a "good life human being." (Weirdly, I once read in another book, the excellent *Precious and Few*, that another author made the exact same mistake I did.)

I had to concede that Margaret's performance had bested mine by far. But no matter. On this summer day long ago in the country, we laughed until we almost cried, a pair of 12-year-old twins bonding in a way that I'm sure helped us survive the oncoming teenager years.

My son, who is now 16, is seriously into classic rock, along with seminal punk bands like the New York Dolls and the

Clash. He listens to the Stones, Bowie, AC/DC, Rush, Dream Theater, Def Leppard and many others. And he loves "Brandy." I asked him what it is about the song that he likes so much. He looked at me and stated simply, "It's just a great song."

And maybe that's it. It's just a great song, now, then and forever—one with the power to instantly bring back innocent memories of bell-bottoms, DayGlo happy face stickers, puka-shell necklaces and singing into a lemon with your sister.

R E F L E C T I O N S
from Looking Glass singer and composer Elliot Lurie

Elliot Lurie, the former singer and guitarist for Looking Glass, the guy who wrote and sang "Brandy," answered some of my questions after reading this essay.

After the group broke up, I made one solo album that did nothing. I moved to L.A. in 1984 and got involved in music for film and TV—what's called "music supervision"—and in 1985, I became the executive in charge of music for Twentieth Century Fox. I left Fox in 1994 and continued as an independent music supervisor. I've worked for Disney a lot; I supervised (and wrote the theme song for) the *Lizzie McGuire* series. I still live in L.A., do some music supervision, some artist management and, about two or three times a year, for fun, I do shows with some musicians from the Midwest. We play "Brandy," other old Looking Glass tunes and a few newer things I've written. I have two kids, a boy, 24, who teaches school in New York City, and a girl, 21, who has had an album out under the name Fan 3.

It's always fun when someone I've known or worked with for a while finds out that I wrote and sang "Brandy." It's an "oh, wow" moment—I guess I don't seem like that guy on the radio. Everyone usually has nice things to say about it and I don't think they're just being polite. I think story songs stick exceptionally well. I also think that the recording was well done and has aged pretty well. One of the things that makes my vocals distinctive is the enunciation. It's the result of a boy from Brooklyn trying to hide his accent and overcompensating—especially those "R"s on "silver" and "summer."

As for the inspiration, I had a high school girlfriend named Randye. It didn't sing as well, so I changed it to Brandy. No, she wasn't a barmaid and I was never a sailor. I certainly didn't have any idea it would still be played, covered, used in films, 35 years later.

As for my most memorable moments from the era, right after the song hit number 1, we were booked at the old Steel Pier in Atlantic City, New Jersey. This was before there was gambling there, and the main attraction at the pier was the famous diving horse. Three times a day, the poor animal would climb a 25-foot flight of stairs and, on command, dive into a pool of water below. We, like the horse, had three shows a day. The promoter's instructions to us were short and sweet, and delivered in a classic Jersey accent: "When you hear that friggin' splash—you hit it!" Ah, the big time.

Spider and a Slugger
(1973)

I loved pro football as a kid, but not so much as an adult. Part of the reason is that we live near Los Angeles, which has lacked a pro team for years, thus making it hard to stay involved as a fan. Another reason is the style of play: the posing, strutting, hot-dogging nonsense; the celebrations after simple tackles; the chest-thumping, in-your-face taunting. . . . What ever happened to players like Johnny Unitas, Roger Staubach, Deacon Jones or Bubba Smith? These were tough, brutally competitive guys—but they were also men of character. Bart Starr, Walter Payton and Joe Montana—players like these seem to be a dying breed, replaced by distractions like Terrell Owens. You remember: the guy who pulled a Sharpie marker out of his sock after catching a touchdown pass, then proceeded to autograph the ball and hand it to his financial adviser, who was sitting in an end zone luxury suite rented by Shawn Springs, the cornerback Owens had just beaten? Can you imagine what Vince Lombardi would have done to a jerk like this? Team play has given way to the "me, me, me, hyper-narcissistic, can-I-get-on-the-ESPN-clip-reel-tonight?" star system that's also infected pro basketball in the last decade.

And while I know there are still good guys playing the game, they don't seem to get the attention that the out-of-control showboats get. Decency used to trump thuggery, but a lot of things have changed today. But for every arrogant tackle I watch who insists on dancing a jig after he's third man on the pile, my mind drifts back to a player from another era and what *he* might think if he was watching the game today. I think of Carl "Spider" Lockhart, my all-time favorite New York Giant.

In 1973, my dad had some connections that allowed us to attend a summer practice where the Giants worked out at Monmouth University in New Jersey. This was before the days when teams charge admission to watch practices. In fact, I was the only kid there that day. We drove down and in the parking lot, we met Wellington Mara, the famed owner of the Giants. He and some other businessmen walked us inside, where they started having a meeting in the lobby of the building, leaving me pretty much to myself.

Sitting on a couch, I noticed a big black guy enter the room, looking around as if he was meeting someone. I recognized him as Rich Glover, the star rookie who had played at Nebraska (we saw him play in person the year before at West Point when the Cornhuskers trounced Army 77–7). There was a ping-pong table in the room and Glover said to me, "You play?" I told him I did and a moment later, we were warming up—Rich Glover and me! As I recall, he won the game, but not by much (21–17?). I could have gone home happy at that point, without so much as even seeing a football. I had played ping-pong with Rich Glover.

My dad and the rest of the men were all getting ready to have lunch, and the man who'd invited us for the day said, "Can't Chris just go out to the field himself?" My dad asked what I thought and I said no problem, so to the field I was led.

Seeing the Giants in their dark blue jerseys and classic blue helmets with the white "NY" on the side was surreal. They weren't in Yankee Stadium; they were surrounding me, in huddles, running plays, punting and driving tackling sleds up and down the field. As thrilling as it was though, it was also awkward because I didn't know anybody. I had no place there. Add to the mix my bright marigold shirt, plaid-checked pants and white leather belt, and clearly I became "what's wrong with this picture?" But before I became too self-conscious (or seriously injured), I was rescued.

"Kid!"

I turned around and saw number 43—Carl "Spider" Lockhart, Giants safety and my favorite player.

"Kid, come on, let's get you doing something! You can't just stand here, this is *practice*."

Spider introduced himself and asked me if I played football. I told him I did, he grabbed a ball and we had a catch—with him giving me pointers with every toss. All warmed up, he brought me to the sideline where linebacker Brad Van Pelt was practicing kicking off a tee. Spider said, "Brad, can Chris hold for you?" Van Pelt said "Sure," and so Spider showed me how to hold the ball in place. I probably winced a bit as Van Pelt stepped up and thundered his kicks just inches from my hand, but what a feeling! My new pal Spider introduced me around, and made me feel like part of the team.

After practice, he told me he'd meet me in the cafeteria where we could have lunch with the rest of the players. I waited there for him while he changed. Soon he arrived, dressed casually in red-and-white-checked pants and a white knit shirt. Spider sat me down right in the thick of things, with Bob Grim, Ron Johnson, Don Herrmann, Greg Larson and all the other guys whose football cards I'd collected. We ate a huge lunch (fried chicken), and then Spider noticed I was holding a Giants media guide. "Hey, let's get that signed," he said, and so he led me table to table.

My favorite. With Carl "Spider" Lockhart.

When my dad

and his associates were done meeting, they found me with Spider, who by then had invited us to watch the Giants play at Yankee Stadium on opening day against Houston. Before it was time to leave, Spider found a guy with a camera and we went outside to take some pictures (Spider even corralled the Giants head coach, Alex Webster, and had him pose with me).

Posing with the New York Giants coaches that day. *(from left to right)* **Head Coach Alex Webster, me and Assistant Coach Joe Walton.**

Spider Lockhart was my favorite Giant. Unprompted, he went out of his way to make sure I had the day of my life. He never stopped talking, he was funny and the other players seemed to love him—he was just one of those guys who seemed to bring a positive spark and energy into everything.

At Yankee Stadium watching the New York Giants in 1973.

We went to Yankee Stadium a month or so later to watch the Giants—we even sat in the press box. I rooted as hard as I could for Spider that day, and for every game he played after that until he retired in 1975. I kept the picture of him and me near my bed for years (it's on my desk in front of me as I write this now).

In July of 1986, I was on a sweltering subway car in New York reading the paper. I got to the sports page and read the headline:

The media guide they gave me the day of my visit.

"Carl 'Spider' Lockhart Dies. The defensive back, who spent his entire National Football League career with the Giants, succumbed to lymph cancer at the age of 43."

What? Number 43, dead at 43?

The obituary told the story of this beautiful man. And I held the paper up to my face to cover the tears that were streaming down my face.

When I watch a player today do his peacock strut after sharing a fumble recovery with three other guys, howling and carrying on like he just won the lottery or cured cancer, I think about Spider Lockhart—and I look at our picture together and smile, just like I did on that summer day long ago in New Jersey.

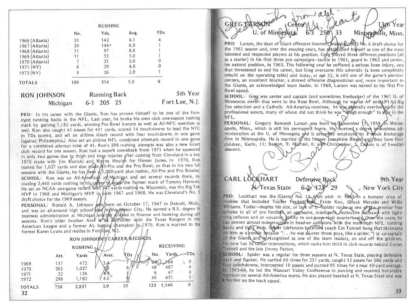

Various autographs inside the media guide.

We want our athletes to live up to their images, I think most fans would agree. After you have kids though, and they are of an age to chase down autographs and try and meet their sports idols, the stakes get raised. We protect the fragile dreams of our children, making sure

Collecting autographs that wonderful summer day in 1973.

what they hold dear remains intact as long as possible. Innocence and wonder have been on the endangered species list for some time now, and I know my wife and I have always worked overtime to preserve the environment around our children; trying to create a loving, supportive, fun household that allows for goofs, stumbles, getting dirty and a simple sense of innocence that kids used to have.

So I'll be damned if I'll let some sports star ruin everything!

We went to baseball spring training in 2001, an annual vacation we did for about seven years. For us in California, the drive to the Phoenix area is a simple, seven-hour cruise through the desert and it's a trip that never failed to delight. We'd wander most of the baseball camps in the area, catching games, but more than anything, watching practices up close. Our main focus was in Tempe, where the Anaheim Angels train, because that's our team. Charlie loved tracking down Tim Salmon, Garret Anderson, Troy Glaus and the rest of his favorite players, especially pre-2002, before they won the World Series, when spring training was still a fairly quiet, laid-back environment. Some days we'd be the only people in the stadium to watch practice. Those wonderful sounds of spring, gorgeous weather and watching our kids do what kids do—chase baseballs, chase players and chase their little dreams on the soft, green grass lawn out beyond the left field wall.

Near the end of the '01 spring practice, the Angels signed slugger Jose Canseco to a short contract. I'd read the stories about what a malcontent he could be, so I held my breath when Charlie, then about seven, told me how badly he wanted to try and get Jose's autograph. So what made Charlie like him? Not his legendary homerun prowess, which was not yet known to be tainted at this point. We had a video, a baseball bloopers tape, which featured perhaps the mother of all mishaps: the ball bouncing off Canseco's head in right field and going over the wall for a homerun. We'd watched that the way some had watched the Zapruder film—endlessly and analytically. From that, Charlie thought Jose Canseco was one of the greatest guys in the game—a legend.

We saw him enter the tunnel and head toward the field. While I stayed in my seat, Charlie darted over to him, about 50 yards away. I saw them have an exchange and Charlie hustled back, thrilled.

"What happened, fella?" I asked. "Did he sign your baseball?"

"No," Charlie gushed. "He said he was too busy but maybe sometime later he'd be able to. Isn't that great?"

"Yeah," I mustered. "Great!"

My first thought was, "We are the only two people in the ballpark right now—would it have killed you to sign this little kid's baseball? This kid who says 'please' and 'thank you,' and isn't pushy? This kid who collects your baseball cards?" But then again, maybe he was just trying to focus. After all, he was trying to get a job, and you can't fault a guy for concentrating on that.

Soon, Canseco was at the plate. It reminded me of an old *Munsters* episode where Herman tries out for Leo Durocher's baseball team. Munster hits balls that travel miles out of the park, breaking windows all over the city. The balls Canseco hit disappeared over the horizon, completely out of the park, one after another.

Little did we know that in just a few years he'd bring the sport to its knees, ratting out teammates and exposing the underbelly of baseball's seamiest side. I'm still not sure what I think about all of that. By doing the wrong thing (ratting), he did the right thing (exposing)—a tough call. But on this day, he was just a steel-armed slugger, hitting balls so hard that if they'd exploded (like Munster's did), I would not have been surprised.

After the hitting exhibition, the squad packed it in to leave for a game across town in Scottsdale against the Giants. As Canseco left, I knew Charlie was a little sad. He watched Jose head toward a protected exit, erasing any chance that he might be able to get the star's attention. Heading up the stairs, I said, "It's okay, pal." Charlie said, "I know, he's just busy." Right after that though, we heard a whistle. I mean a *whistle*, when someone can use his or her thumb and forefinger to blow one that raises the roof. We both turned, and there was Jose Canseco, whistling and waving to us—or rather, to Charlie. "He wants you, buddy," I started to say, but Charlie was on his way down the stairs in a flash before I could finish my sentence.

When I got down by the field, I heard Jose say to Charlie, "Hey, I told you when I was done it'd be okay, and you were taking off!" He chatted with Charlie, asked him how old he was, where he went to school and what position he played. He gave Charlie his autograph, took a picture with him and then excused himself. At home, we watched the video of the ball bouncing off his head, and Charlie

Jose Conseco and Charlie at spring training in 2001.

With Coach Tony Dungy and Charlie in 2008. (Memphis, Tennessee.)

said, "Wasn't he great, Dad? See, I told you he was nice."

And despite all we know now and all the other things that have happened with Jose Canseco, he was a nice guy that day. A very nice guy.

Football fan update—Three relatively recent events helped pull me back into the fold and remind me why I loved the game so much in my youth. First was the 2008 Super Bowl, when the New York Giants, somehow, defeated the heavily favored New England Patriots. But was it really that shocking? Maybe not. The Giants took the old-fashioned route that day in Phoenix, blending teamwork with grit and tenacity to stun the almost-perfect Pats. Eli Manning seized the moment and did what his dad taught him to do—be smart and play his heart out.

Second was a trip to Lambeau Field in Green Bay. Have you been there? If so, then you know what I mean. If not—then go.

Third was a chance meeting in 2008 with Coach Tony Dungy. He was incredibly gracious with us, especially to my son. He was down-to-earth, and a gentleman. It reminded me that, for all the goons in the headlines, the game is more about (or should be about) pros like this—men of character and class. Dungy was the next generation of Tom Landry, George Allen and Vince Lombardi, and a throwback to the days when I couldn't wait to throw a jersey on and practice for the "Punt, Pass and Kick" competition or beg my dad to go outside and have a catch in the snow. The days when Spider Lockhart might even take you under his wing.

Hooray for Hollywood
(1974)

Part 1

We first visited California in 1974. My father, a big-shot advertising executive (think of the series *Mad Men* on AMC, and that was his existence in the 1960s into the '70s), had a business trip out west and decided that it could also double as a summer vacation. He'd have his scotch-and-Marlboro meetings, but my mom could keep my sisters and I occupied during the day. When his meetings were done after a few days, we'd then have about a week together in what was still, blissfully, "La La Land."

In the early 1970s, before Woody Allen defined the city as a bunch of sprout-eating, EST-addicted basket cases, Los Angeles was still Shangri-La for many an East Coaster. So this would be a trip into the mystic, where shows like *McMillan & Wife* and *Kojak* were made, the city where Charleton Heston endured a cinematic *Earthquake* ("in Sensurround!") and where Lucille Ball heisted John Wayne's footprints from the Chinese Theatre. This was a pre-gangsta "El Lay," where bouncy, blonde beach girls and endless summers and the Dodgers and swaying palm trees and the Strip and the Bowl and a million other fantasies were ready to be picked like so many big yellow lemons in those lush Beverly Hills backyards. Los Angeles, the mere idea of it, seduced a young New Yorker like the first copy of *Playboy* he ever saw. So pretty on the outside . . . and can you even imagine what's under the cover?

We left New York from John F. Kennedy International Airport on this, our first really big trip, aboard one of those ridiculously spacious 747 jumbo jets. Remember? The planes that had those jazzy piano bars in the upstairs lounge where adults could gather to drink, smoke and socialize while the kids read books, played games or watched a movie downstairs. Our folks were up there soon after takeoff and I had to go upstairs for a moment to get some cash to purchase the movie. It was another world. A guy at the piano could just have well been Burt Bacharach, caressing the keys in that mellow and sensitive 1970s way, laughing and eyeing broads in between sips of his Martini & Rossi on the rocks. He asked for requests. "How about 'Georgie Girl'? Or 'What the World Needs Now Is Love'? Or, hey, maybe 'Come Fly With Me?'" Men with '70s sideburns and lots of cologne lolled about with pretty women in stylish clothes and careful makeup. There was lots of smoke and the sound of ice tumbling into glasses. Warm, cozy and intimate, it was clearly the place to be—a bohemian sky-pad for swinging suburban jet-setters.

Downstairs (where I'd soon return), efficient, perky stewardesses—who all looked sort of like Joey Heatherton—prepared meals, gave the kids plastic flight wings and made small talk with single male passengers.

Back in my seat, maybe 30 minutes into our flight, a familiar male face emerged from first class and was about to pass me en route to the stairs and the good times happening above, where more than occasional bursts of laughter kept wafting down. I stared up from my seat and he stared back, because he knew he was being stared at. "Hey, pal," said Paul Newman, unshaven in blue jeans and a blue denim shirt, with blue eyes to match. I'd just seen *The Sting* and right before that, *Butch Cassidy and the Sundance Kid*, so this was weird. He loped upstairs while I tried to process the moment. I'd just had contact with an A-list movie star, and we weren't even over Akron yet.

The flight was smooth and laidback. My sisters and I

watched a movie. But we were antsy. We wanted to get to California, to Disneyland and Universal Studios and Malibu and Hollywood.

As we were getting ready to land at Los Angeles International Airport, I remember the song "Tumbling Dice" playing on the in-flight headsets. I adored the Rolling Stones, and this song seemed the perfect soundtrack as we approached paradise. Swaggering and slightly mysterious, it lulled me into a bit of a hypnotic trance as we flew in over the fabulous Forum. I could even see the Hollywood Hills, with "Tumbling Dice" fading out as we approached the ground. Then reality hit when I could see the airport. "There, look, it's that weird space-age building that I saw on *The Rockford Files*—the one that looks like a giant spider!" We had arrived.

At the baggage carousel, there was a commotion. Important-looking executives were waiting for someone, checking their watches, acting edgy, along with a limousine driver. Who were they waiting for? A moment later, Paul Newman was walking briskly toward us (and them). Now though, he wasn't the casual, denim-clad Paul Newman I'd encountered over Akron. This was *Paul Newman* in a sharp black tuxedo, freshly shaven and wearing dark movie star sunglasses, all Hollywood sparkle and power. He'd transformed in the plane. I must have been gawking because as he passed, as he had done on the plane, he acknowledged me. "Bye, pal!" And then he was gone, whisked up and away by the forces of show business to some other astral plane—maybe an awards show or something better—transported from us mortals.

Do people who live here ever get used to this, I wonder?

Heady as all this was, it was time to focus. There were bags to claim, a car to rent and a trip to make to the Century Plaza hotel, where we'd be staying.

Riding north on the 405 freeway, we all craned our necks for some taste of Los Angeles. There were palm trees, but not much else. No movie sets or gorgeous blondes, no beaches or mansions or anything of the sort. Instead, it was just sort of a bland freeway. Was this it? Had our trip peaked at the baggage carousel? Is this place just one big tease?

My mom is adept at spotting celebrities the way expert birders are in the bush. Keen eye for detail (even at a distance), cool, calm, constantly analyzing and never afraid to make adjustments in her appraisals. "That's Jill St. John—no wait, Stefanie Powers." "See that man by the fountain? He was Glenn Ford's brother in. . . ." So it was an easy one for her as we pulled up at the hotel—one of her all-time favorites, standing alone and apparently waiting for a ride.

"Kids, in the front of the hotel: Gene Kelly."

Now, I did not get as excited as I did with Paul Newman, but still, Gene Kelly is Gene Kelly and so, once more, here we were looking at a bigger-than-life celebrity in a normal, pedestrian setting. Would he start swinging on a lamppost and begin dancing like he did in *Singin' in the Rain*? Nope. He just got into a car that pulled up for him. Like a normal person.

Inside the hotel, my sisters and I explored the lobby like maniacs while my folks checked in. This was our first big vacation, and we were going to squeeze every second out of the place. The Century Plaza was a lovely hotel, bustling and full of important, interesting-looking people. While my parents were checking in, I had a chance encounter with one of these important, interesting looking people.

I was running perhaps where I should not have been running, and certainly not looking where I should have been looking. A portly gentleman was coming in the front door and, looking back over my shoulder, I *plowed* into his gut. Bouncing back off of him, I knew in an instant that was he seriously annoyed by what happened. Paul Newman probably would have just said, "Hi, pal!" or maybe, "Watch it, pal!" but not this guy. This guy looked down sternly and, in a deep, foreboding, truly ticked-off voice said, "Young man . . . where are your parents?" It was hard for me to react with the swift, polite answer he expected, and understandably so. It was hard because the portly guy I had just bounced off of was Alfred Hitchcock.

If you're wondering how a 12-year-old could be so sure, I grew up in a "movie household." We watched lots of great movies—many older classics, comedies, musical, silents, art house films—whenever they were on TV as part of shows like *Million Dollar Movies* and other late-night movie re-run packages, complete with lots of discussions, debates and critiques. My parents loved good books, music and, especially, movies. Because of this, my sisters and I were fairly adept in our film knowledge, and I'd actually seen Mr. Hitchcock just days before, being interviewed on PBS, so his face was fresh in my brain. (And I was a big fan—the first thing I'd wanted to do was to go to Universal Studios just to see the Bates Motel set.)

I remained mute while looking up at the jowly Englishman, who seemed more a stern schoolmaster than a great filmmaker. But I'm pretty sure in my star-struck haze that I gestured over to my parents, who were still checking in. Leading me by the scruff of my neck, the Master of Suspense marched me to them, like he was leading me to the gallows. I clearly remember the double-double take they did as we got close. I can also still hear that wonderful, British-syrup drawl, saying (this is pretty close), "I find it inappropriate for a young man to be creating such chaos in a public place like this and do trust he'll be watched closer."

While I waited for someone in the background to yell, "Cut! Print it! Perfect!" Hitchcock actually gave me a little tousle of my hair. Then he ambled away, leaving the scene on a lighter note than he had entered it. But this was not a movie; this was simply Los Angeles, revealing herself one luscious layer at a time. And I was totally infatuated.

My parents and I looked at each other in that moment, dumbstruck and giddy, knowing, I think, that we had a story for life. Even the guy checking us in seemed a little star struck.

A few years ago, I was at the Century Plaza, not running into stomachs, but attending an advertising industry awards show. I'd written some commercials that were nominated and after they lost, I headed to the lobby to have a drink with a colleague. For old time's sake, I told him this story while walking through the entire scene, right where it happened. It was fun for a moment but, all of a sudden, I missed being a kid. I missed seeing my family together right there, before my folks got divorced. I missed the era of Gene Kelly, Alfred Hitchcock and Paul Newman. I missed the old, laid back-L.A. and airplanes that had piano bars and smartly attired stewardesses who said, "Coffee, tea or me?" (Even if they never really said that, I missed the made-up cliché of them saying that.) Certain stories, it seems, may have more power than we give them credit for. They become markers in our lives, capturing and preserving some wistful shreds of innocence or thrill or nostalgia or melancholy. And those places where said stories occur, like the hotel lobby, are the chambers where all of our old ghosts are kept, just waiting for us to take a peek back.

Part II

I still remember many details about that visit to California. Whenever we go to Disneyland (frequently), my kids still ask about that vacation and where certain things happened. There was Universal Studios (where James Garner waved to our tram), Trader Vic's restaurant (my mom: "Kids, don't look, but there's Peter Falk"), plus Zuma Beach, the Tar Pits, Grauman's Chinese Theatre and more—even a chic Beverly Hills boutique my mom shopped at that had just hosted Elton John and Bill Wyman. Good stuff, but it wasn't all bread and roses, as they say. My twin sister and I had a Hollywood moment that wasn't just unpleasant in 1974, but haunted me later, too.

Early one morning, while my dad was at a meeting, my mom took us to the Farmers Market, the famed Los Angles landmark featuring shops, food stalls, restaurants and kitschy gift shops in an open air marketplace. The Farmers Market is still a place that, although touristy, still attracts some genuine old-time L.A. characters, and it's always been a favorite haunt of mine.

So we had breakfast and shopped around a bit, buying postcards and other mementos from our trip. Window-shopping down one row of stores, my mom's antenna went up. She had one in her sights: *Hollywoodus celebritus.*

"Kids, that man walking toward us? McLean Stevenson."

Sure enough, it was Lt. Colonel Blake. He was even wearing a fishing hat like in *M*A*S*H*. Wow, some actors even dressed in character while in public, no doubt as a means of seamlessly entertaining fans like my twin sister and I, who, against my mom's command, made a dash to greet the actor. He was alone on this quiet weekday morning, and something was wrong. He didn't greet us with open arms and invite us to the set. He didn't smile like Paul Newman or even tousle my hair

The Farmers Market, site of the McLean Stevenson blow off.

like Hitchcock. Nope, as my sister and I said, "Hi, Mr. Stevenson," he waved his arms like he'd just noticed a tarantula on
it, "Get the hell away from me!" With that, he shuffled past us,
leaving us numb in his wake.

"You can't win 'em all," was the moral, I guess, and my
mom was quick to point out that he's entitled to his privacy and
may have simply been having a bad day. Still, there was something scary about one of your favorite TV characters yelling at
you like some crazy toothless uncle who's just been startled out
of a nap. I know exactly where the site is today at the Farmers
Market, but I avoid it—too ugly a memory. I wanted McLean
Stevenson forever out of my brain after that, and I'd be lying if
I said that next season on *M*A*S*H*, when his chopper disappeared, well, no tears were shed in our house.

But as I said, the specter of Stevenson would return. In
the early 1990s, my wife and I were at the Santa Anita racetrack attending a celebrity softball game that some friends were
playing in. By now, I'd worked in advertising for a number of
years and had amassed a stable of older comic actors for radio
commercials I was writing. On this night, many of our pals,
from Harvey Korman to Don Adams would be taking part in the
game and they invited my wife and I to watch and then have
dinner. Looking at the program before the game, whose name
did I see but McLean Stevenson?

I recounted the Farmers Market tale for my wife and
then I saw him. He was walking across the infield, maybe 50
yards away from us, shuffling along just like 20 years earlier.
A young kid ran up to him, carrying a program and holding up
a pen. We were too far away to hear, but we saw everything just
fine. Stevenson shooed the kid away, just like he'd done to my
sister and me, leaving the confused kid alone in he dust. Time,
ugly time, stood still.

I wondered how many other kids there had been over the
years. Was McLean Stevenson a serial bubble-burster, haunting kids all over the country—if not the world?

I wanted to go comfort the kid, but my wife said to let it

go—the kid would survive. In fact, he may even be better for it—tougher in a world full of surly C-list actors.

After the softball game, we had dinner at the club in the track. McLean Stevenson was several tables away, yukking it up with some friends. I told the story, at my wife's encouraging, to the people at our table. These men, all good pals with McLean, laughed and said, "Hey, go tell McLean—he's a good guy—he'll get a kick out of this. Really, he's not that bad." I was about to go over, but it didn't seem quite right. To have a laugh at my own expense and that kid in the infield? Didn't seem worth it, but I was getting egged on by the table. Peer pressure from 70-year-old comics! What if he shooed me away again? Or worse? Still, it seemed I had little choice but to go. Then the actor, Don Adams, looked up at me. He'd been quiet up this point. He said, "I wouldn't tell him that story, either. You can't be a prick to kids. Adults, maybe. But kids, no way." In other words, "Get smart." So I took his advice. I sat back down and enjoyed the rest of the evening. And stayed as far away from McLean Stevenson as I could.

Ladies and Gentlemen: The Rolling Stones
(1975)

O n the TV show *Don Kirshner's Rock Concert* in 1973, I saw the images that would change my life. The Rolling Stones playing the songs "Angie," "Silver Train," "Dancing with Mr. D" and then "All Down the Line" from the movie *Ladies and Gentlemen: The Rolling Stones*. I was entranced. I'd already started listening to the band, but *seeing* them sealed the deal. I was helplessly stuck in their storm, where I have remained ever since. The Stones are danger, sex, mystery, confidence, intrigue, playfulness, power, rebellion, excess, fury, charisma, flash, glamour, passion, love—they are everything to me. I like many other bands and performers, but nothing like this. The Rolling Stones represent the soundtrack to my life, the sirens in my head, the musical elixir that always makes everything better.

A ticket to the show at Madison Square Garden.

May 1

To announce their 1975 Tour of the Americas, the Stones, in lieu of appearing at a scheduled press conference, pulled up outside the hotel at 1 Fifth Avenue on the back of a flatbed truck playing an eight-minute version of "Brown Sugar." Right after that, tickets went on sale. My father, God bless him, procured the house seats at Madison Square Garden that his ad agency had. Six great seats, priced $12.50 per, were ours. That next month, the Stones moved their army up north from the city to Newburgh to an airplane hangar not an hour from our house in order to rehearse and build their newfangled, six-pointed, star-shaped stage. Soon, we'd be seeing them in the flesh. And I would never be the same.

June 22

This was *our* show—their first of six nights in New York. My parents were going take me, my twin sister Margaret (we were 13 at the time), my little sister Lee (then 10) and my friend, Bryant. At the last minute though, my 30-ish cousins, Helene and Chip, were given the nod to take us. My folks thought they'd enjoy it more, and they were thrilled.

The program from that night.

Headline in the *New York Times* about the show: "Rolling Stones begin six nights at Garden with finely crafted show before sold out house of 19,500."

Quote from writer John Rockwell in the same article: "The show on Sunday was tighter and more finely crafted than any in the first three cities. Mr. Jagger looked as if he knew exactly what he was doing, and he did it with his customary confidence."

He sure did.

My picture was even on the front page of the *New York Post*, in the background as Mick tossed a bucked of water on the crowd! This remains the most important and influential show I've ever seen. The 1975 Rolling Stones were sloppier than they had been in previous years, but in a way, that was always sort of the charm of the band. I remember almost every

First concert, June 22, 1975.

second of this show today.

It was one of the first, truly big, "spectacle" tours of the era, featuring that six-pointed, star-shaped stage that opened up, flower-like, to reveal the band at the beginning of the show. The lighting was extremely advanced for its time, featuring bold, neon-like colors throughout the two-and-a-half-hour show, and the sound design was revolutionary. But for all the elaborate staging, effects, and pomp, it all came down to the music, and the Stones more than delivered.

First concert, June 22, 1975.

The band that night featured Ronnie Wood on guitar in place of Mick Taylor (Wood was "on loan" from the Faces at that point), and the Stones were furthered augmented by Billy Preston on keyboards and Ollie Brown on percussion. If simply being in the same space as them wasn't enough, the set list that night elevated the evening into one of majesty. Starting off with "Honky Tonk Women," and wending through "Angie," "Wild Horses," "You Can't Always Get What You Want," "Tumbling Dice," "Happy," "Brown Sugar," and many more, this was an experience that affected all of my senses, like a major earthquake that is still producing aftershocks.

I have a copy of the audio from the show and I listen to it frequently. This night cemented my love affair with the Stones and also became the show I compared everything else to. I will never recover from it. During "Angie," I said to Bryant, "We're breathing the same air as they are." And there they were, in the flesh: the Rolling Stones. I'd never be the same again for having seen this; I had my music set for life.

That's me in the crowd!

John Cheever

(1975)

Literature has been the salvation of the damned, literature has inspired and guided lovers, routed despair and can perhaps in this case save the world.

—John Cheever, *Home before Dark*

n a California bookstore recently, I saw a copy of *The Short Stories of John Cheever*, my all-time favorite collection of short fiction. On the table near it was a book that I wrote called *James Dean Died Here*. Light years apart in terms of impact and importance, seeing the two books near each other still gave me a special feeling, a deep connection to a past chapter in my life.

It was 1975 up in Westchester County, New York, in a town called Ossining. Ossining's original name, "Sing Sing," was named after the Native American Sint Sinck tribe from whom the land was purchased in 1685. As you might know, Sing Sing is also the name of the famed local prison. We lived in the rural part of town, in the forest on a winding, idyllic country lane called Spring Valley Road. (Other roads in the area were Hawks Lane, Apple Bee Farm Road, Cedar Lane . . . you get the picture.)

I was about 13 years old and had decided that I wanted to be a writer (especially if the baseball player thing didn't work out). When I announced this to my parents, my mom suggested I write a neighbor of ours to see if he might be able to supply some professional guidance. His name was John Cheever, and all I knew of him was that my parents loved his writing and several of his books were on the shelves in our living room library (*The Wapshot Chronicle* is the one that jumps out in my mind). My mom's idea seemed reasonable enough so I wrote Mr. Cheever a short note asking if I might be able to ask him a few questions some day. Just a couple of days later, the following letter arrived at our house:

> *Dear Chris Epting,*
> *It is nice to know that there is another writer living in the neighborhood. I will call you one day soon and then maybe we can take a walk and talk about writing.*
>
> *(signed) John Cheever*

And the very next day, he called my house.

"Yes, Chris," a rich New England-accented voice began, "this is John Cheever."

What a unique way to be introduced to one of the greatest fiction writers in American literary history.

Armed with a few school writing samples, I went to his house the next day and spent several hours there. I listened to him, I asked questions, I watched him smoke tons of filterless cigarettes, I drank Coke and I listened to his Beatles records with him. But then it was time for Little League practice. It was okay, I'd be back many other times in the next several years to talk about writing.

John Cheever became a mentor to me until his death in 1982. He'd review my work (scribbling copious notes in red felt tip

John Cheever's signature on a book I have.

John Cheever's house. This is where we'd often meet for our discussions. (Ossining, New York.)

marker across my pages), take the occasional walk with me and, once, even personally called a professor at my college to recommend me for a much-in-demand writing course. Naturally, the call helped secure my place in the class (it had been his idea to call after I described the situation) and it wasn't until later in life that I could appreciate the absurdity of the moment: a pompous college English professor with his own dreams of becoming a great American novelist getting a call from one of the true lions of American fiction to vouch for a student.

John Cheever lived in Ossining from 1951 until the time of his death. Over the years, the Quincy, Massachusetts native became iconic in his adopted city. He taught at Sing Sing prison, was part of a regular salon-style dinner group for years and even did readings at the local public library. Cheever was such a regular at the Highland Diner that his photo hung there, shrine-like, for years after his death. He was everywhere, and he was nowhere; seen all over town, but

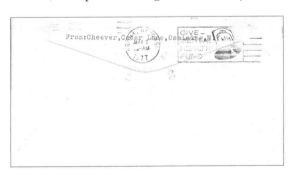

One of the many letters I received from John Cheever.

just as happy in his beautiful colonial home on Cedar Lane with his lovely wife, Mary.

Once I'd known him for a couple of years, it finally hit me who he was—and what he represented to people. I was in the supermarket with my mom and at the checkout stand, there was that elegant, weathered face on the cover of *Newsweek* magazine. I was seeing Cheever later that day, so I brought the copy with me. In his office, I showed it to him. He just nodded and I asked him something. I explained to him that when I first visited, I was not familiar with him. But now, over time, and especially with this magazine, it was clear to me he was very important. So I wanted to know: Why grant me, a kid in the neighborhood, all of this precious time?

He laughed a little at that and explained that since his drinking problems in the last few years, he had looked for therapeutic outlets that might help him focus—and that helping a young writer was almost like medicine. (I learned later that he was completely dry the last seven years of his life—and those were the years I knew him.) In addition to visiting at his home, I called him from college to chat from time to time. I'd bump into him taking long walks down Spring Valley Road on lazy summer days (or riding his beloved bicycle) and he'd always stop to talk and catch up.

I spoke to John Cheever less than two weeks before he died. I was away at school and, while I knew he was ill with cancer, I didn't know just how sick he was. There was an article I wanted to write about him and on the phone, in a ravaged voice, he told me as soon as he was feeling better we could talk more about it. Then I turned on the news one morning soon after and saw he was gone.

But as I've learned since, he's still here—as all the

greats remain. His stories continue to charm and captivate new readers every day. At the beautiful new Ossining Public Library at 53 Croton Avenue, next-door to the former library site that Cheever would visit, Ossining's "Chekhov of the Suburbs" is immortalized. The main reading room in the library is named for him (and Jane Clark, a longtime library staffer and friend of Mr. Cheever, proudly keeps his legacy alive with photos, letters and wonderful personal stories about him).

In his lifetime, Cheever won the Pulitzer Prize, the National Book Award, and the National Medal for Literature. His short stories and novels, including *The Wapshot Chronicle*, *The Wapshot Scandal*, *Bullet Park* and *Falconer* (inspired by writing classes he taught at Sing Sing), remain vital examples of some of the world's best 20th-century fiction.

If you ever visit Ossining, wherever you are in the village, know that he was probably right nearby at some point. If you make your way to the serene Teatown Lake near his home, be aware that he paused there along the road by the water more than once to sit by the rocks and talk to this young writer about craft and critique, while also mixing in a fair amount of baseball chatter. (I still recommend John Updike's piece describing Ted Williams's last at bat to friends because Cheever told me about it on Spring Valley Road—after I told him we'd lost our all-star game earlier that day.) Further on down the woodsy road, at the Teatown Lake Reservation, the ancient stone walls where Cheever would stop and rest are still there and everything remains as it was when he was here—exactly as I remember it as a teenager.

There's still a diner at 191 N. Highland Avenue where Cheever could frequently be found. As the local library recounts:

> Cheever was a regular at the Highland Diner, where he'd arrive with a book or newspaper and look around for someone to talk to. . . . He knew and was liked by so many people in the town

that his family used to call him the "Mayor of Ossining." He never ran for office, of course, but there was an abortive movement in the wake of the Pulitzer to name a street after him. Cheever was pleased and self-deprecatory about this at the same time. He and Mary and the children sat around the dinner table thinking of what else might be named after him. "Let's see," he proposed, "how about the John Cheever Memorial Dump?"

And Sing Sing prison, where many a con was sent "up the river" (the expression refers to the Hudson River on which the prison sits), is still in business. Located at 95 Broadway, today there's even a prison museum on site (a safe distance from the criminals). This may be the most telling Cheever-related landmark in Ossining. While recovering from alcoholism and drug addiction in the mid-1970s, Cheever wrote *Falconer* by specifically drawing on his experience as a writing instructor here. This was a breakthrough book for him, and so one must consider the influence the prison had in helping to re-establish Cheever's force as a writer.

He taught here and, obviously, he learned here, too.

Back in the bookstore in California, I look down at John Cheever's face on the cover of his book. I can hear his voice and I can see him lighting up another cigarette and asking me, "Did you see me on *Dick Cavett* with John Updike? What did you think? Is that something teenagers watch these days?"

The Cheever mailbox.

I placed his book back down on the table, but I moved it right next to mine—connecting us one more time.

Recently, I drove once more past the Cheever's house on Cedar Lane near Route 9A. Out on the road in front of their property, the old gray metal mailbox I remembered with the name Cheever hand-lettered in black paint had been updated. Peeking down the driveway and looking at the house set back against the woods, I could picture him getting into his red Volkswagen Rabbit to drive me home after that first visit. Then I thought back to what he told me at that meeting:

"Keep a journal, start today and don't stop. It forces you to write and that's good. Writers write, they don't *talk* about writing, and a journal strengthens the muscle. So go. Write."

I thought to myself about how lucky I was to have known someone so gifted and inspirational, someone who took the time to share some stories and advice—someone who gave some critique and company to, as he put it, "another writer living in the neighborhood."

REFLECTIONS
from Mary Cheever, Summer 2009

It's surreal to be back on the porch where I'd sometimes sit with John Cheever. It's a perfect lazy summer day and the yard glows green from all the recent rains. The Cheever's Dutch Colonial farmhouse (built in 1928 to resemble a house hundreds of years older) looks just as it did when I was last here almost 30 years ago. Set back in the woods, it still feels like a writer's retreat. On the side of the house is the maple tree John Cheever would often sit under when thinking and writing.

Just inside the front door, his chair still sits by the fireplace, surrounded by his books. It's like he is still there, no doubt because his widow, Mary Cheever, still misses him a great deal. At 92, she maintains the Cheever legacy with grace— proud of her husband's literary accomplishments, but honest about his demons. On this day, with my wife, children and her live-in helper, Alexis, Mary and I caught up.

"John was an egotist, so of course he loved talking to you about himself," she laughs. "But he loved talking about writing, too, and his belief that it was very hard work. At least it was for him."

We get to talking about some of John Cheever's best stories, including a favorite of mine, "Christmas is a Sad Season for the Poor." "That was written about the apartment where we lived in New York City," she says wistfully. "Including our doorman and everything."

I ask Mary about the group of writers Mr. Cheever would regularly lunch with at the Villa Morelli restaurant in Croton-on-Hudson. "Writers? More like reprobates!" she corrects me. "Though there may have been a few writers there from time to time."

Does she think this digital era, with texting and other unconventional technological writing techniques, might hinder the development of a new crop of great writers? "There will always be great writers, the biggest challenge will be getting their work out there, making it sure people can find it and vice versa."

Mary invites me to sit in John Cheever's chair, and I accept. "It was good he spent some time with you for

My family on that familiar porch with Mary Cheever.

With Mary Cheever during the summer of 2009.

those years," she says. "Young writers were important to him and I'm sure he'd be happy to know you brought one of your books to keep here in this room. He enjoyed your company back then because, unlike many others at the time, you asked for nothing of him besides some guidance. He liked that earnestness and innocence. He felt like he was making a difference with you."

Note—Lest you're wondering, some of you may be aware that after his death, it came out that John Cheever had secretly been leading a bisexual life, including his having had a relationship with a younger male writer. I was asked about this by a couple of reporters when the news first came out in the 1980s, and what I said then holds true now: In all the time I spent with Mr. Cheever, he was simply nothing less than a good, serious (if somewhat aloof) teacher.

John Cheever's favorite chair still sits in his den.

The Tin Man
(1975)

For remember, my sentimental friend, a heart is not judged by how much you love, but by how much you are loved by others.
—The Wizard of Oz, *The Wizard of Oz*

No, Oz never did give nothing to the Tin Man
That he didn't, didn't already have
—America, "Tin Man"

That I've always been interested in celebrity culture probably plays a part in this next story.

A product of the '70s TV generation, I was living in a time when our celebrities were bigger-than-life and still veiled with some sense of mystery. There was no tabloid TV and very little tabloid print—it was basically *People* magazine from about 1974 on, and that was it.

As I got older and began making commercials, I started working with more and more actor types, many of whom I grew up watching and appreciating. (More on that in another essay.) As the years went on, many of these people became friends, which gave me yet another, more intimate, view of celebrity culture.

But way back in 1974 at the age of 12, I had an experience with an actor that became, for me, the gold standard of all meetings.

For many of us, *The Wizard of Oz* is a seminal film. It

helped define good vs. bad, reality vs. fantasy and even black-and-white filmmaking vs. color. But I think more than anything, it presented us with a series of characters that each of us ended up choosing from and identifying with. Between Dorothy, the Scarecrow, the Tin Man and the Lion, most of us (in my circle anyway) felt a stronger kinship with one of those characters more than the others, sharing some common bond, values and/or personality traits.

For me, hands down, it was the Tin Man because he was so sentimental—just like me.

In 1974, the Broadway production of *The Wiz* starring Stephanie Mills (and the magnificent, late, great Tiger Haynes as the Tin Man) was in the midst of a huge run. (About 10 years later, Tiger would become a good friend as you'll read later—life is weird.) We went to a Wednesday matinee, my mom, my two sisters and I. After the performance, we went to the famed Sardi's restaurant for an early dinner.

As we were starting to eat, my mom (with the uncanny gift for recognizing people) mentioned quietly that the Tin Man was sitting at a table nearby. Jack Haley himself. Taught, as we were, to not bother people in public, I was told I could not rush over to Mr. Haley and bombard him with questions. But as I negotiated the finer points of a possible compromise with my mom, my younger sister slipped over to the table. Next, I saw

her engaged in what looked like friendly conversation with Mr. Haley and his female companion (who ended up being the actress Penny Singleton from all of those old *Blondie* movies). So I ditched the negotiation process and bee-lined over myself. By the time my

Sardi's, where we met Jack Haley in 1974. (New York City, New York.)

mom came over to gather us and apologize, Mr. Haley had already been as gracious as he could be. He jotted down his home address on a piece of paper, gave it to me and said, "You write and ask me whatever you'd like." The Tin Man who, despite lacking the aluminum makeup and oil can hat, still had the twinkling Tin Man eyes and kind smile.

So when I got home that night, I composed the mother of all fan letters. I wanted to know everything: how they shot the movie, where they shot the movie why they shot the movie, where the munchkins came from, how the effects were created, etcetera. I had the Tin Man's home address after all. And he said it was okay to write him.

The photo Jack Haley sent me.

Weeks went by and one day, when my mom was picking us up at school, she had an oversized manila envelope that had come in the mail. Return address: Beverly Hills.

I opened it carefully. In it were several production stills from *The Wizard of Oz*, all signed individually to my sisters and me. But more important to me was a two-page, single-spaced typed letter to me from Mr. Haley, answering in great, pleasant detail every question I'd asked of him (and then some). It began, "Dear Chris, thank you for your list of interesting questions regarding the making of *The Wizard of Oz*. I've done my best to answer them as thoroughly as possible." Which he did—from who hired the Munchkin actors to where they stayed in Culver City to what it was like to be made up as the Tin Man. He closed by saying we could visit him if we were ever in California.

The Tin Man.

"Do You Feel?"
(1976)

I had a crush on a girl in high school and she, like many other high school girls, was a Peter Frampton nut. This was in the midst of the *Frampton Comes Alive!* insanity, 1976–1977, when that double live record represented everything to everyone. For guys, it was the catchy riffs and snazzy solos on songs like "Something's Happening," "Doobie Wah" and "Do You Feel Like We Do?" (featuring that mysterious talk box). For girls, it was "Show Me the Way," "Baby I Love Your Way" and Frampton's shoulder-length curls, sparkly eyes and charming smile.

So when I heard that Frampton actually bought a house right down the road from us, I knew I had a pretty good in with this particular girl.

The house could not be seen from the street. It sat back in the woods, and I read in *Time* magazine that Frampton bought the estate because it reminded him of being in England. After determining which driveway was Frampton's (through a friend's mom, the realtor who brokered the deal), I casually invited "Kate" over to my house so that she and I could take a romantic stroll down Spring Valley Road, over to Glendale Road where we'd no doubt spend quality time getting to know each other before we stalked our first

Circa 1976.

The Frampton house driveway. (Ossining, New York.)

rock star. This polite, modest suburbanite showed up wearing more makeup than an 8th Avenue hooker and I realized she was preparing to meet him, painting herself the way a tribal woman might before being sacrificed to some God in a volcano.

As we waited outside the gates (looking back, it's hard to say for what exactly), the only sign of life was a red sports car that screamed past us, waited for the electronic gate to open, and then sped up the hill. Kate soon grew bored of this and went home, less interested in me than in meeting Peter Frampton.

Several weeks later, I was in a mall jewelry store in the nearby town of Mount Kisco. I wanted to buy Kate a pair of earrings to surprise her for her birthday (though she'd shown scant interest in me, I really liked her). At the counter, I notice a pretty blonde woman talking with the salesman. Next to her was a petite-sized man with sunglasses silently looking at jewelry. He spoke, and though he said, "Penny, what about these?" as opposed to, "Bob Mayo on the keyboards! Bob Mayo!" like after the solo in "Do You Feel Like We Do?" I knew it was Peter Frampton. So much for stalking—he was being handed to me! There was nobody else in the little store, and so I did the bold thing—asked him to sign an autograph for "Kate." Penny (Mc-

Call, his then-girlfriend), gave me an odd look, but he could not have been more gracious; he was totally down-to-earth and pleasant. I briefly told him it'd be given with the earrings and he said, "Good luck, mate."

As I left the store and looked back, I could still see the two of them in there. Dozens of teenagers walked by and nobody noticed the small man in tight jeans and T-shirt with sunglasses and long hair. Many of them had probably just gone to see him at Madison Square Garden weeks earlier with the rest of us.

Earrings and signature in hand, I made plans to present them to Kate. Days later, as I had her open her eyes (this was at a tennis club), she all but jumped out of her skin when she saw the autograph. The earrings, not so much. She also told me excitedly that she'd just started dating a guy who also loved Frampton, so I'd really made her day. So I was never really in the running. It was the Frampton, not the Epting. Good luck, mate!

PS—Months later I saw Kate. I asked if she had the new Frampton record (*I'm in You*) and she said she'd moved on. Seemed she'd seen him at the Gemini II nightclub hanging out one night, and asked him for a kiss. He told her, "Sorry, darling, but you don't know where I've been." "What a jerk!" she said. Yeah. What a jerk.

(from left to right) **My friend Stanley Sheldon (Frampton's longtime bassist), his son Alex, my friend Elizabeth Shaboo and me.**

PPS—Frampton's then-bassist Stanley Sheldon, whom I eventually became friends with, as you'll read later, joked recently about the house: "I did spend a lot of time there . . . seems I do remember a few people skulking around."

REFLECTIONS
from photographer Mark Weiss

The photos here were taken by a teenager who actually did make it up to that house: famed rock-and-roll photographer Mark Weiss. It was his first official gig shooting a big star in a non-concert setting and it represents the launch of one of the most renowned photography careers in rock-and-roll history. Recalling the day, Mark told me the following for this book:

Frampton by Weiss, 1979.

"Peter was very low-key. He was still recovering from a near-fatal car crash down in the Bahamas and here I am, still a teenager, on this big first assignment. So it was a little weird at first. But we got loose eventually up at that house, he

Famed photographer Mark Weiss and Peter Frampton.

started jumping on his trampoline, having some fun, and then I had him pose with his dog, Rocky—who he wrote the song, 'Rocky's Hot Club' for. That photo became the official PR shot for him and I even posed with Peter after that—which is something I ended up doing with many of the rock stars I shot over the years."

Calling Heather
(1977)

Seventies television and movies became sort of a primer on dating, crushes and first loves for many adolescents. You had the exploits of teen idols Keith Partridge and Arthur Fonzarelli dealing with too many girls, and Richie, Potsy and Ralph dealing with too few. You had Bobby Brady seeing fireworks when he got his first kiss from that neighborhood girl Millicent, as well as *Summer of '42*, *American Graffiti* and a host of other angst-ridden, teenage pop culture scenarios to help guide one through the tangle of emotional first steps. By this time in life, I'd known several girls slightly beyond the "friends" stage, but had to connect on the deep sort of level of say, Joanie and Chachi (or even Mork and Mindy, for that matter). But, armed with what I'd learned on TV and in the movies, I was ready to head to deeper emotional waters. The only thing was, would anyone be there to wade out with me?

The summer of 1977, my family had joined a small tennis and swim club called Chilmark, and it opened my sisters and me up to a new bunch of kids away from our school—which I liked.

These were good kids for the most part, from similar backgrounds and disciplines (or lack thereof). My twin sister fit in right away, as she always did. For me, it was a bit more work, as usual, but the fact that I was a decent tennis player helped me. I played on the club team, hung out there almost every day and adapted easier than I expected. Our family became friends with another family at the club. They had three girls, one of whom was just a year younger than us: Heather. She was lithe, willowy (a ballet dancer) and possessed an attitude that I found quite appealing; she wasn't a snob per se, but she had high standards about things and wasn't afraid to express them. I liked that. I thought her parents were terrific, as well, and much like mine in that they were smart, well read, fun—and good parents.

Nothing happened between us that summer, perhaps because of the fact that our families were friends, thus keeping everything at sort of a "friend" level, but we played tennis together occasionally and made small talk, and all in all I found Heather to be good company.

There was actually another girl at the club that I liked, and I planned on biting the bullet and asking *her* out. As another wonderful summer was about to end, I went out and bought tickets to a Broadway show called *Gemini* that had opened recently. When I finished hitting tennis balls with her one day at the club, I boldly invited her to go to New York with me to see the play. She had been friendly enough with me all summer that I actually thought this would be a no-brainer—she'd actually hinted at how badly she wanted to go see a show. However, she told me she couldn't because he had a "serious" boyfriend outside of the club. Huh?

Was I was simply a clueless judge of character?

Out of touch with the rhythms of adolescence?

An idiot?

Regardless, I was frustrated once more—and now had these (expensive) tickets. The date was approaching and I didn't know what to do.

My mother suggested I invite Heather. After all, we were friends, Heather possessed a sophistication the other girls didn't have and so an evening at the theater might be something that appealed to her. It seemed like a good idea—a "friend" date no doubt, but still, it might be fun.

The "friend factor" did nothing to appease my anxiety when I called her. In true nervous teenage fashion, I dialed each number but the last digit several times, hanging up and redialing—unable to complete the call. Finally, I spun the rotary dial one last time to complete the call and in a moment, she answered.

After stammering out the invitation, I was surprised to hear an enthusiastic . . . "yes."

It was that simple.

And not just that—she started talking to me. Actual conversation. And I spoke back.

It began simply, discussing the past summer. Then the upcoming school year (we went to different high schools). The conversation easily evolved into movies, TV, books (she read books!), her dancing, our families—I had never imagined someone could be so interesting, or interested in talking to me. Seamlessly, the hours began to pile up. 11 PM. Then, midnight. By then, both of our families had gone to bed, and I was sitting on the kitchen floor, entranced at the ease of conversation.

As the night progressed, the call became friendlier, warmer and even a little flirtatious. Blissfully, 1:00 AM became 2:00 AM became 3:00 AM. We talked about our upcoming date and decided that we should have dinner afterwards as well, so the evening was expanded to include Sardi's, the famous Broadway haunt. In the midst of the epic talk, Heather even coined a hybrid word to represent the lofty standard to which she aspired: "sophisti-couth." And I was thoroughly charmed.

Me, around the time of this story (c. 1977).

We then dared each other to stay on the

phone until dawn—and the "all-night phone call challenge" was on. We laughed and struggled to keep things going, digging deeper and deeper for topics until we practically ran out of breath. Then, I saw soft pink-and-peach-colored light starting to peek through the woods outside. And I heard birds chirping—some real, some

Heather (c. 1977).

perhaps imagined. We'd done it. We'd spoken all night long.

Heather started to hear stirring in her house, so we decided to say goodbye. Or goodnight. Or good morning. We'd become a little punch-drunk. Still, we signed off with the promise that we'd speak *later that same day*. I skipped sleeping that day, so intoxicated was I as a result of "the call"—and I counted the hours until I could phone her again and hear her voice.

The world seemed different now—full of a promise that had not existed the night before. The call had literally changed my view of the distaff world, having revealed someone of meaning, substance and, the more I thought about it, very good looks. That was interesting to me—I'd almost forgotten how pretty Heather was, so beguiling was her personality over the phone.

Heather and I went to the show and had dinner afterwards, and it was easy, fun and natural, the way I'd hoped it'd be: a first date for the ages that ended with a kiss. Just like in a movie or TV show.

We saw each other for about a year, shared all sorts of emotions in a short time span, and if I'd been as mature (or sophisti-couth) as she was, it might have even developed deeper. Still, it's always been a chapter of adolescent life that I have considered pivotal—made possible by that marathon phone call.

That was the night I saw, for the first time, the excitement, the promise and the beauty of what happens when sparks fly for all the right reasons—made even more special by the fact that it was unexpected.

And I know, for sure, that all of those shows I watched helped prepare me for the moment.

R E F L E C T I O N S
from Heather McVeigh

Today, Heather lives happily in Briarcliff—not far from where all of this took place—with her husband and their two sons. And she offered this on our marathon chat, after reading the previous piece:

"You definitely captured our call. You brought me right back to sitting on my bed with the old, heavy, gold-colored phone, which had the round disc in the center, and had 'RO2-0120' typed on it. You do have quite the memory. I'm glad you said you were keeping somewhat of a journal, because though I remember a lot, you have me beat!

"Your words are very sweet and flattering and remind me of just how innocent we were and how much fun we truly did have. Most boys your age weren't asking girls to Broadway shows, so I appreciated that you were a little 'different,' too. Thank goodness for Chilmark. It really was a very special little place."

Hey! Ho! Let's Go!
(1977)

On a wintry night, on the Lower East Side of New York City, I saw what would become one of my favorite bands for the first time. A friend's older brother took us into a cave-like club called CBGB, another first for us, and it was the coolest place I'd ever seen: long like a tunnel, dark, hot and loud. I'd seen pictures of Iggy Pop and David Johansen and Nico and Patti Smith hanging out there, but in the dark I couldn't tell if any of them were there. It didn't matter. *We* were there, warm, long-neck Budweisers in hand, and from the other end of the tunnel came the roar of the Ramones.

The place was packed, but we inched our way toward the three-chord thunder. On the small stage, there they were, already famous in New York, in their blue jeans, T-shirts and leather jackets. Maybe 10 feet away, they raced through their set at a ridiculous pace, like cartoon characters. The next night, the Ramones opened for (I think) Blue Öyster Cult at the Nassau Coliseum on Long Island. We went. It was strange. This was no place for the Ramones, and so when Joey announced to the near-empty arena that they'd be heading back to NYC that night for a late-night set at CBGB, we trucked back into Man-

With my pal Bill Smith (c. 1977).

hattan to see them (the set also featured the band Suicide). We even had drinks with them afterwards, as was sometimes possible. CBGB was an amazing place; it was ground zero for Television, Blondie and Mink DeVille. But it's the Ramones, the ultimate American bubblegum punk band, that I always associated with the place most. I saw them there a few more times that year, but that first night was the game changer. At a time when disco was starting to surge, the year of *Saturday Night Fever*, the Ramones gave us hope in the simple promise of rock and roll as a liberating force on a cold, clear night that still seems like a movie scene rather than real life.

Today, Joey, Johnny and Dee Dee Ramone are all dead. CBGB closed on October 15, 2006. It sat empty for a year or so, and now it's a boutique run by high-end designer John Varvatos. It's weird to go back in the building, because it has not changed much and the architects tried to keep some of the integrity of the former space. Original graffiti still scars the walls, and an

old Ramones "Gabba Gabba Hey" sign rests right by where the stage used to sit. I stood there recently, trying to soak up the ghosts with my teenaged son, after regaling him with tales of the old place. I closed my eyes and recalled the raw sounds of the Ramones, Richard Hell, Johnny Thunders and other mu-

CBGB as it looked in the early 1980s. (New York City, New York.)

The exterior today.

The inside of CBGB today—
it's a clothing boutique owned
by designer John Varvatos.

sicians I'd seen here back in the 1970s. What I wouldn't give to have my old college radio pal, Jimmy Garland, right next to me, yelling through the smoke and yellow lights as Richard Lloyd took the stage to play "Alchemy." What I wouldn't give to see Johnny Thunders hiding out in the corner. What I wouldn't give to come in from the cold once more and see the Ramones at CBGB.

My passport photo (c. 1977)—
nice hair!

REFLECTIONS
from Television guitarist
Richard Lloyd

Richard Lloyd, the innovative guitarist and founding member of the band Television, was also instrumental in the birth of CBGB. He told me this:

"After Tom Verlaine and I decided to form this band, Television, and after we convinced Richard Hell to play bass in the band, we needed a place to play. We rented our own club, CBGB; we built the stage in the place for crying out loud. That created the scene on the Lower East Side. We'd actually booked the place—for three years, our manager Terry Ork and I booked all the music at CBGB. We'd hear these demos and say, 'Yeah, the Talking Heads should be playing here. Yes, the Ramones should be playing here. Yeah, let Blondie in.' But Hilly Kristal, the club's owner, was so nice and generous; anybody could play there—once. But we were the catalysts there—the chemical that doesn't itself change a lot, but it allows other chemical reactions to take place."

Taken By the Dead
(1977)

n the 1970s, I had a love-hate mindset when it came to the Grateful Dead. That is to say, I "loved to hate them." It was something I just could not grasp: the seemingly endless jams; the quiet, laidback vocals about Tennessee Jed or a friend of the Devil; and those fans, in some cases high school pals of mine who'd seemingly joined a cult called the Deadheads whose ritual included torturing me with lectures on why I'd be better off leaving my Rolling Stones and New York Dolls and Todd Rundgren in favor of Jerry, Bob and Phil. And how I "just didn't get" why dropping acid at the Nassau Coliseum before the band launched into "Dark Star" was such a cool thing.

A friend of mine, Stephen, loved the Dead. He was 16 like me, and invited me to a show at the Englishtown Raceway with his girlfriend and another girl he wanted to fix me up with. Neither of us drove yet, so he told me his dad (a good guy) would be driving us. I hemmed and hawed. An outdoor Dead show? In the humid, end-of-summer muck? A mini-Woodstock in New Jersey with all of those filthy, disgusting, mud-covered faithful? The New Riders of the Purple Sage and the Marshall Tucker Band (whom I liked a lot) were also playing, and the girl was supposedly pretty, so I caved.

We parked miles from the site, trudged in the rain past thousands of abandoned cars and VW vans, stepped over bodies and eventually found a place about 1,000 yards away from the stage—which was the size of a Chicklet square, the tiny kind. My "date" seemed to hate me, given that I couldn't just

The Grateful Dead in 1977. (Englishtown, New Jersey.)

give in to the moment and enjoy the fourth-world conditions around me (I opted for a Woody Allen-type cynical, observational repertoire that my friend's dad found hilarious). Even Stephen seemed to regret inviting a flat fourth wheel like me, but I couldn't help it—I was miserable. In the mud, the fans danced to the opening bands, spiraling around in an acid haze. They puked. They made love. And they got high. In the middle of it all, on our small raft of a blanket, sat the five of us— straight, sober and a little cranky.

Once the Dead came out, I decided to wander to the stage. It was only a couple of miles away and I needed some exercise. I got semi-close—maybe 30 yards (this is before big screens or anything)—and I watched the band with a critical eye—just how bad were they? Just how many jokes would I get out of this? How crazy would I make my Deadhead friends with my witty observations? Well, once I settled on a spot and took some time to watch, I found myself . . . completely entranced. They were playing a song called "Estimated Prophet," and, like snake charmers, they hypnotized me. All of a sudden, I *got* it; I understood an aspect of this band I'd never understood. The teamwork and the spirit—the intricate yet throwaway together- ness of it all—was stunning. They were monsters, these guys. The real deal. What had I been missing? How could I have been so naïve? This was not at all what I expected. These guys were a rock-and-roll band, and an amazing one at that. Having seen the light, I wandered back to find my little tribe, satisfied. Stephen's dad wanted to leave early to beat the traffic, plus we had miles to walk to try and find the car in the dark. My "date" completely ignored me for the balance of the night ride home, but that was fine. I was thrilled. I had discovered a marvelous band, on my own, in the mud and the rain at a New Jersey racetrack.

Keith Richards
(1977)

A kid in my high school sat a few of us down in the cafeteria with some highly top-secret news. A friend of his mother, a realtor, had just leased a house in nearby South Salem to none other than Keith Richards. For the next two years, we'd stake out the house on an almost weekly basis.

The house sat right near the road and us 17-year-old Stones freaks had it under surveillance constantly. When *People* magazine featured Mick and Keith on the cover, inside was a picture of Keith and his son Marlon on a tire swing that was right by the driveway. We snuck up and looked inside a greenhouse window that had been turned into a photo developing room—incredibly, there were pictures of Jagger there on the front lawn of the house.

We'd dream up excuses to go to the door—for instance, the day after the band's 1978 *SNL* appearance we thought he might be there, so we went hawking my little sister's candy bars for school. A nanny answered, called Marlon over to order a dozen or so bars and paid (inside, a huge portrait of Keith hung over a fireplace).

"Keith home?" I meekly asked.

"Sorry," she smiled sweetly. "He's in the city."

Cars with tinted windows came and went as we spent nights in our cars outside the house. We crept onto his lawn one night and swiped an axe—not a guitar—but a real hatchet. But he was too elusive for us.

By 1979, we were graduating high school, moving on—

but we made one last stand at the Keith house to see if he was there. The ruse that day was that our car was out of water and overheating. A buddy and I knocked on the door, and a young guy—maybe a year older than us—wearing a frock and holding a sheep-herding staff came around the house. He kindly gave us water, knowing (I think) what we were up to.

The house we'd stalk. (South Salem, New York.)

"Keith's not here, guys," he said. "He's in Europe."

Foiled again.

Not long after this odd meeting, something terrible happened at the house. As papers around the world reported, a 17-year-old boy named Scott Cantrell shot himself in the head in actress Anita Pallenberg's bed with a gun owned by Keith Richards. According to reports, Cantrell had been employed as a part-time groundskeeper at the estate and was rumored to be involved with Pallenberg in an intimate relationship. At the time of the shooting, Richards was in Paris recording with the Rolling Stones, but his son with Pallenberg, Marlon, was actually in the home when the tragedy occurred. Pallenberg was arrested, but Cantrell's death was ruled as a suicide in 1980, despite ongoing rumors that Pallenberg and Cantrell had been playing a game of Russian roulette with the gun. Fortunately for Pallenberg, the police investigation confirmed that she was not in the room or on the same floor of the home when the fatal shot was fired.

The kid who gave us water that day was Scott Cantrell, an oft-forgotten Stones casualty who got too close to the fire.

David Johansen
(1978)

"adies and gentleman, from Staten Island, New York, the David Johansen Group!"

In the summer of 1978, those were the words that kicked off a live broadcast of the David Johansen on, I think, WNEW-FM ("Where Rock Lives"—or lived, anyway).

David Johansen, the former lead singer of the New York Dolls, had released his first solo record and was performing all over the New York area to promote it. I was a sophomore in high school, so I'd missed the Dolls era, but I adored their two studio records and was always fascinated by Johansen. He was like an

The David Johansen Group in 1978.

approachable version of Mick Jagger and his picture was always all over *Rock Scene*, the scrapbook-styled rock magazine that featured the work of Lisa Robinson, Lenny Kaye, Bob Gruen and many other NYC-area rock critics and photographers.

With Brian Carr and David Johansen in 1985. (New York City, New York.)

The Johansen show on the radio that night blew me away. The passion, the energy—it was raw, fiery, New York City music that celebrated everything I loved (and hated!) about the city. It was Johansen, but it was also his band that excited me. Guitarists Johnny Rao and Thomas Trask, bassist Buz Verno and drummer Frankie LaRocka, with the addition of former New York Doll Sylvain Sylvain on third guitar, looked like *Mean Streets* extras and they played it tough and soulful behind Johansen's street-smart theatrics and showbiz swagger. Later that year when I heard they'd be playing the nearby Gemini II nightclub, I had to go. It was December when they played up by us in the suburbs, and I could not believe I was going to see this band in person—but it almost didn't happen. See, about two feet of snow blanketed the city that day and night. Still, my friend Patty LaRocco commandeered her family's old blue Cadillac and somehow guided the boat into Yorktown Heights, into the empty parking lot at the Triangle Shopping Center where the club was located. Would the band even show up? The club was open, a good sign. Only a handful of people there, but in the back, near the pinball machines, I saw David Johansen, in a black leather sport coat and pork pie hat, just as he appeared in the pages of *Rock Scene* magazine. His band surrounded him, much the way a Mafioso don is surrounded by his consigliere. Amazing. Evidently, the show would go on.

Shortly after, the band was introduced in front of the sparse crowd, and for 90 minutes or so they tore it up, playing like their lives depended upon it. It didn't matter that the crowd numbered only in the dozens, Johansen and company spoiled us that night and watching them from just a few feet was a rock-and-roll fantasy come to life; a stripped down, furious show that brimmed with desperate soul and Johansen's trademark vaude-ville touches. It was brilliant. They wrapped up, the doors blew open and they disappeared into the snowy night, presumably driving back down to New York City.

About six years later, when I lived in Manhattan, I heard about a little once-a-week show Johansen was doing at a blues bar called Tramps down near Gramercy Park. From the *New York Times*, September 14, 1984:

> The urbane vocalist who was perched on a bar-stool at Tramps the other day, dressed in the tux-edo and black bow-tie that are regulation garb for saloon singers, looked familiar. Long, long ago, in the early 1970s, he made his professional singing debut as the lead vocalist for the legend-ary and somewhat infamous New York Dolls, the progenitors of punk rock. His later rock career as a solo artist is a matter of public record.
>
> To rock aficionados, that singer is David Johansen. But this new person, with his slickly oiled hair and a repertory of songs associated with Fats Waller, Bessie Smith and Wynonie Harris, calls himself Buster Poindexter.
>
> "It all started because there wasn't any-thing to do around here on Monday nights," the pseudonymous Mr. Poindexter recalled between sets. "When I was on the road touring, as David Johansen, of course, I would occasionally bring

a couple of guys from my band down to the Holiday Inn lounges and ask if we could do a couple of songs, and the whole thing kind of grew from there. It was originally just a way to do fun songs, songs I like, songs for adults."

This was the birth of the Johansen over-the-top alter ego that was the rage through the '80s until he shifted gears again, interpreting folk and blues tunes, and then again, completing the circle, back as the front man for the New York Dolls. And I think I went to Tramps about 50 times to watch the evolution.

Later, my son embraced the David Johansen Group, and the Dolls, in a big way.

And so we had to go see the new-model New York Dolls. I'd interviewed Dolls guitarist Sylvain Sylvain for my radio show, so we went backstage to say hi after the show. And then, there was Charlie with them. Talk about connecting the dots: from the Dolls to that winter night long ago in 1978, through the Buster Poindexter era and now back to the "new" New York Dolls. It's weird (and wonderful) when your child starts listening to—even embracing—your music. But when you get to hang out together with those who made that music, forget about it—sensory overload—especially for sentimental saps like me.

R E F L E C T I O N S
from New York Dolls guitarist Sylvain Sylvain

Guitarist Sylvain Sylvain started playing with David Johansen back in the early 1970s. Since then, on and off, the one-time fashion designer has been a part of numerous Johansen projects and today finds himself right back at the beginning, alongside

Sylvain Sylvain, my son and David Johansen backstage at a New York Dolls show in 2008.

the singer as a New York Doll. Here's what Sylvain told me about Johansen, which helps frame what makes him such an important artist:

"David's amazing because he can morph into these rock-and-roll characters and make each one his own. Like you and your son, we see lots of people on the road with all this Johansen baggage, these incredible memories from days gone by, usually starting with the Dolls and then working through all the other records and styles. Whatever he decides to do, he has this knack for interpreting it in a unique way that's totally his. He's amazing."

My First Celebrity Interview: Herman Munster
(1978)

n official definition of one of television's all-time greatest characters, from a press release at the time:

Herman Munster, 5th Earl of Shroudshire (born "Herman" alone), is a fictional character in the CBS sitcom, *The Munsters*, played by Fred Gwynne. The patriarch of the Munster household, Herman is an entity much like Frankenstein's monster, along with Lurch on the show's competitor, *The Addams Family*.

Whatever. To me, Herman was simply one of the silliest, most earnest and loveable characters in the history of television. He was a big baby of a beast who, though he scared whatever he came in contact with, was gentle and kind-hearted to a fault.

In my junior year of high school, 1978, we had a class that did critical analysis of several films. One of the assignments was to write a piece on the actor or actress of our choice; someone we felt brought their craft to a higher level. I chose to write about Fred Gwynne—that's right, Herman Munster. I was a *Munsters* nut as a kid and since I knew Fred Gwynne lived nearby, I thought I'd up the ante and actually interview the subject of my report in person. My mom had pointed him out a few times in the supermarket and it was always kind of weird to see him out of character—I hadn't seen him yet in the classic *On the Waterfront*, but there was a *Munsters* episode where, after getting struck by lightning, he looks "normal." (It was Fred Gwynne, sans makeup). The episode spooked me a little as a kid, so disturbing was it for me to see the "real Herman," so when I saw him in person, it brought back the strange memory of the episode.

Gwynne's phone number was listed, so I simply called him one day and he answered. As you may remember, his voice was as distinctive as James Earl Jones's, so it was bizarre to be talking with "Herman." He said he'd be happy to talk and he invited me over. I brought my tape recorder, and for the half hour I was there, he was fantastic—funny, engaging and a great storyteller. But there was a problem—his language was incredibly profane. He wove F-words so seamlessly into conversation that, after a while, I almost started doing it, so natural did it seem. There was nothing offensive about it—evidently, he just spoke like that.

After listening to the tape at home, I had a dilemma: out Herman Munster as foul-mouthed (though charming) actor, or sanitize the piece and protect the once green-faced TV icon? Once protective of your heroes, always protective, I guess, because I scrubbed the interview down and presented Fred Gwynne as a bland, banal, innocuous character.

My teacher, after reading the piece, called me in one day after school. He said he loved the effort of getting Gwynne. But he was surprised. "I'd always heard he was a salty, funny, sort of outrageous guy. So I was a little disappointed to see that he's so normal."

Scarlet Letters
(1979)

'll never forget the first "official" piece I ever had published. I've spoken to other writers over the years that feel the same way about the charge you feel once your name appears in print. Not letters to the editor, school papers or being quoted in an article, I'm talking about writing a piece for a commercial publication and getting paid for it. For me, as a teenager, I equated the sensation with that of entering a secret society, a vaunted cosmic arena where the likes of Ben Franklin, Mark Twain, Ernest Hemingway and Dorothy Parker all hung around together swapping witty anecdotes and showing off their collective rapier wits; a velvet underground where Bukowski, Kerouac and Ginsberg held court while creating brilliant literary madness into the night. Being published was your ticket to the other side, away from the unwashed, *unpublished* masses, and into a private world where only a select group of chosen thinkers has earned the privilege of entry . . . right?

I mean, it didn't matter where you were first published, be it *Colliers*, the *New Yorker*, the *Atlantic Monthly* or . . . the *Rock Music Machine*.

Never heard of the *Rock Music Machine*? It was a free publication distributed throughout the suburbs in northern Westchester County where I grew up. It covered local bands along with bigger bands that occasionally came through, and if a big band did play the area, odds are it would have happened at the Gemini II nightclub—which is where this story begins.

Tucked in the back corner of the Triangle Shopping Center in Yorktown Heights, the Gemini was a haunt for many of us who grew up in the mid-to-late 1970s in the pretty suburbs of Westchester, less than an hour from New York City. They had a big, cutting-edge video projection screen, a set-up that involved three light cannons (blue, green and red) firing images against what looked to be a small movie screen suspended over the bar. On that screen would be music performances cribbed from shows like *Don Kirshner* and *The Midnight Special*, with a steady stream of bands like Blue Öyster Cult, Black Oak Arkansas, David Bowie and the Rolling Stones in heavy rotation.

The Gemini had a front door policy more porous than the U.S.-Mexican border when it came to keeping out slightly underage patrons (toting ridiculously doctored fake IDs), but more importantly, they had live music. There were other local places, like the Fore-n-Aft way up in Brewster and a few others, but nothing like the Gemini, at least not in Westchester. This was a large space that held up to about 400 people, with two bars, a mirrored disco ball and a terrific stage-sound-lights setup that produced many sweaty, beer-fueled rock-and-roll nights for a lot of us. There were local bands, popular area-acts such as Rat Race Choir, Fountainhead and Southern Cross, up-and-comers like Twisted Sister, cover bands such as the Crystal Ship and occasional legends such as Rick Derringer, Edgar Winter and David Johansen who would pack the place.

The Richie Scarlet Band (c. 1979).

There was also Richie Scarlet. Scarlet was a local, jet-black-haired singer-guitarist in his early twenties who had this amazing trash-glam look and energy that created a buzz as soon as he started playing regular shows with his band at the Gemini. If Keith Richards and Steven Tyler had a baby, it would probably have looked something like him (right down to the blonde streak of hair Scarlet had, just the way Richards had dyed it in 1972). His songs were flashy and cool, not unlike early Aerosmith and the New York Dolls; his stage presence was electric and his guitar playing, superb. He felt like the real deal, an embryonic rock-and-roll star in our midst, and many of us

A copy of the Richie Scarlet 45 for "Nothing Is Sacred."

got stuck in the orbit. We felt like we were watching an arena-ready legend in the making and so we caught his show as much as we could as high school seniors in 1979.

Watching Scarlet gave me an idea—why not pitch an article about him to the magazine? I wanted to write, and I doubt there was an issue of *Creem, Circus, Rolling Stone* or *Rock Scene* that I had missed since about eighth grade, so I was familiar with the formula. I looked up the name of the publisher on the masthead, called him, and he invited me to come pitch my idea in his office the next day. This was easy!

I expected *Rock Music Machine* headquarters to be a decadent, rambling rock-and-roll pad where musicians lolled around giving interviews and getting high while up-and-coming rock journalists like me and Cameron Crowe bashed away on typewriters, bottling up all that rock-and-roll lightning in print form so that legions of fans would be able to vicariously live out their dreams via our exclusive access to the rock gods. Instead, it was one tiny room where the publisher, a bald, heavy-set, fast-talking forty-ish guy, chain-smoked while making cold calls to try and sell ad space in the magazine. However, he was familiar with Richie Scarlet and said, "Great! Get me an interview and we'll put him on the cover. I love that guy! And I'll pay you 20 bucks, no expenses." I had my shot. All I had to do now was pitch Mr. Scarlet. On my way out the guy yelled, "Hey, know anybody that wants to buy the inside cover ad? I'm getting screwed over here!"

A few nights later, after watching yet another blistering set at the Gemini, I made my move. Scarlet had emerged from the tiny "backstage" area (basically a beer case storage closet), eyeliner still running from his intense performance, and was at the bar getting a beer. A small gang of admirers, mostly female and pretty in that then-popular tube-top-powder-blue-eye-shadow-suburban-slut look, buzzed near Scarlet like summer June bugs around a fluorescent porch light. I edged my way in, tapped Scarlet's shoulder and, over the music that was thundering over the house system, told him my idea. As I spoke, he put his ear right to my mouth, nodding the whole time. Then he cupped his hand and spoke into my ear. "Cool, call me." He bummed a pen from the bartender, wrote his number on a napkin and pushed it in my hand. As I left, one of the girls followed me outside.

"Is that his number?" she whined. "I've been trying to get that. Come on, give me his number." Then begging. "Please? *Puh-leeze!*" This was a taste of what it must be like to be Richie Scarlet—this was a taste of rock and roll.

The next morning, I called Richie and from his groggy whisper, I assumed I'd woken him up. He said no problem, when did I want to come over and interview him? He told me he rented the basement of a house in Mahopac, which was just a few towns over from me. I had started teaching tennis at a camp right near his house so we made a plan for the next day.

After teaching tennis, I got changed before heading over for the interview. After all, I couldn't show up wearing Adidas shorts and a white Lacoste shirt, not in the presence of the serpentine, black-leather-and-mascared Mr. Scarlet. No, to win his respect (and thus secure a more telling interview), I'd wear my New York Dolls T-shirt and, incomprehensibly, tight, white

Jordache jeans (what was I think-ing?).

He lived in a pleasant split-level on a woodsy street that ran alongside a lake. Did the neighbors know about this? They allowed this debauched, sinewy, black leather-clad rock-er to live amongst their pretty coeds, cheerleaders and field hockey players? Richie Scarlet? Maybe they didn't know. Maybe he was under the suburban radar. As he'd told me, he rented the basement apartment. That must be it—they didn't know he lived there.

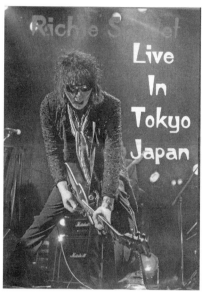

Richie Scarlet: Live in Tokyo, Japan DVD.

A separate door to the side of the house allowed me in from the thick July heat and down into his cool, dark, cave-like dwelling. He met me just inside the door—not the raucous madman I'd seen so often at the Gemini, but a soft-spoken, laid-back scarecrow who was killing time with Iggy, the giant pet iguana he allowed to run free on a giant fishnet that had been tacked up canopy-style across the ceiling. For about an hour, with my tape recorder running, he answered my questions in a sensitive, world-weary tone that was more like an aged vet-eran rocker as opposed to the sparkly, vibrant young force that he was. He even went to an upright piano to play me a sweet ballad called "Eyes of an Angel," sort of like when Nigel Tufnel sits down at the piano in *This is Spinal Tap* to caress a shim-mery melody, thus proving he's not just an insensitive heavy metalist. (Nigel's tune was called "Lick My Love Pump.")

Still, this was "another shade of scarlet" (what I con-sidered titling the piece) and it was my look from inside the hurricane that was his life at that point. This interview would set the rock world on its ear, and might even propel *Rock Music Machine* into that pantheon of truly *important* rock rags. I had struck glitter and gold. After the interview, a woman in the house (the owner, if I recall) took a picture of Richie and me to run in the magazine and then I rushed home to peck out my opus on a Selectric typewriter. For a couple of days I sweated over the interview, adding plenty of my own thoughts about Scarlet's life as he sat perched on the cusp of certain rock immortality. This was it. 1979's defining piece of rock journalism. Would I even need college after this? What would Clapton, Townshend and Jagger do without me? Who would tell *their* stories?

I submitted the piece (entitled "Richie Scarlet—Rock Star on the Rise") and while the publisher made no changes, I'm not even sure he actually even read the whole thing (though he did call me on the phone and yell, "Know anybody that wants to buy the back cover ad? I'm getting screwed over here!").

A week later, there it was on the cover, distributed for free (along with the Penny-Saver and Recycler) in almost every 7–Eleven, mini-mart and liquor store in northern Westchester. There was a huge picture of Richie performing and a tiny inset shot of the two of us. Wherever I saw it, I'd stand by the rack, waiting to be recognized, perhaps by the girl buying a fistful of Slim Jims to go with her bottle of Boone's Farm Strawberry Hill Wine and pocket-sized canister of spearmint-flavored Binaca. Never happened, but hey, I was still published.

With Richie, the day of the big interview in 1979.

Soon after, I went to see Richie Scarlet play and proudly brought him some copies of the piece. The second he saw me, he came over and gave me a hug. "Loved the piece, man, great job." Wow, he'd already seen it! That rest of the summer, whenever I saw him play, he'd usually give me a little wave or wink from the stage, always impressive if I had a date with me. "Yeah, Richie and I worked together on a project recently."

The Gemini II is gone, but the building remains today. (Yorktown Heights, New York.)

As it turned out, after returning to earth, I did leave for college that fall. The rock gods would just have to wait. And while I wrote extensively in my college paper, nothing ever matched the thrill of that first piece.

I also didn't go back to the Gemini much after that. There were new priorities in life, and music was changing. The classic stuff I loved was being swapped out by more and more big-haired metal bands, which didn't really do it for me.

Years later, after going to a movie at a nearby theater, I walked over and found the club was gone, transformed into office space. I looked in through the window and pictured everything—the stage, the bar and the backstage dressing area. My mind drifted back through the fog of time and somewhere in the distance, I could almost hear a bouncer saying (after studying my fake ID up close with a police flashlight), "What Zodiac sign are you, asshole?" I could hear Rick Derringer tearing through "Rock and Roll, Hoochie Koo," David Johansen pounding out "Funky But Chic" and Richie Scarlet playing for his life (and for us) on those sweltering summer nights back in 1979.

As the years went on, I'd occasionally think about Richie Scarlet (especially whenever I'd find an old, yellowed copy of that article in a box in the garage or someplace—I must have collected 2,000 of them).

I've never played guitar on a stage in front of a lot of people, so I'm not sure what that feeling is like. But I imagine it's exciting, and sort of dream-like—just like the first time a writer sees an article with their name next to it.

R E F L E C T I O N S
from musician Richie Scarlet

I tracked down Richie Scarlet today and shared the previous piece with him. Still a busy, successful guitarist and singer, he remembered this period vividly—right down to his pet iguana.

"Chris, this took me back in a way that's hard to describe. You captured that period in my life that was so insane, but so memorable to me because I was doing exactly what I wanted to be doing. It was before I learned all about the 'business' of rock and roll, when I was just feeling it, playing what I wanted to be playing and not worrying about anything. Man, those late '70s were something. I had managers that wanted to mold me into the next this or that but I had none of that—I always stuck to my guns.

"Starting in the 1980s, I became sort of a hired gun for guys like Alice Cooper, Sebastian Bach, the Outlaws, Ace Frehley from Kiss and plenty of other guys who I still play with today. Sometimes I wonder if it hurt my solo career, but hey, you've gotta make a living. I still find time for my solo stuff and I've gotten to see the world many times around so, thinking back, I'm pretty sure I made the right decisions. It's like God had this plan for me and I'm just going along with it and staying true to myself creatively. That's what it's all about for me. But man, thanks again for the trip back. Reading the story made me remember exactly how it was, which was very cool."

Chapter Two

parachute pants

CHIA PETS

denim jackets

Rubik's Cubes

RAINBOW BRITE

Care Bears Atari Trivial Pursuit

"Where's the Beef?"

Pee-wee Herman Pac-Man SIMON

Apple computers

KOOSH BALLS

Members Only jackets

neon everything Hackey Sacks

SPANDEX

Cabbage Patch Dolls Nintendo

having your collar up

Vans shoes Ray-Ban

Swatch watches

Miami Vice Shasta soda

Teenage Mutant Ninja Turtles

Sony Walkmans

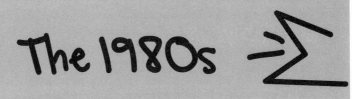
The 1980s

Doc Martens

Garbage Pail Kids

GOBOTS

legwarmers worn over jeans

moonwalking

roller skating rinks

MOLLY RINGWALD

Garfield

JELLY SHOES

MTV

My Little Pony

CONNECT FOUR

Thriller

break dancing

Dungeons and Dragons

hair metal bands

mullet haircuts

video arcades

John Hughes films

Spuds Mackenzie

sunglasses

California Raisins

Transformers

BIG HAIR

"Just Say No"

And my personal favorites from the era:

TV Shows
Square Pegs (1982–1983)
Newhart (1982–1990)
Highway to Heaven (1984–1989)
Moonlighting (1985–1989)
Ray Bradbury Theater (1985–1986, 1988–1992)
Crime Story (1986–1988)
It's Garry Shandling's Show (1986–1990)
Mystery Science Theater 3000 (1988–1999)
America's Most Wanted (1988–present)
The Simpsons (1989–present)

Movies
Atlantic City (1980)
Raging Bull (1980)
Raiders of the Lost Ark (1981)
This Is Spinal Tap (1984)
Lost in America (1985)
Hannah and Her Sisters (1986)
Hoosiers (1986)
Moonstruck (1987)
The Princess Bride (1987)
Cinema Paradiso (1988)

Albums

Scary Monsters (and Super Creeps)
   by David Bowie (1980)
Bella Donna by Stevie Nicks (1981)
Discipline by King Crimson (1981)
Swordfishtrombones by Tom Waits (1983)
Skylarking by XTC (1986)
Flash Light by Tom Verlaine (1987)
Strangeways, Here We Come by The Smiths
   (1987)
I'm Your Man by Leonard Cohen (1988)
Nearly Human by Todd Rundgren (1989)
New York by Lou Reed (1989)

Killed By the Dead
(1980)

n college, I knew this group of Deadheads. It consisted of three average guys who'd wear things like beaded headbands and hippie vests and one gorgeous girl, Jill. She was a lithe, blonde stunner with massive blue eyes—a thoroughly beguiling beauty. They'd hang out at the school radio station while I was on the air (which was a lot). Then sometimes we'd go get a bite to eat at the student union when I was done. They were a nice, laid-back lot, always talking about the Dead, and one got the feeling that all of the three guys were making a play for Jill. If one got the feeling that I was also making a play for Jill as well, one would have been right, because I was. One day while we were all fumbling over ourselves trying to impress Jill (they with their Dead knowledge, me with "comedic" observations about student life), it came out that this quartet was planning a long, strange Dead road trip over spring break, driving to Chicago, Cleveland and a few other places where the band was playing. They'd be heading out in a van, and I'll admit I was a bit jealous thinking that someone might finally win Jill over and make her their conquest. Oh well. I wished them a good trip, and in a day or so, packed my car and headed home for a week.

Weeks later, back at school, I saw the group at a table in the student union. Only now, they were a trio. Jill was not there and the guys looked glum, morose, even.

"What's up?" I asked. (Translation: "Where's Jill?")

Within minutes, they told the tale. At tour stop number

one, Chicago, a roadie approached Jill.

"Would you like to meet Bob Weir after the show?"

The guys were thrilled. "We're gonna meet Bob Weir!"

Well, long story short, Weir didn't want to sleep with the guys, just Jill, so she was plucked from their small world of student unions and vans, and placed on the fast track of a bona fide Dead tour. The guys were left to shuffle back to school while Jill took an extra week away to travel with the band. The guys were shattered. Their band, their *raison d'être*, had swiped the one thing that truly defined them—their girl, Jill. They were shell-shocked. No more *American Beauty*; no more *Workingman's Dead, Blues for Allah* or *Aoxomoxoa*. It was over.

I saw Jill a week or so later at school. She no longer hung out with those guys. Or me. Or anyone else. She had reached some higher plane and was no longer part of our gene pool. She knew things we'd never know, having morphed into a groupie goddess who no doubt had other conquests ahead of her. I recovered soon after. As for the guys, I wouldn't be surprised if they were still at that table, confused, broken and adrift—killed by the Dead.

The World at Ease
(1981)

In 1981, a cable television company opened in nearby Yorktown Heights. I'd read about something called "public access television," whereby the company had to allow the public a certain amount of airtime. But they also had video equipment that was available, including a camera, lighting, even a small production studio. I'd always wanted to create and host a talk show that would allow me to travel around and conduct unstructured interviews with interesting people, sort of like Charles Kuralt did.

When I visited the studio, the man who ran the place, an avuncular military veteran named Ed Champagne said, "You should meet this kid, Tony Sonnanstine. He wants to be a cameraman and maybe you guys could work something out." So Tony and I met. And we got along. And for about three years, the world was our public access oyster.

It all started with a show idea I had called "The World at Ease" (title based on a popular documentary show, *The World at War*—I humbly thought my show could counter all the mayhem with some relaxed, NPR-style conversation). Together, the

A promo photo for my show.

Another promo photo for my show.

two of us traversed the tri-state area (and beyond), learning more about production (and life) than I think we could ever be aware of. I'd arrange the interviews, cold calling celebrities, artists, writers—whomever I could get on the phone. Then Tony would grab the gear and off we'd go. We'd edit the shows later and each week we'd start all over again. Eventually, they made it on to Manhattan cable TV in New York City, which expanded our audience, thus making it easier for me to get guests.

Looking back, it's amazing that Tony and I were able to pull off what we did, but there were no rules yet; we made a lot if up as we went along and it ended up providing some amazing experiences that we'd both use later on in life. It was a crazy time for me, juggling way too many college credits (23 in one semester and 28 in another—an Emerson College record they told me) and constantly scrambling to try and get guests, tape shows, edit, etcetera. But what wonderful, colorful chaos.

Some stories about just a few of our dozens of segments:

Tony tapes me doing a "stand up" near the USS *Intrepid* in the early 1980s. (New York City, New York.)

John Waters

With director John Waters.

ack then, you could look John Waters up in the Baltimore directory. My attitude was then as it is now: if you want something you have to make an effort and go for it—it never hurts to ask. I was a huge fan of his, from *Pink Flamingos*, *Desperate Living* and what was then his newest shock masterpiece, *Polyester* (presented in "Odorama"—actually a card with scented numbers on it, and the audience was cued on what number circle to scratch and sniff during the movie). So I called Mr. Waters up at home, asked about an interview and he told me to meet him in New York the next week at the office of New Line Cinema. Tony and I trudged down, me from college in Boston and Tony from nearby Westchester County (during the school year, I'd get burned out from a lot of this, but still, it was worth it). We met John in a small conference room at his film company's offices, and for more than an hour we chatted and he told stories. He was amazing: open, funny and outrageous in this polite, buttoned-up way. We actually sort of hit it off, to a point where he told me about a party they were having in the city the next week for Divine, the transvestite superstar of so many Waters classics. So I drove back down to New York to the club where this get-together was taking place. John remembered me right away, introduced me to Divine, Edith Massey and the rest of his off-

With Janice Montecalvo and Divine in 1982.

beat troupe of players. Andy Warhol was there ("Don't you just love Hollywood?" he said to me at the bar), and as the night wore it became Fellini-esque as other legends of the New York underground came to see Divine, John and everyone else. For me, this was a trip into a netherworld I'd never have the chance to see were it not for my little cable TV show, and I remember thinking that night, "I have to keep doing this public access cable show because it is providing me private access," which I really enjoyed.

The Cramps

In bed with one of my favorite bands then, the Cramps.

My memory is a bit thin on this episode, though I do remember that I ended up interviewing the great L.A.-based band the Cramps on their hotel bed in Boston at about four in the morning before they left for the airport for a dawn flight back to the coast. And I have a picture to prove it.

Quentin Crisp

I saw the famous British writer Quentin Crisp on David Letterman one night and I found him fascinating. He was funny, erudite, and a wonderful storyteller. I'd known that he became a gay icon in the 1970s after his memoir, *The Naked Civil Servant*, focused attention on his flamboyant lifestyle and his flair for exhibitionism. I didn't care so much about that—I just thought he'd make a great guest because of how entertaining he was and so I called him (he was listed in the Manhattan white pages).

With author Quentin Crisp.

"Oh yessss?" he hissed devilishly as he answered the phone.

I explained my idea, and he invited me and my cameraman Tony (along with my then-girlfriend Janice, who shot some wonderful photos during this time while taking part in the production of the show) over to his tiny apartment down on Great Jones Street in lower Manhattan to tape a segment. The delicate, elderly thin-faced man with purple-streaked hair greeted us at the door. It was so small in there I had to sit on the bed with him to tape our interview and, like John Waters, he told interesting story after story. After this interview, Mr. Crisp would call me at school and at home, just to talk late at night. I'd listen as he'd critique films he'd seen and books he'd read (or was writing), and talked about how he may have spent that particular day. It was interesting, to say the least.

He also seemed lonely, and whenever I was in his neighborhood, as a courtesy, I'd call to see if I could drop off some milk or bread or any other staple. If he were home, he'd take me up on it. Crisp loved chatting with the girl I was dating once I graduated from college (he'd give her

A look at how crazy my days were back then. Interviewing actors Fred Gwynne and Jose Ferrer and author John Cheever on a single day.

hair and makeup advice—he was quite flamboyant) and even invited us to some risqué off-off-*off*-Broadway plays with him, which we escorted him to. Over time, we lost touch and then I moved to California. But I always took note when I'd see him on TV or saw something in the paper about him.

When I read of his passing in 1999, I thought back to those days of knocking on his door to drop off groceries and visit. Somewhere packed away in a box, I have a copy of his book, *How to Become a Virgin*. In it he inscribed, "Chris, if you want to become a virgin, simply go on television." I never quite figured that one out.

The Lords of the New Church

My God, this was one of my favorite episodes—an on-the-road documentary with the punk rock supergroup, the Lords of the New Church. The band featured punk pioneers Stiv Bators (the Dead Boys) and Brian James (the Damned), with Dave Tregunna (Sham 69) and Nicky Turner (the Barracudas). From Boston to Providence to New York City, we rode along with these guys, interviewing them and shooting concert footage at each club where they played. It was insane. Stiv and I sort of bonded and spent hours talking together. I once had to help the road manager carry him from the stage when the crowds became semi-violent—it was really fun and out of control. They wouldn't leave for the club until after Johnny Carson's monologue, which we'd watch at the ho-

In a hotel room with punk supergroup the Lords of the New Church.

tel. These funny Brit-
ish guys *loved* Carson's
monologue. The funniest
memory I have with them
happened when we were
all crammed into a taxi
in Boston going back to
their hotel after dinner.
At a red light, the Chicago song "If You Leave Me
Now" came on the radio.
The milquetoast ballad
droned on for a minute
or so before everyone in

With punk legend Stiv Bators.

the car erupted in spontaneous laughing spasms so harsh—I
thought Stiv would choke to death—the song's lameness striking everyone at the same moment.

Once we got to New York, we all went to see Johnny
Thunders at the Mudd Club, and Stiv kept telling me how upset
he was by all of the drugs Thunders was taking (which seemed
strange, given the amounts of cocaine Stiv was ingesting right
in front of me). I had so much fun with these guys, though. It
was their first tour together and there were lots of challenges.
They asked us a million questions about what it was like to
grow up in the States and when it came time to say goodbye,
these tough, black-leather punks got very sentimental—we left
among hugs and sweet goodbyes.

I remember hearing the news in 1990 that Bators had
died. He was hit by a taxi cab while walking across a street in
Paris, where he was living at the time. The reports said that he
was rushed to a hospital, but up and left after several hours of
waiting, without seeing a physician. He died later in his sleep
from injuries sustained in the collision. It was an odd, seemingly preventable death that made me sad and brought back
that funny memory of Stiv and the guys cracking up in the taxi
when that lame Chicago song came on.

Johnny Thunders

N ew York Dolls fan that I was, I arranged to interview Johnny Thunders once in Boston, just after I'd graduated. He

Johnny Thunders in 1982.

was so out of it, though, that I
stopped the tape (Tony wasn't
at this session—I had a kid
I went to school with shoot
it). I didn't want there to be
evidence of Thunders in this
condition—he could barely
speak—yet he was amazing
onstage that night, playing
with a fury and finesse that
didn't seem possible while he
was on the nod backstage dur-
ing our "interview." But he almost collapsed at the end; I carried him from the stage to a cab in front of the club and when he
asked me for some money, I gave him what I had, about $10.

Todd Rundgren

N ext to the Roll-
ing Stones, Todd
Rundgren was (and still
is) my favorite musician.
I think he's also one of the
most under-appreciated
artists in history, but that
would be a whole other
book. Todd Rundgren and
Utopia shows through the
1970s and early 1980s are

**With Todd Rundgren in a hotel
lobby in 1981. (Rochester,
New York.)**

some of my most precious memories. How he's not in the Rock and Roll Hall of Fame. . . . How's he not?— I'll shut up. But doing *The World at Ease* gave me some big thrills includ- ing the chance to work on some Todd Rundgren projects, culminating in this one.

A shot from a TV show I did on Todd Rundgren.

He and Utopia were playing a club called Metro in Boston. I'd al- ready interviewed Todd for my program, had been up to his Utopia Video studio in Woodstock* a bunch of times while working on a school proj- ect and I did a piece with him for a show on the ABC affiliate in Boston. I sug- gested that the club tape this performance. After all, they had a five-camera set-up and they loved the idea, but they left it to me to call Todd's people and

After my big directorial debut.

*Those were the days when there was a very cute little girl, four or five years old, named Liv running around Todd's place. Who knew that one day, she'd grow up to be Liv Tyler? You might remember the story of how Liv's beautiful mom, Bebe Buell, raised Liv with the assistance of Todd, who for years had a relationship with Buell. As it was revealed later though, Todd wasn't her biological father as we all believed back then—it's actually Aerosmith lead singer Steven Tyler.

make the arrangements—so I did. Chris Anderson, Todd's well-known sound guy got back to me and said it was a go. He sent me the set list and I wrote a basic shooting script for the show.

A backstage pass for the big night I directed the taping of a Todd Rundgren/Utopia show at Metro in 1982. (Boston, Massachusetts.)

When the night came to do it, the guy at club who ran all of the video set-up didn't recognize any of the songs (he'd expected a vintage Todd Rundgren set, which this was not to be) and so he told me I could do it. It was the biggest thrill of my life, donning the headset and calling the shots for a show (that actually ended up being released commercially years later—*Utopia Live in Boston*). Being a big fan of an artist is one thing, but when you actually work on something that contributes to their catalog, it's like you have a bit of a link. And again, without my little show, the opportunity never would have presented itself.

With author Jim Carroll.

Jim Carroll

One night I got to interview (for the second time) one of my favorite writers, Jim Carroll. He had also started fronting a rock-and-roll band by then and this was backstage before he played. I had brought along my copy of his classic book, *The Basketball Diaries*, and I asked if he'd do a short reading from the book for my show. He did. Then we watched the Celtics-Knicks game on TV backstage before his set began and this former NYC high school star analyzed almost every play. He had run out of cigarettes when it was time to play and asked if I could go down the street to buy him two packs of Marlboros. As big a fan of his as I was, I was actually honored to be asked and when I came back he was already onstage. He motioned for me to flip him a pack, which I did, and then right before he did the next number, "City Drops into Night," my favorite song, he thanked me on mic. Little moments like that made me crazy—in the grand scheme of things, no big deal, but for a fan, totally unforgettable.

Taking My Turn

think my favorite *World at Ease* was this one, because the experience went on for years after the interviews. *Taking My Turn* was an off-Broadway musical revue put together by director Robert H. Livingston, composer Gary William Friedman and lyricist Will Holt. The show was inspired by the reflections of people who were growing old. It was uplifting, revelatory and a celebration of age, wisdom and maturity. And what a cast. It included Margaret Whiting, the veteran pop singer; Cissy Houston (Whitney's mom—I met the teenaged Whitney the day I interviewed Cissy) and Marni Nixon, who had dubbed the singing of such movie actresses as Deborah Kerr (*The King and*

An ad for *Taking My Turn*.

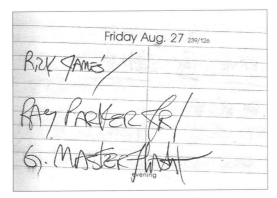

Friday Aug. 27 239/126

Rick James'

Ray Parker Jr /

6. Master Flash

evening

More craziness: Rick James, Ray Parker Jr. and Grandmaster Flash—all in one day!

Gannett/Howie Swetz

Christian Epting ... on camera.

Riding the video vortex

By Noreen O'Donnell

Two futile trips across the country taught Christian Epting how hard it is to get a job on a television show. So he returned to Goldens Bridge and started his own.

Videopinions, Epting's half-hour show, airs once a week on both Westchester Cable

An article back then about what I was up to.

I) and Audrey Hepburn (*My Fair Lady*)—she's also the mom of pop star Andrew Gold. And there was Tiger Haynes.

Tiger was perhaps best known for his dazzling portrayal of the Tin Man in the original Broadway cast of *The Wiz*. Originally a member of the seminal vocal group, the Three Flames, he was also seen fairly regularly on TV on programs such as *The Cosby Show* and *In the Heat of the Night*. Later in life, he also appeared in several high-profile films including *All That Jazz* and *Moscow on the Hudson*. He was a bawdy, outrageous man with more personality and lust for life than anyone I've ever known. Both my family and I came to love Tiger deeply and, again, our relationship became one more example of how my little cable show delivered big in my life. One quick anecdote about Tiger: We'd have dinner many nights after his show and I'd also bring family members to see *Tak-ing My Turn*. His favorite word was "m———r" and he used it as a noun, adverb, adjective—you name it. When my Uncle Fred and Aunt Mildred were set to meet Tiger after a matinee, I told him, "Look, these are elegant people, watch the language, huh?" Tiger was impeccable with them—classy, reserved, charming. As they walked away from the front of the Entermedia Theater, Tiger yelled, "Good meeting you . . . m———s!" to their dismay. That was Tiger.

A promo photo for my show.

R E F L E C T I O N S
from Tony Sonnanstine

As The World at Ease *wound down near the time I graduated school (and thus needed to start making money), I created a show called* Videopinions, *which was a review show of music videos. To make some money, I sold time on the show to help cover costs, and then wrote and created the commercials myself for my sponsors. It wasn't enough to live on, but it helped me cut my teeth in the advertising business—and came in handy later in life when I was writing commercials for a living.*

And Tony was certainly affected by the experience. Since then, he's made his living as one of the best cameramen in the business, traveling the world for CNN and many other outlets doing what he does. The education Tony and I got was price-less—as were the adventures.

I tracked down my former production partner in crime

for a look back on this time, and this is what he had to say:

The times that I spent shooting stories with Chris started me on the path that I have been on for the last 30 or so years. Working with him was one of the cherished memories that I have from my youth.

With Tony, reunited in 2009.

The show that we used to do together, *The World at Ease*, was a half-hour-ish program about things that interested me and Chris. One show that I really remember was the one with Quentin Crisp (not just because I had the lamest sideburns that ever walked the earth) because he was on Letterman at the time and he was famous, but he lived in a cold water flat. That was one of the first times that I realized that fame doesn't really equate with riches. It opened my young eyes to the real world.

The shows that we did were fun and interesting. One time, we interviewed John Waters and I remember one of the things that annoyed him was when he is in a cab and the driver would talk to him on the assumption that if you're a guy, you're into sports. He was wondering about the commonality of sports and why that would be the "guy touchstone" (that is, for you kids, when cabbies were mostly white men). It's funny that after 20-plus years, I would remember that line.

The programs that Chris and I did still resonate with me to this day. They gave me a look at the world and the people that had their place in it, and it gave me the courage to find my place in the world.

Albee Darned
(1981)

The playwright Edward Albee was speaking in Boston during my junior year in college and I was anxious to hear him speak. *Who's Afraid of Virginia Woolf*, *The Zoo Story* and *The American Dream* were just a few of his most famous plays and up until that point, I had really enjoyed reading much of Mr. Albee's work. In particular, I enjoyed his Theatre of the Absurd leanings and sharp, biting dialogue. This was 1981 and he had just adapted *Lolita* from the novel by Nabokov, as well as just finishing a play called *The Man Who Had Three Arms*. He's quite famous as you might know, and so the huge auditorium was packed but for a few seats in the very last row when I got there, just a few minutes from the lecture start time. The clear autumn night was unusually cold, and so I was bundled up. The room was warm, though, so I used the aisle seat for my jacket, gloves and sweater. It probably looked like I was holding the seat for someone,

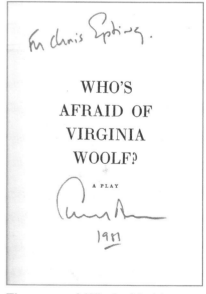

The copy of *Who's Afraid of Virginia Woolf* playwright Edward Albee signed the night of this story.

but I was there alone and so when an older, distinguished-looking gentleman with glasses and salt-and-pepper hair peeked in the door, looked around at the packed hall and then down at the seat, I offered it to him—and he happily took it.

Looking around the hall he nodded his head and said to me, "Good crowd."

I was looking over my copy of *Virginia Woolf*, on the seemingly impossible chance that I might get it signed. Not with this mob. But I surveyed the crowd and I had to agree. The place was crackling with a pre-Albee buzz that was genuinely exciting.

"Who's speaking tonight?" he asked me.

And then I realized that it was the great playwright himself, running late and catching his breath before he had to head down to the stage to be introduced. Everybody around us was too caught up talking about Albee to realize that Albee was right next to them.

"Just some hack," I said, in a lame attempt to be funny. "I don't think he's supposed to be very good but we'll see."

"That we will," Albee agreed.

He got up to head down toward the stage and, before leaving, said quietly, "Want me to sign your book?" So he did, and then he ambled down to the stage where he met the moderator, was introduced and then gave a wonderful speech to a rapt, standing-room-only audience.

So pay attention. You never know who might be sitting right next to you (and keep a pen handy).

Norman Mailer
(1982)

s a junior at Emerson College in Boston, I had another run-in with a famous writer. It happened at a movie theater at Coolidge Corner, near Brookline, Massachusetts where my apartment was. The Coolidge Corner Theatre was (and is) a classic, a 1933 Art Deco cinema house that always showed something small, interesting, foreign, offbeat or all of the above. I forget what it was that I was going to see, but it didn't matter. What did matter was that Norman Mailer was also going to see it, just another quiet matinee-goer joining the perhaps 10 of us who were ducking out of the afternoon sun to enjoy a film. He was right next to me in the lobby, he seemed to notice that I recognized him and so he nodded without smiling. I couldn't help myself.

"How does it feel to have helped a killer get out of prison so that he could kill someone six weeks later?"

That's what Mailer had done. In 1965, a 21-year-old man named Jack Henry Abbott was serving a sentence for forgery in a Utah prison when he stabbed a fellow inmate to death. He was given a sentence of three to 23 years for this offense, and in 1971 his

The Coolidge Corner Theatre, where I told off Norman Mailer. (Boston, Massachusetts.)

sentence was increased by a further 19 years after he escaped and committed a bank robbery in Colorado. Behind bars, he was troublesome and spent much time in solitary confinement.

In 1977, he read that author Norman Mailer was writing about convicted killer Gary Gilmore. Abbott wrote to Mailer, alleging that Gilmore was largely embroidering his experiences, and offered to write about his time behind bars in order to provide a more factual depiction of life behind bars. Mailer agreed and helped to publish *In the Belly of the Beast,* a book on life in the prison system consisting of Abbott's letters to Mailer.

Mailer supported Abbott's attempts to gain parole. Abbott was released on parole in June 1981, despite the misgivings of prison officials, many of whom questioned Abbott's mental state and whether he was rehabilitated. After leaving prison, Abbott went to New York City and was the toast of the literary scene for a short while.

On the morning of July 18, 1981, just six weeks after getting out of prison, Jack Abbott went to a small café called the Binibon in Manhattan. He argued with 22-year-old Richard Adan, son-in-law of the restaurant's owner. Adan, a budding actor and playwright, told him that the restroom was for staff use only. The short-tempered Abbott stabbed Adan in the chest, killing him. The very next day, unaware of Abbott's crime, the *New York Times* ran a positive review of *In the Belly of the Beast.*

I had read about all of this and it had made me livid. Now I could tell Mailer to his face what I thought of his actions. At first, he looked like he was going to get furious. He furrowed his brow and opened his mouth to speak. Then he caught himself, shook his head and turned to go into the theater. I won't repeat what I said, but it was a less-than-flattering review of Mr. Mailer.

Right after that, I left the theater, walked home and called my dad to tell him what had happened.

"Good for you," my dad laughed. "It's about time someone told that son of a bitch off."

Dimi
(1982)

That same year, I met this guy. He was doing some grad work at Emerson, I think. But unlike many of the other media-wannabe, slick producer-in-training types that were so prevalent at Emerson, this guy was very cool and "anti." I first saw him when I was checking out a film camera and we got to talking. He noticed that I was wearing my New York Dolls T-shirt and he told me how much he liked them. He had spiky hair, was a few years older than me, spoke in a thick Russian accent and hated everything. Except hanging out and talking. He was smart. He drove a Caddy and had a pretty blonde girl-friend.

"I want to be like James Dean," he'd say. "Actors today are pussies. James Dean was a god."

His name was Dimitri Turin and for several months we fell in with each other, double dating and hanging out, having these mad discussions into the night about books, films, politics and his beloved motorcycles. He was sort of crazy and volatile, but marvelous company. He was funny, extremely smart and well read, but did everything to excess. He'd come along when I was doing interviews for my cable TV show and, when I was done, pick little arguments with people like Jim Carroll, Tom Verlaine and Ric Ocasek. He'd suck them into these discussions, which, in Jim Carroll's case anyway, almost led to a fight. Then Dimitri would laugh into the night, we all would, and move on to the next adventure. Several times, Dimitri got arrested for fighting in bars, and even started one with a Boston cop (bad idea), but somehow he always got out of jail scot-free. I'd ask how he did it and he'd just laugh his mad Russian laugh and say, "It's who you know. Let's go drink."

One day in class, a kid said to me, "You know who your friend Dimitri is, right?" I said no and he told me. "The Russian writer, Alexander Solzhenitsyn? That's Dimi's dad. He calls the State Department to get him out of trouble. He has, like, diplomatic immunity or something." I never mentioned it, but one day Dimitri asked me if I knew. I told him I did, and he said, "And you never bothered me about it. See, that is why I call you my friend."

After school, Dimi and I hung out several more times, but soon lost touch. He'd call me over the years from time to time, but never left a number. These were late-night calls from all over the world, from loud taverns and raucous parties. I'd hear him yelling on my answering machine, "My friend, how are you? It's your friend, Dimi! I miss you! I'm in Zurich! REO Speedwagon sucks!" But never any way to get a hold of him.

I did some research a few years ago and discovered that Dimi died from a drug overdose March 17, 1994. I got such a lump in my throat. Turns out, as I learned later, that he'd lived in New York City the last years of his life. When I lived there. I wish I'd known.

R E F L E C T I O N S
from playwright John Baron

The playwright John Baron was one of Dimi's best friends, and attended Emerson College at the same time we did. He wrote this deeply personal piece about Dimi for this book (and is working on a long-form piece about his good friend). He told me the following story dates to a moment in 1985 when he knew Dimi was in serious trouble—the drugs were taking over.

It was a long, long drive home. It was the end of many things, and in many ways, the end of my youth. I was 25, it was 1983 and I had seroconverted (become HIV positive). He said to meet him near the Holland Tunnel at the Shell gas station. There he was, on time, and I was so glad to see him. He was leaning on his motorcycle, a no-frills vintage Norton, smoking a Camel non-filter when I pulled

The motorcycle shop where Dimi worked. (New York City, New York.)

up in the car. He still had his hair spiked up in a random way and wore black pants, a leather jacket and pointy black shoes. I rolled the window down, gave a huge sigh and he smiled as he picked a piece of tobacco from his teeth.

"Follow me. I'm just around the corner."

He was barely 23, but already world-weary from his drug adventures. The evidence was not on his face or even his soul, rather in his head and in his heart, the sights and the pains were, by now, scar tissue.

We brought my things upstairs and tried to be quiet. Dimi was living at a relative's house on the third floor. Once we were settled, he put on some music and we started to catch up. He said he really liked New York, and I had the opposite to say about L.A. He had some work he found amusing and I looked around the room to see old papers, textbooks and note pads. Between puffs of a joint, Dimi was translating World War II documents from German into Russian as we talked in English about old video projects of ours while the Violent Femmes played. I had a let out a laugh glad to be back where I belonged.

The next few weeks had high highs and low lows. The highest high was at a festival in Jersey City in early July. Dimi told me that he had been asked to shoot a video of a speech on Ethiopian hunger relief to be delivered by Esther Haile Selassie (a relative of former Ethiopian emperor Haile Selassie). He asked if I wanted to go and I said sure. We taped her speech and sent if off to WWOR-TV in Secaucus, then went to a gathering at her home. It was so apparent that she and Dimi were the stars of the party. They actually made a striking couple. Dimi with his intense, yet sensitive, looks and Esther's exotic goddess qualities. I just sat back and watched them drink shots of vodka and talk world affairs.

The lowest low ended on the Lower East Side. It started in the Hells Kitchen crackerbox apartment I had just rented on 47th Street between 9th and 10th avenues. Dimi came over, parked his bike on the sidewalk, came upstairs and broke out his works as if it was something he had done in front of me 1,000 times. In reality, this was the first time in our six-year friendship that he had ever shot up in front of me, and I did something so uncharacteristic—I asked him if he had any more. He did, but I didn't shoot it, I snorted it. So this is what it was coming down to: both of us doing heroin in this dark, cramped, ugly room. Right then and there, panic set in and I ran outside onto the sidewalk. He came down a few minutes later and asked why I ran out of the house. I just said, "I gotta go out for a while." I got in a cab and went to a friend's on Avenue B and 11th Street. When the cab turned the corner onto B from 14th Street, there was Dimi's Norton parked in front of a known drug dealer's, I just shook my head and knew then.

Thanks, John. Today, traces of Dimitri remain on the Lower East Side of New York City, at the Sixth Street Specials motorcycle garage. From a MotorcyclistOnline.com article:

During the early '90s, a visit to Sixth Street Specials meant immersion in a wild, bohemian motorcycling subculture. [Owner Hugh] Mackie's then-partner was a mad Russian stunt rider by the name of Dimitri Turin, who loved to wow visitors by riding wheelies on an old Norton Atlas with a hollowed-out pumpkin perched atop his head.

That sounds like Dimi. The bike shop where he worked and hung out still remains. And outside the nearby Sidewalk Café, another haunt of his, there is a mural that pays tribute to my mad Russian friend. That's Dimi: out front, the leader of the pack.

Dimi immortalized on the mural outside the restaurant. (New York City, New York.)

Manute

(1983)

hen I was a senior in college in Boston, my cousin Frankie called me and said, "Drive to Bridgeport with me today."

Frankie, who had begun acting as an agent for college basketball players, was headed to meet a kid he'd just started working with and he wanted me to meet him too. We headed down to Connecticut and Frankie said, "Look, when this guy comes out, no cracks. He hears enough of it."

"About what?" I asked.

My question was answered when I saw 7-foot-7-inch, 180-pound Manute Bol heading toward our car. This Sudanese beanpole, black as Mississippi mud, folded himself silently in the car and off we went to breakfast. Frankie had told me he didn't talk much, but when Frankie was in the men's room I told him about an article I'd just read abut the political unrest in his homeland. That broke the ice and we actually had a nice discussion, even with the little English he spoke. Over lots of bacon and eggs (and many stares from the coffee shop crowd), Frankie laid out what would be next for Manute: playing on the college team, for the Bridgeport Gulls after that, and that Manute would be staying at Frankie's house in Marblehead with Frankie's amazing wife Terry and their four beautiful kids. I stayed out there at their huge place on many a weekend—it was a great escape from school.

Once Manute started staying there, I saw him quite a bit. We'd shoot around in the driveway while curious neighbors wondered what he as doing there (cars would circle endlessly, gawking at him). I got to help Manute a bit with his English and watch this stranger in a strange land adapt to life in America. He was gentle, curious, shy, and he was a family member in the Catapano household. Soon, he'd enter the NBA, and he created a stir whenever and wherever he played. I'd go see him when I lived in New York, when the Warriors or 76ers were playing the Knicks, and he'd always come over and say hi to me and ask how I was. No matter how notable he became, he never

Manute while he played for the Golden State Warriors in 1989.

Another angle from the same game.

seemed to forget those nights up in Marblehead, where he was like one of the kids to Frankie and Terry.

Bol finished his career with a total of 1,599 points; 2,647 rebounds; and 2,086 blocks, having appeared in 624 games over 10 seasons.

I read this recently in *Sports Illustrated*:

Once he'd mastered English, Bol became one of the top trash-talkers in the league. He didn't accept insults from anyone without a retort, especially the dim bulbs on the street that would ask, "How's the weather up there?"

"Who do I look like," he would answer with disdain, "Willard Scott?"

Yes, Manute had a great sense of humor. And there was also this in the piece:

> "One of the remarkable things about Manute was that he was never self-conscious about his height," says Bol's longtime agent, Frank Catapano. "He carried himself with a regal bearing— he never slouched. He didn't consider his height a burden; he considered it a gift from God."

Getting to know Manute was special. One night, he broke a bathroom light fixture by standing up straight—his head hit it. The glass shattered, no cuts or anything, but he panicked and became very upset. "It's okay," I told him. "It can be fixed." Looking for the right words he said, "You have so much in this country that can be broken. Who fixes it all?"

Charles Kuralt
(1983)

"The everyday kindness of the back roads more than makes up for the acts of greed in the headlines."
  —Charles Kuralt, "On the Road"

Whenever I work on my newspaper column today, I remind myself of what the great journalist Charles Kuralt advised in a book of his: keep yourself in the background, don't become the story—because the *story* is the story. I loved watching Kuralt when I was a teenager in the 1970s, starting with his "On the Road" segments and then his marvelous *CBS News Sunday Morning* program. This pudgy, avuncular country gentleman wandering the back roads was, for me, inspirational. In fact, I think he's why I started writing books about discovering interesting people and places along the byways of this country. Watching him introduce the stories on *Sunday Morning* was enjoyable, but I missed seeing him go "on the road" to find the next candlemaker or root beer brewer—sitting on a quiet soundstage made him seem sort of caged, but still, it was Charles Kuralt.

When I graduated from college, I wanted to get my parents a gift to say thanks for the support. For my dad, I wanted to have Charles Kuralt sign a copy of one of his "On the Road" books for him. After all, my dad first introduced me to the charms of Kuralt and he was a huge fan of the broadcaster— I think in part because they shared certain a love of fishing, the great outdoors and that old-school "rugged individualism." My dad, for all of his faults, did pass along some good things to me, including his appreciation of Charles Kuralt.

So I bought the book in Brookline, Massachusetts, not far from my apartment. But now what? I decided to send the book to CBS with a letter that laid out my request: Would Mr. Kuralt sign this book to my dad, perhaps jot a message that conveyed how thankful I was for college? I had the exact postage calculated and taped it up in an envelope so the return wouldn't cost anything. I put it in the mail and crossed my fingers.

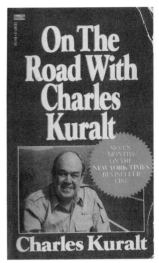

One of my favorite Charles Kuralt books.

Unfortunately, I had this idea late in the game, just several days before my graduation when I wanted to present the book, so this felt like a long shot (I'd included that in my note).

But two days later, via next-day delivery no less, the book was returned to me. I opened it to find an inscription that read:

> *Lawrence,*
> *Please accept this fondly from Christian, and myself. We'd both like to thank you for putting him through college.*
> > *Most sincerely,*
> > *Charles Kuralt*

Inside the envelope was something else: the unopened envelope containing my postage.

Charles Kuralt died in 1997, and two years later it came out that he'd had a decades-long, secret relationship with a woman while he was still married. All of a sudden, Kuralt's integrity and folksy credibility came under attack. The news didn't thrill me, but it was his business, he never flaunted his family or proclaimed any sort of personal devotion, so I found it strange how quickly so many began to dismiss the power of what he accomplished. Sure, I wished it wasn't true, but I tried to put it all aside.

The revelation of the extramarital relationship did eventually take a big toll on Kuralt's image and reputation. However, Kuralt's biographer, the fine writer Ralph Grizzle, who sometimes faced hostility when promoting his book *Remembering Charles Kuralt*, attempted to rehabilitate Kuralt's image in a *USA Today* column called "Forgiving Charles Kuralt." When I read this, it made me feel better, because Mr. Grizzle made a case that I felt effectively answered the critics, while also clarifying the legacy of Charles Kuralt. An excerpt:

> From a moral point of view, if we hold him to strict Christian scrutiny, as we are so prone to do in the South, we must also extend to him the most gracious of Christian virtues. Even Charles's wife, while certainly not apathetic about the affair, forgave him. "He was the best man I ever knew," she announced at a dinner I attended shortly before her own death.
>
> Each Sunday morning as Charles spoke to us seated on a stool, he was perched, in our minds, on a pedestal. Well aware of his own flaws, he never aspired to such lofty heights. He drank too much, he smoked too much, he ate too much and, now, it seems, he loved too much. May we forgive his excesses as readily as we embraced, unknowingly, of course, the emotional deficits that drove him to seek out the people and places that so enthralled him, and through him, us.

Whenever we're rumbling down the road in our Road-trek van, looking at those country miles roll by, I often think of Charles Kuralt. He may not have been perfect, but there were things he did perfectly—celebrating the common man, giving voice to every day people doing extraordinary things and, of course, keeping himself in the background.

R E F L E C T I O N S
from author and Kuralt biographer Ralph Grizzle

Today, 10 years after the revelations about Charles Kuralt, how is he viewed? Even as he was becoming a successful national broadcaster, Charles Kuralt told a Chapel Hill newspaper that he didn't think he'd be remembered for anything. "And if I do any good," he added, "it's just the same thing all journalists hope they do—maybe some good by enlightening people about the times they live in."

Author Ralph Grizzle, who wrote a definitive book, *Remembering Charles Kuralt*, about the "On the Road" host.

Three decades later, in 1996, the multiple Emmy Award-winning journalist told the Academy of Achievement: "I'd like to write something that would live. . . . In television, everything is gone with the speed of light, literally. It is no field for anybody with intimations of immortality, because your stuff, by and large, doesn't live on. It's not easy for me to admit, but I would love to write something that people would still read 50 or 100 years from now.

That comes with growing older. You begin to think, 'Well, what have I ever done to benefit society? What have I ever written that would excite a young reader years from now, the way Mark Twain's journalism still excited me when I first read *Roughing It* and *The Innocents Abroad*?' So we can't all be Mark Twain. In fact, I guess it's fair to say, none of us can be Mark Twain, except Mark Twain. But you do begin to yearn to write something that gains a little permanence."

What's sad to me is that Kuralt never reached his goal to achieve the sort of immortality that Twain did—in large part, I believe, because of the scandal that came to surface following his death. When news broke about his long affair with Patricia Shannon, a book publishing company that had been eager to publish my manuscript *Remembering Charles Kuralt* told me that the reporter had ruined his career. Refusing to believe that Americans could be so shallow, I mortgaged my house to publish several thousand copies of the book—and sold them all within six months.

Now, however, more than 10 years after his death, I believe, sadly, that Kuralt's legacy fails to live on. But then, whose does? Even Twain struggles to maintain a foothold in a national psyche increasingly inundated with data, images and Youtube videos. We loved Kuralt in the last decades of the last century. Many people told me that they skipped church to watch his enriching broadcast, *Sunday Morning*. The show was, of course, a powerful religion in its own right, as was "On the Road," praising unheralded heroes and ordinary people doing extraordinary things. Kuralt was one of those people, just an ordinary guy doing something extraordinary. To forget Kuralt would not only be sad for him but also for us.

Woody, Ack and Rod
(1984)

I was almost a year out of Emerson College and I'd finally landed my first job at an ad agency in New York City, working as a copywriter. (My first 20 years of work were spent writing and directing commercials, and this is where I started.)

The agency also had a production company arm, which was hired to produce the first *MTV Video Music Awards* show at Radio City Music Hall. A few of us in the creative department were brought on to help get things done, and I was fortunate enough to land one of the more interesting assignments: assisting one of the show's co-hosts, the actor and comedian Dan Aykroyd. (To illustrate how much pop culture has changed, the other host was Bette Midler.)

The program from the first MTV Video Music Awards.

For a couple of weeks, I shadowed Dan, wrote some little comedic bits, and stood at the ready as he prepped for the show—all in all a great time because he could not have been any nicer, funnier or more down-to-earth. He was good buddies with the Hells Angels, who were always there to do everything, from fetching him smokes to running errands for his (gorgeous) wife, the actress Donna Dixon. This was sort of a bizarre set-up, but those guys were very cool to everyone around them. "Ack," as a few people called him, had also just co-opened the Hard Rock Cafe, so he was also busy with that.

As the date got closer, rehearsals started, the show got booked, and it was all looking good. Madonna was to perform an as-yet-unreleased "Like a Virgin," which became a controversial, sexually charged performance (the clip of her writhing still gets played and, for a moment, you can see me and Dan Aykroyd by the side of the stage where we watched all the performances together). Also performing were ZZ Top, Rod Stewart, Huey Lewis, David Bowie and Tina Turner—a solid show for the time. Plus, the list of attendees was spectacular. All of rock's royalty, for the most part, would be sitting in Radio City that night.

Throughout show week, celebrities and rock stars came and went to visit Dan, and it was always just a relaxing hang—and fun!—and not an ounce of booze or anything illicit was ever present. Aykroyd, as I understood it, had recently stopped drinking and, outside of chain-smoking cigarettes, he did not seem to have any other vices. Then one day, he said to me, "Look, when Woody drops by, he'll turn this place upside down for a drink. Don't let him bring anything in. I don't want anything in the dressing room." He was referring to Ronnie Wood of the Rolling Stones, who would be presenting

Today, Madonna's dress from the infamous "Like a Virgin" performance hangs in a Universal City store window.

an award with his old Faces bandmate, Rod Stewart. The day of dress rehearsal, sure enough, there he was, Woody, at the dressing room door with his wife, Jo.

Now, I'm a Rolling Stones devotee of a fairly serious order, have been since about the age of 11, so I was decidedly star-struck watching Woody look for a drink in the crowded room. It was sort of funny and intriguing, and I really wanted to meet him.

The well-known film director, John Landis, whom I'd gotten to know during the week, saw me straining my neck to watch Woody, put two and two together and introduced us. He said, "Chris is working with Danny!" Woody pulled me aside, acknowledging nothing Landis said, and whispered, "Mate, where the f——k I can get a drink in this building? There's no bar downstairs, no hospitality set-up—nothing—and I'd like a bloody drink!" (MTV was running a very tight corporate show—no riffraff, no open bar.)

Torn between loyalty to my client and the possibility of being able to help a legend procure his liquid desire, I scanned the room. Mr. Aykroyd was in a serious chat with the singer Ray Parker, Jr. about his lawsuit with Huey Lewis over the song "Ghostbusters," which sounded suspiciously like the Huey Lewis hit, "I Want a New Drug." (Huey Lewis later reached a settlement out of court, and interestingly, both songs were played at the awards by their respective artists.)

Ack was noticing nothing, so I slipped away.

Earlier, I'd seen someone in Bette Midler's outer dressing room filling a cooler across the hall for Bette and her guests. Evidently, no such "Aykroyd rules" applied over there. So I told Ronnie about the stash in the cooler. He began giggling like a kid (looking back, I think he was probably feeling the effects of something stronger than booze), and he whispered, "C'mon, mate," sneaking out the door with me in tow.

In the hall, we got on our knees at his command and crept into Bette's "first" room—sort of a waiting area with flowers and stuff. Looking back, I've wondered why we didn't we just go ask her for a drink. Then again, the espionage approach felt appropriate.

So I crawled in on all fours. I could hear Bette's voice in the next room—much cursing followed by bursts of laughter—as I grabbed a short bottle of Southern Comfort out of the cooler. Bottle in hand, I crawled back to Woody in the cramped hallway. He was smoking a cigarette and cracking up as I tried to shush him. I'd seen Bette get a bit tense during the week, and the last thing I wanted to do was cause a scene that would inspire more friction—and maybe cost me my job, too.

We had the booze, and it was time for a drink—but obviously not in the Aykroyd dressing room. Then, I heard another British voice in the hall, another in the seemingly endless parade of well-wishers on their way to see Dan Aykroyd.

"Well bloody 'ell, wot in God's name is this?" the raspy voice said.

It was Rod Stewart, who had just finished soundchecking the song "Infatuation" down in the hall. In fact, he was still holding a soccer ball, one of many he'd kick into to the crowd during the song the next night when the show went up.

The two exchanged hellos—it seemed like they hadn't seen each other in a while—and I was numb. Could this really be happening?

Woody said to Rod, "C'mon, mate, me and, uh, er, uh . . . me and my mate here, uh, er, um. . . ."

"Chris."

"Bloody right! Chris, here—we're having ourselves a quick one, so come on."

A few seconds later, the three of us were sitting in a cramped utility closet among mops and buckets, passing the bottle. It was like high school, but with iconic British rock stars. For the most part, I simply listened to the two of them and tried not to spoil any of the loose, adolescent energy in the room.

"You seen Billy Idol? "

"'E's good! I mean, you know, I've 'eard 'e's good. Never 'eard him meself, actually. "

"Yeah, you see Prince down there? "

"With Quincy Jones? In purple? "

"Yeah! "

"'E's good! I mean, you know, I've 'eard 'e's good. Never 'eard him meself, actually. But 'e's good, that Prince. "

"See Daryl Hall? "

"'E the one with Oates, then? "

"Right!"

Like some stilted Monty Python sketch gone awry, this went on for maybe 10 minutes, but it felt gloriously drawn out. I was in heaven.

In the near dark, with each pull of Woody's cigarette, I saw those two faces in the glow. I thought of all the album covers, the photos, the shows—and here they were, huddled up in the dark and in the flesh with a 22-year-old copywriter. I bummed a smoke from Woody just to produce more light so I could see them in the orange shadows. Their rooster hairdos were silhouetted against a backdrop of paper towel rolls and stacked pails of industrial cleaner.

They talked, and I was more or less invisible. They were happy to be presenting an award together the next night. Wood complained that he had nobody to play with, but that he wanted to do something. Stewart said, "My guys aren't really playing, they're pretending to, not plugged in, or you'd have been welcome."

We heard the din of the party in Dan's room, and Rod Stewart finally said, "We'd better make an appearance in there—he's expecting me."

The booze had created a lovely, warm buzz in the closet, and I could have stayed in there forever. After all, how soon until they'd both feel like croaking out some old blues numbers? We could use the buckets as drums, play as a trio, but then Stewart opened the door, light spilled in, and we—or I—were back on Earth. A cloud of cigarette smoke spilled out into the hallway with us, conspicuous beyond belief, like a Cheech and Chong movie. I also noticed I was taller than both of them. How could that be?

We went into the dressing room a bit sheepishly, and Aykroyd looked suspicious, but he was so happy to see Rod Stewart that all seemed okay. Woody was back talking to his wife, Rod was talking to everyone else, and I figured the moment was over.

A little while later, though, Woody was at the window—the second-floor perch looking down on West 51st Street—causing a commotion. Many kids had been camping out to stargaze during rehearsals. They had spotted him, and now they were freaking out. Woody was mugging, waving and blowing kisses. Stewart got wind of it and headed toward the window,

Ack's inscription to me after the big night.

but then he said to Woody, "Bring your mate over, our drinking buddy, Chris." Rod Stewart remembered my name! Woody, the scarecrow caricature of a rock star, motioned all excitedly, "Come over, mate!" (I don't think *he* ever really did get my name.)

They forced me in between them, draped their arms about me, and Woody said, "Isn't this nice, mate? Look down there. This is what it's like!"

On the street, tons of people were screaming and waving at them. Stewart whispered to me, sort of *sotto voce* in my ear, "Ridiculous, isn't it? I mean, look how they get. But isn't it fun to see it from this angle? Enjoy this, mate—now you can say you know how it feels."

And yes, it was insane, and glorious, and unforgettable.

The party was breaking up behind us, and again, another magic moment crashed to an all-too-soon coda. Rod Stewart actually seemed really together, almost businesslike to Woody's boyishness. He shook my hand before leaving and said in an official way, "Have a good show tomorrow, mate."

The next night during the show, before Woody presented his award, I fixed his woefully crooked collar (he was completely smashed), and then I appeared in a Milk Bones commercial parody sketch with Dan Aykroyd. Trying to find Ack's mark three floors beneath Radio City Music Hall so he could ride the elevator up to do his opening with Bette was tense and amazing.

"Twenty seconds to air! Is Dan on his mark?"

We bumped into Rod Stewart and his band looking for their elevator in the dark. It was like a scene from *The Poseidon Adventure*-meets-*Spinal Tap*, all of us wandering the bowels of Radio City as the show was about to kick off.

I did 100 amazing things that night, but nothing—nothing—came close to the bottle-swiping, closet-drinking, window-posing escapades the day before with my two "mates."

At the after party (held at the Hard Rock Cafe, of course), Mr. Aykroyd got me a nice table for some friends from work. The Hells Angels were there to make sure we had what we needed. I sat and told this story like a schoolgirl to some disbelieving co-workers. As if on cue, Rod Stewart, passed by the table and yelled good-naturedly, "Don't believe a bloody word!"

I left the Hard Rock Cafe on cloud nine. The experiences of the evening were magical, plus I'd sort of fallen for a girl working on the show and things were looking good on that front. Yes, at this point, I was on a high I had not really ever felt in life.

Goodbyes in front of the Hard Rock featured huge hugs from Aykroyd and his wife. I got to kiss Tina Turner—heady stuff.

I got in my car to drive back to Westchester County at about four in the morning. It was ethereal—I was hearing little birds chirp in my head—and I had the first New York Dolls tape cranked up on this clear, cold fall night. I felt invincible.

I headed over to the Westside Highway to go north. Near 12th Avenue, there was chaos on the street. Cops were in the middle of busting a bunch of hookers (who hung out there every night to hook the businessman heading home to New Jersey and Westchester).

The NYPD Blues were fanning out, and ladies of the night in huge stiletto heels were attempting to escape, scattering like clumsy birds. It was like those nature videos where the lions stalk and then easily overtake the gazelles and yaks. The girls had no chance.

One of the women, a sort of pretty blonde maybe in her mid-twenties with a bunch of miles on her, got stuck in my headlights and looked at me like, *"Help."* On the spur of the moment, I opened the door, yelled, "Get in!" and then we were off. I gunned it hard up the avenue. I figured, I'm invincible tonight, I'll spread the magic around, I'll *save* this damsel who deserves better. Hey, I had seen *Taxi Driver!*

As I sped to hit the sequence of green lights, she was focused on looking out the back window at her past. Hitting every pothole on the westside, I started making a pious speech (as I do sometimes) about how she's better than this and, you know, it's never too late for a fresh start and, hey, we all make mistakes and, uh, this world is hard but, look, a jerk like me was just recently in a closet with Rod Stewart and Ron Wood so, like, I know what bright horizons are out there and anything's possible—

She finally turned toward me, staring at the steering wheel, a deep concern in her eyes. "Did you escape from a mental hospital?"

She was looking at the bracelet I had on. It identified me as full access at the show, but she was right, it did look like a hospital ID bracelet. That, coupled with my plaintive speech about life's eternal promise, must have been too much for her.

She started to panic and said, with more than a bit of fear, "Let me out of here!"

I pulled over, saying, "No, no, no, really, I just worked

the MTV awards. I ate a milk bone with Dan Aykroyd on TV.
Me and Madonna are sort of pals now, and I'm a gentleman, so
let me get your door and, like—"

But by now she was convinced I was nuts, maybe even
the Son of Sam, and my little mission of mercy had gone awry.
Somewhere near Riverside Drive, she dashed out of my car,
slamming the door as hard as I'd ever felt and bolted into the
night.

I sat there—the New York Dolls still droning on, only
now not sounding so exhilarating. My night had done a 180 the
likes of which I haven't replicated since.

Dog, Gone
(1985)

"I think we are drawn to dogs because they are the uninhibited creatures we might be if we weren't certain we knew better. They fight for honor at the first challenge, make love with no moral restraint, and they do not for all their marvelous instincts appear to know about death. Being such wonderfully uncomplicated beings, they need us to do their worrying."

—George Bird Evans, *Troubles with Bird Dogs*

Dogs have always figured heavy in the American pop culture experience, and with good reason—*they're dogs* for crying out loud. Where would we be without them? As a kid, I loved the array of cinematic and television (and even comic) hounds that existed. There's Lassie, of course. And Old Yeller, Toto, Pluto, Goofy and Richie Rich's dog, Dollar; Batman and Robin's pooch, Ace; Scooby-Doo, Dino from *The Flintstones*, Lady and the Tramp, Snoopy, Benji, Rocky's dog, Butkus—right on up through Spuds MacKenzie, Eddie from *Frasier*, Hootch, Beethoven, Gidget the Taco Bell dog and Marley. Think of all the famous dogs that have wormed their way into our collective hearts over the years.

My favorite of all was Rin Tin Tin. Originally brought home from France by an American soldier at the end of World War I, the famed German shepherd soon became a movie star after appearing in 1922's *The Man from Hell's River*. Over the years, there would be more than one heroic dog cast as Rin Tin

Me with Rin Tin Tin in 1975.

Tin, and I'd watch reruns of the old movies and also the popular 1950s TV series *The Adventures of Rin Tin Tin* in awe of that proud, noble German shepherd. They even brought back a short-lived version of the series in the mid-1970s, and through a connection my father had, we went to a reception at the Waldorf Astoria hotel for the newly-cast dog. (I was sick as a dog that day, suffering from mononucleosis, but there was no way I would have stayed home.) Beyond Rin Tin Tin, it was hard not to love German shepherds for another reason, or rather, five reasons, as I'll explain in a moment.

Recently, I'd almost forgotten what it was like to have a dog. Then, three years ago, we adopted a mutt so the kids would be able to enjoy the experience of a family hound. (This, on top of our beloved cat, Veronica, plus a snake, a bird, a turtle, fish, a rabbit, a lizard and a few creatures I have probably, deliberately, forgotten.) We named her Marilyn at Claire's suggestion, because her mascared-looking eyes evoked Marilyn Monroe. From day one, Marilyn has been everything you'd hope for a dog to be: excessively loving, loyal, protective, playful . . . like I said, I'd almost forgotten what it was like to have a dog, and most days when I see Marilyn, I am reminded of the dogs we had while I was growing up. In order they were:

Cleo—a proud, brilliant German shepherd who lived a long, full life;

Casar—a slightly bumbling, loveable German shepherd we rescued from terrible abuse, who became mine;

Opal—my younger sister's show dog, a graceful

German shepherd we believe was abducted from our property;

Kas—my German shepherd-golden retriever mix I got in college. Perhaps the sweetest animal that ever lived, killed by a hit-and-run driver (who, to this day, I still hope met some harsh, karmic fate);

And last, but not least, Bunter, whom I'd like to tell you more about now.

Bunter had replaced Opal, so he was my sister's. She'd present him from time to time in dog shows, but for the most part he was the pup that had to fight Cleo and Casar, the old timers, for attention. In time, Bunter grew into a hulking, impressive animal; he was all muscle, courage and obedience. He looked over Cleo and Casar as they became elders, and if you were a UPS or mail person, God help you. That said, if people understood dogs, Bunter's ferocity was easily handled—he'd become a big puppy in a moment. As he got older, he settled in as the leader of the pack. After my folks divorced, we moved to a smaller property. Gone was the 10-acre lot of forest and streams where the dogs would patrol and hunt. Cleo and Casar soon passed away, leaving Bunter as the last shepherd standing. We still had a decent-sized yard, even a small pond, so he was content. For the too-short span I had Kas, they became pals, which was fun to watch.

Me with Casar in 1975.

Kas, on my college couch in 1980.

Then my younger sister left for California to go to school.

I had graduated college and was working in New York, so Bunter sort of fell to me. By that time (the mid-1980s), my mom and both sisters had moved to California, leaving me, my grandmother and Bunter. Every day when I'd come home from the city, he'd be waiting to play. Even though he was getting old, he still loved running and, since I was home a lot, he started sleeping on the foot of my bed. He guarded over me like a sentry at night; any sound and he was up, pacing and curious. When all was clear, he was back on the bed across my legs. He'd wake me up in the morning by licking my face, wait outside the door when I showered and watch my grandmother make her wonderful meals. She'd fix him plates of pasta with homemade sauce and pour chicken broth over his meal—no dog ate better than Bunter. We'd go for walks up in the woods and over time, I started to see him slow down a bit.

"That's okay," I thought, "just age setting in."

But when he became very sluggish, I took him to the vet, who told me that Bunter had advanced cancer. I couldn't believe it. This noble, beautiful animal was very sick, and I didn't know what to do. The vet told me that because of how strong a dog Bunter was, he could actually live awhile. He also said he could be put down if I so decided. I couldn't do that.

But I did not know what to do.

A few days later, the vet called me with the name of a woman up in Brewster, New York, just a few miles away, who had a large property. She took in sick dogs if they were well behaved and tended to them in their final days, making sure they were comfortable and affording them as much quality of life as she could. The vet

Bunter in 1984.

thought it might be perfect for Bunter because he'd be getting round-the-clock care (my grandmother had moved to California by now and so it was just me and Bunter in the house so, by day, he had no care).

I called her and arranged an appointment. Bunter and I drove up and ambled around the farm-like property. The woman, a wealthy former model who looked sort of like Bo Derek, watched him carefully.

"Look at how all of the other dogs on the property watch him," she said. "He's majestic, like a lion. They're keeping their distance out of respect."

She was right. The dogs sat up silently as he walked by, like a king had entered their territory—or like Rin Tin Tin had walked into the scene.

Throughout the property, there must have been a couple dozen dogs being tended to by a few of her helpers. The dogs each slept in cozy horse stables, as she showed me. After maybe an hour of watching Bunter, "Diane" told me he was welcome to live out his last few weeks, months—whatever— here at her farm.

I thanked her and drove home with Bunter to think about it. I spoke to him all night like he was person; I spoke to my family, and we decided it was the right thing to do. The next day, I drove Bunter up there and got him settled. He was in a bit of pain, but Diane had vet-approved medications for all of the dogs up there and she said she'd take care of him. (By the way, she charged not a dime for any of this.)

For several weeks, I'd visit after getting home after work and could tell Bunter was fading. He knew the sound of my car and would walk to the door of his stable, tail still wagging. We'd walk by the lake, he'd rest his head in my lap for a while, then I'd go home.

One day, Diane called me at my job in Manhattan and told me that Bunter had become very weak and that it might be a good idea to head up that night. So I did.

When I saw him in the dusk, I knew. We made it down

by the lake as the sun set for our last time together. As tears streamed down my face, he stared out at the water, impassively. Eventually, he leaned into me and licked my face. In the dark, we walked back to his stable. I fixed his blanket and pillow, sat with him a bit more, said a prayer, gave him a hug and a kiss and said goodbye. I felt sort of like Travis in *Old Yeller*, right before the inevitable. Bunter stared at me as I left, which made me linger near the door. Blinking through tears, I blew him one last kiss.

The next day, Diane called me to say that Bunter had died in the middle of the night. We made the arrangements with the vet to have him cremated, and that was that. This grand, faithful, spectacular dog was gone.

Do dogs have any comprehension at all of the tethers they attach to our hearts? I'm not one of those people who puts dogs on the same level of humans, at least I never was before, but you know what? I do wish more people could make us feel the way dogs do sometimes—I do respect the power of dogs to make emotional attachments with us that are rewarding, lasting and even profound. I watch Marilyn with the kids and I am reminded of this every day.

As I write this, Marilyn is stretched across my feet. But she seems to sense that this is an emotional dog story I'm working on (are there any others?). Now she's getting up. I think she knows I'm a bit sad at this moment because she's just propped her paws up on me like she does, as if to give a hug. Here, I'll take her picture for you at this moment.

She knows what's going on. I'm telling, you—she knows.

Where would we be without dogs?

"Louie, Louie"
(1985)

A small story involving a big rock star.

In 1985, while working in New York City and commuting from home up in Westchester County, I met a guy named Stanley Sheldon one night at a local bar. Stanley, as you may know, was the bass player on the classic album *Frampton Comes Alive!*, among many other great records. We got to talking and it turned out he played tennis, so literally within days, we became tennis partners. Soon after, we became pretty good friends, too. At that time, Stanley was quietly working on a solo record with Lou Gramm, lead singer of the band Foreigner, who was huge at that time—one of the biggest bands on the planet. Lou lived nearby and once I met him at his house when I picked Stanley up there. Lou Gramm!

One day, Stanley says to Lou, "Hey, Chris knows some great record stores down in Greenwich Village. Weren't you looking for something?"

Lou, normally quiet, perked up. "Really? Any way in the world you could get me a copy of the 45 of 'Louie, Louie' by the Kingsmen?"

The lead singer of Foreigner wanted me to find him

Bleecker Street Records, where I found "Louie, Louie" for Lou. (New York City, New York.)

"Waiting for a Girl like You," one of many hit Foreigner singles.

a record? You got it, Lou! Next time I was in the city, I went to my favorite record shop and found an original 45 copy. I told the guy at the counter, "Yeah, well, this is for someone pretty important." Silence. "A pretty big rock star, sort of a friend of mine—well, friend of a friend." Silence. I love New York.

So I got the record to Stanley, who said he'd get it to Lou. I was kind of hoping I could make the presentation, but whatever. That was that.

About 10 months later, Stanley and I went to see Foreigner at the Brendan Byrne Arena in New Jersey. Lou had arranged passes for Stanley, who brought me along (Joe Walsh opened and Steve Winwood was backstage). The show was great and the sold-out crowd went nuts. Afterwards, Lou was being led offstage by a massive bodyguard (Bob Bender, formerly Mick Jagger's keeper, who I chatted with during the set). In the tunnel was rock star bedlam: sweating musicians running with security guards yelling to get the hell out of the way as if a bunch of presidents were coming through. I saw a small piece of Lou in the scrum. But then the entourage stopped—because Lou stopped. I'd met him once, almost a year earlier, yet he caught my eye in the hallway and stopped to grab my hand.

"Hey, man, that 'Louie Louie,' I cannot thank you enough. Thanks so much!"

Huh?

In the locker room a short while later, he repeated the thank you.

"How'd you put that together in that crazy moment? What made you think of that?" I asked.

"Hey, that's 'Louie Louie,'" he said. "I don't forget stuff like that."

I thought that was the coolest thing in the world. I saw Lou a few more times with Stanley after that, and I always thought of that record incident.

R E F L E C T I O N S
from Foreigner singer Lou Gramm

Lou Gramm left Foreigner in the late '80s and now fronts the Lou Gramm Band. In the late '90s, he endured brain surgery to remove a tumor and he has worked his way back into the fold by performing all the big Foreigner hits along with some stellar new material. I was with my wife and two kids in the beautiful mountains of Big Bear City, California, during the Fourth of July in 2009. That night, before the fireworks, the Lou Gramm Band performed a hits-heavy show on the lake. Backstage after the show, somehow, Lou still recalled the moment, finishing the story before I had a chance.

"'Louie, Louie.' Man, I loved getting that 45. Greatest rock-and-roll song—and I still have the record. Thanks again, by the way, for picking that up. Those original rock-and-roll records are still untouchable, man. And that's still one of those songs that makes me remember why I wanted to do this all in the first place. Hey, did I pay you for that back then?"

Lou Gramm on stage in July 2009.

No worries, Lou.

We visited for a while, Lou signed records and CDs for the kids (huge Foreigner fans), and my wife (mega-huge Foreigner fan) recalled seeing him at Angel Stadium years before with the band. It was incredible night for lots of reasons.

Catching up with Lou. You know—Lou Gramm.

Our family with Lou Gramm in July 2009. (Big Bear City, California.)

Game Six
(1986)

ometimes history just breaks out around you, and if you haven't left to beat traffic, you're forever attached to it.

Saturday, October 25, 1986, the New York Mets were to play the Boston Red Sox in Game Six of the World Series. The Mets were down 3–2 in the series and so a Red Sox victory would earn them their first title since 1918. The woman I was dating at the time worked for ABC, and a couple of days before the game said she could get a pair of seats for either Game Six or, if there was to be one, game seven. I suggested Game Six just in case in the Mets lost, which would negate the next game. Never having been to a World Series game before, the "a bird in the hand" adage seemed a better bet. The Mets were my favorite team and the '86 model was a fun one to watch—scrappy, tough and disliked by much of the league. The Sox featured Wade Boggs, Jim Rice, Bill Buckner and pitcher Roger "The Rocket" Clemens, who won 24 games that year. The Rocket was on the hill for the Red Sox and though he pitched well, the game was tight throughout.

Boston jumped out to a quick 2–0 lead. The Mets tied the game in the fifth inning, but in the seventh, an error by New York Met Ray Knight led to Marty Barrett scoring to give Boston a 3–2 lead.

Top of the eighth, the Red Sox had Dave Henderson on second with one out. Sox skipper John McNamara sent rookie Mike Greenwell to pinch-hit for Roger Clemens. Greenwell struck out, leaving their man stranded on second base. The

Mets scored a tying run on Gary Carter's sacrifice fly in the bottom of the eighth and the game entered extra frames after a scoreless ninth inning.

In the top of the 10th inning, Dave Henderson hit a solo homer, and Barrett singled in Wade Boggs to make it 5–3. The life was sucked from Shea. A cold, blustery night became even more miserable heading into the bottom of the 10th. People began shuffling out. A depressing silence settled in.

The first two batters up for the Mets, Wally Backman and Keith Hernandez, were both retired. We were one out away from the first Red Sox title in, what, 714 years?

Gary Carter was up. With two strikes, a close ball was called and, though almost nobody in the ballpark saw it, a message on the scoreboard in right-center field momentarily flashed: "Congratulations, Boston Red Sox, 1986 World Champions." Yikes. But Carter singled sharply. A breath of life. Darryl Strawberry was due to hit next, but Mets manager Davey Johnson had taken him out earlier in the game as part of a double switch. So Kevin Mitchell was sent to the plate to pinch-hit for pitcher Rick Aguilera. Mitchell singled to center field. Hmm.

Next up was Ray Knight, who quickly found himself down 0–2 in the count. One strike away, once again. But he singled to center, scoring Carter and pushing Mitchell to third base. The score was now 5–4 and the tying run was just 90 feet from home.

Now the stadium was rocking and creaking and moaning like some awakening dormant spirit, dragged into the light from some deep slumber. The noise grew as the surreal fact became clear: this game was not over. Shea was alive because the Mets were alive. Pitcher Calvin Schiraldi was pulled, replaced by veteran righthanded reliever Bob Stanley. Mets outfielder Mookie Wilson stepped in. On the seventh pitch of an epic at-bat, on a 2–2 count, Stanley's throw cut too far inside and got away from catcher Rich Gedman. Wilson, in an acrobatic act, leapt to avoid getting hit by the wild pitch, then waved wildly to Mitchell, who scored from third. Tie game (and Knight moved up to second on the play).

Shea Stadium was now in full lather, the upper deck literally bouncing up and down. Whatever happened though, the Mets would not lose this inning. With a full count on Wilson, the 10th pitch of the at-bat, Mookie grazed a slow roller up the first base line. Gimpy Boston first baseman Bill Buckner moved toward the ball, but it rolled under his legs. Wilson would make it safely to first and, as the baseball Gods somewhere scratched their heads, Knight scored from second and the Mets won, completing one of the most famous comebacks in World Series history.

Many of us remained in that stadium for almost an hour following the game. There were tears, hugs from strangers, and hoarse joy in the midnight hour. In the disbelief and mind-numbing beauty of what had just unfolded, we all realized we were now eternally joined—a community flash-frozen in time forever. We had witnessed the impossible, together, as Met fans (with a smattering of depressed Red Sox fans).

The Mets won the series in seven. How crazy is it that a Game Seven victory seems anti-climactic? But that was the power of Game Six. I have watched the replays from that game hundreds of times. The next day, over lunch, my dad told me I might have seen the most memorable play in World Series his-

The former site of Shea Stadium, where Bill Buckner became the famous goat in World Series history. (New York City, New York.)

tory. My mom said she wept while watching it on TV. For me, Game Six has become a learning moment in life; an event so momentous and profound that it actually changed how I think. On that night, the concept of eternal hope, faith and belief in the notion of never giving up, even when things seem at their darkest, crystallized for me. Yes, Bill Buckner was unfairly tagged as a goat after this. He was far off the bag, Wilson probably would have made it anyway and Stanley was not even at the bag yet to cover. But that's another lesson from that night: Life ain't fair.

My prize—a ticket to Game Six.

I've never been at a sporting event as impactful as this one and I doubt I ever will be again. I sat though another amazing Game Six, at the 2002 World Series when the Anaheim Angels staged another improbable comeback to stun the Giants. This was huge, made more so because I was with my son (then eight). It's a close second in terms of emotional weight and life-lessons playing out on the diamond— but 1986 was too unique an animal to ever consider it being matched, at least for me.

I look at my ticket stub today and marvel that I was actually there. But I was. And in a way, I think a part of me is still there.

Speaking of still being there, I went back to the site while writing this book, and it was a bittersweet trek. Unlike old Yankee Stadium (which, as of this writing is still standing next to the new version), Shea Stadium was torn down quickly and unceremoniously in the blight of a wet 2008 winter. Where the ballpark once stood is now the parking lot for the new Citi Field. Brass markers indicate where the bases would have been. Standing near home plate, memories flood back, and not just of Game Six.

Site of the old home plate at Shea Stadium.

I looked up to where the middle deck would have been along first base and imagined the first game I ever saw in my life—with my dad in 1970, Mets vs. Cardinals. I look up toward left where our day camp group would have sat, up there in the air, for a 1971 doubleheader. I see where my wife and kids and I sat in box seats. And then I look up and behind where home plate would been, where I was on the chilly night in 1986, that night when I learned that anything is possible in life. My kids run around where the bases would have been. I stand near second, where the stage was for that famous Beatles show in 1965. Behind me, music rumbles from inside Citi Field. It's Paul Mc-Cartney and band, soundchecking for the show they'll be doing the next night. (What were the odds of that?) Lastly, I go stand where the ball rolled through Buckner's legs. In my mind, I see Wilson wildly hustling to first. I see Knight grabbing his helmet as he approached home, as if he was unable to grasp what had happened, holding on to his head as if to make sure it wouldn't explode in joy, as we all did that night.

R E F L E C T I O N S
from songwriter, author and baseball memorabilia collector Seth Swirsky

And what about the actual baseball in question?

It's owned by popular author, songwriter, musician and renowned memorabilia collector Seth Swirsky. Seth revels in the stories behind these pieces, exuding passion, knowledge and reverie. He gets giddy when he talks about the items in his possession, especially the 1986 "Mookie ball." See, Seth is not some dispassionate collector/investor. Rather, he is a fan with an earnest, loving interest in the history of the game.

This is one of the most amazing artifacts I've ever held. This one piece alone represents the highest high and the lowest low any fan could feel, depending on who you were rooting for. In this ball, you can feel the history and impact of what happened that night in 1986. It also has the elements that, for me, set any good baseball artifact apart from the rest—it has evidence on it that identifies where it came from and what happened to it. For instance,

Seth Swirsky's famed baseball.

the ump that picked it up put a little "X" on it to make sure it was marked positively as *the* ball. Keith Hernandez kissed the baseball that night, leaving a little tobacco stain on it—think about that! The umpire that night gave the ball to Arthur Richmond, the Mets traveling secretary, and he passed it around the locker room. Mookie signed it that night, creating even more compelling evidence. On the 20th anniversary of the game in 2006, I talked to Mookie in the Mets locker room. He wanted to see the ball, as did all the other players; to see it, to touch it, to reconnect in a meaningful way with that moment—that amazing moment.

Jagger Dances
(1986)

February 15, 1986, Jerry Hall hosted *Saturday Night Live*. Stevie Ray Vaughan was the musical guest, and I wanted to go because there was a rumor that Mick Jagger might perform unannounced with Vaughn's band. A friend of mine who worked at NBC arranged a ticket for me. During the dress rehearsal of the show, it was clear that while Jagger wouldn't sing that night, he would appear during Jon Lovitz's "The Pathological Liar" sketch. Regardless, I grabbed a seat down low for the live airing of the show, which—while somewhat stage obstructed—allowed me to see a little of what was happening behind the scenes (including a costume dress falling off the statuesque Ms. Hall during a commercial—whoo-hoo!).

When she introduced the band for their first number, "Say What," I realized I had chosen the perfect seat. Not 20 feet away from me, obstructed from the view of the crowd, was Jagger. He was alone, listening to the music and *dancing*. Classic moves that harkened back to the 1969 Jagger, the 1972 Jagger and the 1975 Jagger. Leg kicks, hand swoops, pointing, clapping, laughing—Jagger in his own world, getting off on Stevie Ray and Jimmie Vaughan, at one with the blues, dancing up a storm. Nobody seemed to notice as all eyes were on the stage. But it made me realize that even behind a false wall and stepping over cables, there is no more compelling figure in rock and roll than Mick Jagger, whether in front of 50,000 screaming fans or all alone, off to the side, in the shadows.

A "Meeting" with Jagger
(1986)

hen I worked at Ohlmeyer Advertising in New York, my friend Brian Carr and I would often take walks at lunch. We worked on Madison Avenue near 58th Street, so we'd head up Park Avenue over to Fifth Avenue—just shooting the breeze. Often, we'd see a celebrity or two, but like it is in New York, it was never a big deal.

One day, I said, "Let's head up Park."

"No, let's go over to Fifth. We see better names over there," Brian said.

"I bet you a buck we'll see someone bigger on Park."

"I'll take the bet—but over on Fifth."

Done.

Walking down Fifth Avenue on this beautiful spring day near 63rd street, a cab screamed over to the curb. A leggy blonde and a shorter, scruffy guy with long hair popped out and start walking.

"That's Jerry Hall and Mick Jagger," Brian said. "You owe me a buck."

Okay, okay, whatever. But it was *Mick Jagger* for crying out loud. So we followed. They walked two blocks south, then headed east over to Madison and went north. Not a soul recognized them. I wanted to stop people and make them notice, like the guy who hassles Woody Allen in *Annie Hall*—"We got Alvy Singer over here!"—but I refrained.

We kept our stalking distance at about 20 paces, and still, of the hundreds of people, nobody knew who they were.

But the pair also had it figured out, ducking their heads and window-shopping, blending in like chameleons in the rain forest. We kept the subjects in our scope and decided we need a plan to create contact.

"Look, let's pass them," I proposed. "We walk maybe 20 steps ahead, turn abruptly and, as if we're late for a crucial meeting, I'll say, 'Aha! That *meeting*!' and then—*bam*—we'll run right in to him."

Brian said it's the stupidest plan he can imagine. But it's all we had. Loping past Jagger, I could hear him talking. The voice! We got past, and I counted down. One, two, three—

"Aha! That *meeting* we're late for!"

I turned dramatically and there he was. We were face-to-face (he's slightly shorter than me) and we bump, and I realized, he thinks I'm blowing his cover.

"Oh, hi, Mick," I said, as if we were both clocking in at the same time at the meat packing plant.

He muttered something like, "Come on, man," and they disappeared around the corner. Like a birder sneezing in the bush, I'd scared him away. But, I'd made contact. Sort of.

Back at the office, Brian and I breathlessly recounted the episode.

"It was amazing," I said. "He was just walking slowly and casually, not a care in the world."

Barbara, a woman I worked with, said, "Well, he didn't have a big important meeting to get to like you guys did."

Chris Mullin
(1987)

From the *New York Times*, December 20, 1987:

Three summers ago, as Chris Mullin lived what he described as the American Dream, the making of the United States basketball team and its gold-medal victory at the Los Angeles Olympic Games, the members of that memorable group left their signatures in the pub that provided a stop along the way.

Mullin left something more. It was the summer before his senior year at St. John's University, a time for his national reputation to grow. A world that had been limited by design to a campus near his family's Flatbush home was beginning a drastic expansion. Where most teammates wrote their uniform numbers, or thanks, next to their names on the wall, Mullin and several others each wrote this:

If the beer is cold, we'll win the gold.

In the past 10 days, Mullin has begun an attempt to revoke his membership. After two missed practices and a suspension from the Golden State Warriors, which had been preceded by a series of unheeded warning signals, Mullin checked into Centinela Hospital in Inglewood, Calif., in an effort to redirect his life.

I was a big Chris Mullin fan, especially when he played at St. John's. "The Redmen," as they were called back then (before political correctness forced them to change it to "Red Storm," whatever that is), under coach Lou Carnesecca, were always competitive, disciplined and tough. Especially Mullin. A sturdy Irish kid from Brooklyn in the role of spot-up shooting guard, Mullin owned the city for a couple of years before moving on to the NBA where he had a more-than-solid career. But alcoholism had entered his life, and once he moved to the West Coast to play pro ball after college, it took over, as it almost always does.

After the news broke, a friend and I were, ironically enough, discussing the issue over a beer at a bar in New York on a frigid December night. It became more of a debate, as I defended Mullin against my pal who said he'd sacrificed his shot and should be banned from the game. The bartender, quietly drying glasses at the end of the bar, kept looking over at us as

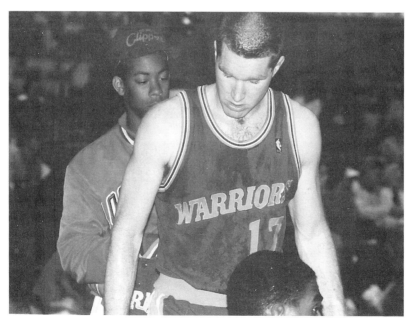

Chris Mullin as a player for the Golden State Warriors.

we made our points. Mullin, I argued, was not a troublemaker—just a kid who drank too much in college and lost control. He was a solid team player, a guy with good character who simply needed help.

"*Can* him," my friend said. "Help him out, sure, but he doesn't deserve to play pro ball. He deserves to be canned."

I tried arguing the point further, but my friend silenced me with a final, "*Can* him!" before heading to the men's room.

The young bartender came over, filled my glass and said, "Hey, that's on me." Noticing he ignored my friend's glass, I said "Thanks," with a bit of a question mark. "Hey," the bartender continued. "I appreciate you sticking up for Chris. He's my brother and things are a little rough now, but he'll be okay."

Turns out he was more than okay. Mullin went on to play under Larry Bird with the Indiana Pacers, ended his career with almost 18,000 points and, as of this writing, he is the executive vice president of Basketball Operations for the Golden State Warriors.

Way to go, Chris.

This Is Hollywood
(1988)

Hollywood is such a strange place. It's not even really a place, it's more a state of mind (or an illusion or a mirage or whatever you want it to be). Except, it's not a place where you see stars. That's always the big misconception when friends or family come out west to visit.

"Let's go to Hollywood so I can see a star."

You explain that Hollywood, "the place," is simply a run-down tourist trap, and that stars are found in Beverly Hills, on Melrose and in rehab facilities, botox centers and Scientology apartment complexes. In the late 1980s, my Aunt Lee— a great lioness of a woman, all Long Island glamour, big Liz Taylor sunglasses and makeup—wanted to see Hollywood. She also thought we might see a big star there. As much as I explained in the car that the stars only existed on the sidewalk in Hollywood, she persisted.

As we walked along decrepit Hollywood Boulevard, she asked, "Where are the stars?" Near the wax museum, "Where are the stars?" Past head shops, tattoo parlors and hookers, "Where are the stars?" I'd just patiently explain, "No stars here, Aunt Lee." We compared handprints and footprints at Grauman's Chinese Theatre and then, making our way back to the car across Hollywood Boulevard, Aunt Lee asked once more, "Aren't there *any* stars in Hollywood?"

"No, Aunt Lee. For the last time, *there are no stars in Hollywood*!"

Then, as if on cue, walking up behind us, Jack Lemmon

said to me, "Well I don't know if that's necessarily true."

Aunt Lee barely flinched, cool as ever. "See, you were wrong. I knew there were stars here. This is Hollywood."

And Jack Lemmon smiled back at her and nodded. So I guess I was wrong all along.

Six Degrees of Jack Riley
(1989)

ack Riley is one of my best friends in the world. TV fans will remember him as morose psych patient Elliot Carlin on the first (and, in my opinion, best) Bob Newhart series, *The Bob Newhart Show*, from the early 1970s. Jack and I became friends by doing commercials together for about nine years, starting in 1989. He, actor Thom Sharp, engineer Jeff Serr and I would meet in the old CBS building in Hollywood about 50 weeks a year and record about 12 radio spots for CompUSA, the computer superstore, each week. It was one of the longest-running campaigns in history (I personally wrote/directed more than 4,000 commercials for this campaign), and in that time I had a front-row seat to one of the best comedy teams ever: Jack and Thom. Our foursome became very tight over the years and my friendship with Jack led to many other important relationships over the years. Jack, in addition to being sweet, funny and hilarious, knows more inter-

With Thom Sharp and Jack Riley. For nine years, I worked with these guys every week.

The Reruns. Who do you recognize? Harvey Korman? Ronnie Schell? Chuck McCann? Any others?

esting people than probably anyone else in Hollywood. It was because of Jack that I played for years on a softball team called the Reruns, comprised of many funny actors, writers, directors and the like (and coached by the great Ronnie Schell).

The great Jerry Houser walks past as I wait on deck during Reruns softball (c. 1992).

In 1992, after one of our recording sessions, Jack told me about a dinner happening that night in honor of Dick Yarmy, another actor, who was very ill. Jack said that for the past few weeks some pals were having dinner with him at a restaurant in the San Fernando Valley to make his last days funny and meaningful. Knowing how much I loved old-time showbiz, Jack invited me. I arrived a little early that night and was having a drink at the bar. Then, one by one, they started entering and heading for a private back room. Harvey Korman, Steve Allen, Sid Caesar, Bob Ridgley, Howard Morris, Gary Owens, Don Adams (Dick Yarmy's brother), Chuck McCann, Bill Dana, Shelley Berman, Pat Harrington, Pat McCormick, Don Knotts—plus famous writers and directors like Howie Storm and Sam Denoff. Thom and Jack finally arrived, too, and led me into the room. The night was amazing. The best stories and the biggest laughs, punctuated with arguing, insults and mayhem, and Dick, weakened by cancer, seemed like he was already in heaven—smiling and peaceful. I met him and he told me to come back, which I did the next week and the next. A few weeks later, Dick Yarmy died.

After the service, Jack told me the meetings would continue and I was free to attend. Back at the restaurant, the group toasted Dick and decided to call the group Yarmy's Army. They also decided to soldier on, because in making Dick feel better, they realized they were making each other feel better, too. As the weeks went on (and the meetings became monthly), things began to take shape. New faces like Tom Poston, Tim Conway, Phil Hartman and Paul Winchell would arrive—you never knew who might turn up. But official members were also named, and I was honored to be included as one. Being in my early 30s then, I was sort of like the cub reporter for the group, and I knew many of the old bits, which the guys seemed to like.

I was writing so many commercials then, that I decided to start casting many of the guys in radio spots. After all, these men sounded great and

Jack holds the newborn Charlie.

they were stage- and club-trained over the years—they understood acting and delivery because it was in their blood—and my writing became revitalized when I knew I was writing for them. The "Chris Epting players," as they became called at the production studio, had a grand old time in these spots—and then we all started becoming friends. After our son Charlie was born, you never knew who might be at the door to "see the baby." Bill Dana? Pat Harrington? It was nuts. They appreciated the work, I know, but for me it was like saying thanks for all the work they'd done previously.

John Astin with Charlie in our kitchen in 1996.

The improbable events continued for years. John Astin went so far as to come to our house one night to prepare dinner for us after my wife became ill after having our daughter Claire. He and his wife Valerie took over the kitchen and waited on us hand and foot, creating a memorable night we still talk about. Imagine, Gomez Addams tossing pasta in your kitchen and yelling, "Tally Ho!" as it lands in the

Jean, Charlie and comic legend Bill Dana in 1994.

Pat Harrington holds the baby.

bowl. And, like so many other things in my life, it all stemmed from my friendship with Jack. (My twin sister Margaret even met her husband through Jack—he's a conduit for my entire family.)

But the best Yarmy's Army experience for me was when the group, as an entity, decided to put on a benefit show. They rented the big Arlington Theatre in Santa Barbara. My wife and I went up a

Pat McCormick and Sally Struthers with Charlie and Claire just after Claire's birth (they brought the giant duck that day).

day early to watch rehearsals, and like excited little boys putting on a play, they worked as hard as I bet they ever worked in their lives, refining their sketches, bits and songs. It was wonderful to watch and the show was such a smash that they eventually took it on the road. The group still meets, but it is smaller. Many of the Army have passed and they are all toasted at the start of each meeting. I haven't been for a while since we moved to Huntington Beach, but I must go again, before it's too late. Yarmy's Army helped my writing, my thinking and how I look at life. To be around that much talent and collective experience, it can only make you better.

A flyer from the first Yarmy's Army show. These men made my life better.

With Jack Riley and Fred Willard.

A party Jack had in 1993 out at a beach house in Oxnard, California, also affected me and my family significantly. My wife and I drove up to the house and once we got there, I met someone I'd always been a fan of: Fred Willard. From the Ace Trucking Company to *Fernwood 2 Night* to *America 2-Night* and many other things, Fred always left me in awe. His calculated cluelessness was funny on so many levels, it was hard to measure, and in person, while funny, he was also just sort of a nice guy. We got to talking baseball and, as it turned out, we both shared an odd interest—tracing the places where old baseball stadiums used to exist. Like kindred spirits, we realized we'd been following each other unknowingly, to where the Polo Grounds used to be, and Ebbets Field, Forbes Field and Sportsman's Park. This night began a meaningful friendship with Fred and his wife Mary. We all became very close—they are lovely people—but an incident stands out in regards to our shared interest.

One day, Fred and I headed to a seedy part of Los Angeles, where old Wrigley Field used to stand. We'd brought photos to line up so we could

(from left to right) **Mary Willard, Charlie and Fred Willard in 1993.**

re-shoot the angles in a then-and-now fashion, we had books, and we even brought our mitts to have a catch there. Well, there's a mental hospital on part of the site now, and Fred wanted to try to get on the roof to take more dramatic photos. A guard came out to see what we were doing and Fred asked earnestly, "Might it be okay if my friend and I go on the roof and get a few shots off?" The guard was incredulous.

(from left to right) **Brian Riley, Jack Riley, Martin Mull, Pat McCormick, Ken Gal, me and Thom Sharp.**

"Get a few shots off?"

"Just a few," Fred laughed. "Then our job will be done!"

The guard went and got another bigger, more official-looking guard. "What's this about taking shots?" the guy demanded.

We explained what kind of "shots" we meant (remember, this was mental hospital) and our request was quickly rebuffed. As Fred says, nobody has ever heard the words yelled, "Can I help you, sir?" more than us, given how many odd spots our former ballpark missions have taken us. Fred is a gem. Especially when he is looking for a former diamond.

Getting back to that beach party, I met someone else there whom I've remained close with: Sally Struthers. We chatted for a long time on a couch that night and she said she wasn't working as much as she wanted, that the industry was changing a lot and it was becoming harder. I asked if she'd ever wanted to do some voiceover work and she said absolutely. The next week, we did a few spots for something I was working on and she was incredible—the best I'd ever worked with. So we did some

With my beloved friend Sally Struthers. She's the best, period.

My nana with Charlie. At her funeral, Sally helped get me through the eulogy.

more, and more, and were having a ton of laughs, too. I invited Sally to our son's christening (which was spiked by Yarmy's Army guys—Jack actually mock baptized Pat McCormick at the reception) and she came. I'd wanted my mom and sister to meet her because I knew they'd get along great—and they did. Before long, Sally was an official Epting family member. She is Aunt Sally to my children today and they adore her because she is the funniest, silliest, most loving aunt anyone could ever have.

But many family members of mine love Sally for something particular she did. In 1995, my grandmother died. Her name was Margaret Gallo, and she was the family matriarch. She was also my heart and soul, and to this day I cannot accept that she is no longer here. She was a resilient, loving little Italian lady who was strong, tough and wise—beyond words. Before I gave my nana's eulogy, I asked Sally at the church if she had any tips for getting through it (Sally had also gotten to know Nana well).

"Don't look at anybody crying," she said. "You'll break down. Stay focused on what you want to say. Look over at me, I can help be your strength."

When I started speaking in front of the assembly, I looked at Sally. She was sobbing, like everyone else. But she nodded at me with encouragement and did in fact help me get through it. After the service, we went to a restaurant, but it was early, there were tons of people in from back east, and my mom and I didn't know what to do with everyone once lunch ended. We were obliged to plan something, but we were still reeling from the loss. Sally saw us talking and came over to see what was up. I told her and she pulled me aside.

"Come on," she said. "You and I are going to my house, ordering a ton of Chinese food and everyone here is coming over. We're throwing a party for Nana."

And that's what we did. Sally took over. She opened her big, beautiful house, she entertained and she celebrated the life of my grandmother for all of these people, most of whom she'd never met. The party went long into the night, and made an impression on my family that will last forever. Sally and I ended up on her trampoline that night just looking up at the stars, exhausted.

"Thanks, Sally," I said.

"No problem, honey," she said. "This is my family, too."

And it is.

Reminded of this day recently, Sally dismisses the notion that she did something substantial. "That's what you do out of love," she says.

PS—I just remembered this. One time, Jack and I were at lunch at a place in Hollywood and there was a commotion at the door—screaming, shrieks—but no worries, it's just the arrival of Sam Kinison.

He spotted Jack from across the room and yelled, "Oh, ohhhhhhhhhhh! Jack Riley!" before rushing over to bear hug Jack. It was then I learned that Jack's reach knew no bounds. Jack had helped Sam when the upstart comic was a wet-behind-the-ears preacher new to town. Sam never forgot this apparently and insisted he join us for lunch with his party. Next to me, in between bites, Kinison said, "Do you know how great this man is? Do you? *Do you*? He's a comedy genius, a *god*. Oh, ohhhh-hhhh!"

A few months later, Kinsion died tragically in a desert car crash. His clear love and respect of the witty, understated jazz hound known as Jack Riley told me a lot more about him than any of his brilliant comedy shtick. I'm telling you, everyone loves Jack. As they should.

R E F L E C T I O N S
from actor Jack Riley

I knew when I asked Jack to comment on what it is that makes him so beloved among friends (and so remarkably connected with interesting people) that he'd be modest, and even a bit dismissive of the premise. That's Jack. Still, I pressed him for at least a sentence. With a slight, dry chuckle, he obliged.

My secret is, I leave [my friends] alone and I don't demand anything from them. I find that's the best way to keep friends. Also, I never notice that I do anything unusual, but if you say so, I'll take it. I've been lucky myself, meeting and working with some wonderful people in my career starting with Tim Conway back in Cleveland, but especially Bob Newhart. I was always a huge fan of his and working on *The Bob Newhart Show* for all those years changed my life. Today, he is a legacy. And I drive a Legacy. So we have something in common.

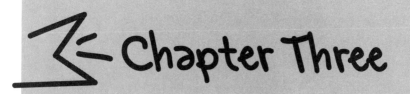

Chapter Three

claw vending machines

Pogs

PUSH POPS

THE MACERANA

chat rooms Teletubbies

Beanie Babies

"I'VE FALLEN AND

blockbuster sequels

stoner and slacker humor *(Beavis and Butthead, Bill and Ted's Excellent Adventure, American Gladiators,* **etcetera)**

rollerblades

Starbucks coffee

LAPTOP COMPUTERS

Sweatin' to the Oldies

extreme sports

grunge music and

the Reebok Pump

PRODIGY

The 1990s →

THE INTERNET

Power Rangers

bleached hair

the Thighmaster

the Sony Discman

Barney & Friends

I CAN'T GET UP!"

fanny packs

yuppie culture

SUVs

The Original Buns of Steel

Sony Playstations

Furbies

GIGA PETS

Napster

Goosebumps

"fashion"

tattoos

AOL

And my personal favorites from the era:

TV Shows
Twin Peaks (1990–1991)
The Larry Sanders Show (1992–1998)
Weird Science (1994–1998)
Space Ghost Coast to Coast (1994–2004)
NewsRadio (1995–1999)
King of the Hill (1997–2009)
Freaks and Geeks (1999–2000)

Movies
Goodfellas (1990)
Slacker (1991)
Glengarry Glen Ross (1992)
Dazed and Confused (1993)
Jurassic Park (1993)
Schindler's List (1993)
Quiz Show (1994)
The Usual Suspects (1995)
Fargo (1996)
Waiting For Guffman (1996)

Albums
Blood Sugar Sex Magik
by Red Hot Chili Peppers (1991)
Metallica by Metallica (1991)
Out of the Cradle by Lindsey Buckingham
(1992)
The Downward Spiral by Nine Inch Nails
(1994)
100% Fun by Matthew Sweet (1995)
Mellon Collie and the Infinite Sadness
by The Smashing Pumpkins (1995)
Being There by Wilco (1996)
Homogenic by Björk (1997)
OK Computer by Radiohead (1997)
Time Out of Mind by Bob Dylan (1997)

"Into the Night"
(1990)

A favorite song of my wife's is "Into the Night," by Benny Mardones. It was one of the first really big ballads to dominate the 1980s and became such a monstrous radio hit that Mardones has since actually re-recorded the thing a couple of times and it always ends up being a hit. It's one of the most-played songs in American radio history and, lest you forget, it tells the dramatic tale of professed saviorhood and rescue; of plucking a 16-year-old girl from the depths of her virgin despair and delivering her to a new plane of love and understanding.

Or something like that.

To my wife, a 16-year-old girl living in Peoria, Illinois, the song represented something profound and dreamy, offering slivers of hope and promise—a ticket out of adolescence. Remember the lyrics?

She's just sixteen years old
Leave her alone, they say
Separated by fools
Who don't know what love is yet
But I want you to know

If I could fly
I'd pick you up
I'd take you into the night
And show you a love

Like you've never seen, ever seen

So one night, my wife Jean and I are having a drink in a haunt of ours, a restaurant called the Brentwood Inn in Los Angeles. It's an old-fashioned place with a well-oiled bar that is always studded with local characters (and the occasional celebrity—two most notables for me, Jim Backus and Sean Penn, the latter of which I drank with several times here, right after he split with Madonna). My pal Ernie (an amazing writer) tended the bar there, and one night he whispered to me, "You know that guy over there?" At a table near the bar was a longhaired guy and his date. The guy was boisterously telling stories, a little loudly, but no, I didn't know him. Ernie, whose musical tastes were beautifully avant-garde said, "Says his name is Benny Mardones. Been here a few times this week. Says he's a singer but I don't know him." Looking at him closer, I saw it was in fact Benny Mardones (I'd seen him play years earlier and he has a unique face, so it sort of rang a bell).

The next time Benny came up to the bar to have Ernie freshen his drink, Ernie introduced us. A moment later, Benny brought his girlfriend over and grabbed the two barstools next to us. The guy was incredibly chatty and funny, we're not talking music at all, just comparing New York to Los Angeles (he's from the East Coast, as am I), talking politics, TV—general bar talk. Well into our conversation, a few more rounds of drinks worth, I let out that Jean's favorite song is "Into the Night." And Benny stops. Cold. No more chitchat. Oh no. I've blown it. By acknowledging who he is and what he does, I've disrupted his anonymity. Plus, he's had

The Brentwood Inn, where the impromptu concert took place. (Brentwood, California.)

a few. Would I get a drink in the face? A punch in the face? Would he just turn and leave with his beautiful date, offended at my utter lack of tact?

He was tough to read.

But not for long.

Benny stood, cleared his chair back and stood right before my wife. Taking her hand, he began to sing that song, with more passion, gusto and intensity than the original—and that original packed a punch. Jean blushed as Bennie howled through that plaintive chorus, like he was performing at Madison Square Garden—*wailing*. Ernie, drying glasses at the end of the bar, just watched, smiled his bemused smile and shook his head. Just another night for him.

At the song's end, Bennie yelled, "I'm hungry!" so into the night we went with he and his girlfriend, to Izzy's Deli for a 2:00 AM meal followed by more cruising around listening to ear-splitting versions of Benny's soon-to-be-released record in his car. Benny dumped us off by our car later on and then peeled out in a cloud of blue smoke, into the pre-dawn darkness, leaving Jean and I both to wonder if what had just happened had *really* just happened. Who was that masked, crazed balladeer? Well, it was Benny Mardones. And after that, "Into the Night" became one of my favorite songs as well.

R E F L E C T I O N S
from singer Benny Mardones

I tracked down Benny Mardones for this book, recounting for him what happened back then.

"Usually when I meet someone who says, 'I met you about 20 years ago,' I say, 'Do I owe you an apology?'" Then he laughs. Hard. "Challenging times back then, man. My memory

Benny Mardones's smash album *Never Run, Never Hide*.

is bad. But that sounds like it was a fun night we had!"

But even though Jean and I were lost in the blur and haze of his memory, it isn't like Benny doesn't still spoil his fans. The story I told him led him to tell me this.

One night recently in Buffalo, wintertime, I finished [a show] and I walked offstage. I went out to the parking lot and there was a woman crying. She was standing with her husband or boyfriend or whatever, and I said, "What happened?"

The guy says, "Tonight was my wife's birthday and we got stuck trying to get here with the snow coming down and we were hoping to catch the last couple of songs and it meant a lot, too, because she adores your music. Could I pay you maybe $50 just to sing a couple of lines to her?"

I told him, "Put your money in your pocket," and said to the band, "Guys, get back in before they take the stage down. We're going up for one more song."

They say, "What? The show's over."

I have the tech guys plug everything back in, and then we have to wait for the audience to file out, like 1,000 people. So 10 minutes later we're ready to go, I put them in the front row, then I went onstage and sang "Into the Night" for her. And then I sang "Happy Birthday." And it made me feel probably as good as it made her feel. The husband was crying and shaking his head saying, "I can't believe this happened, I'll never forget this as long as I live." I said, "Well that makes it worth it right there. Without my fans I'm nothing, I may not even be alive today, so I never miss a chance to thank you to people.

We like Benny Mardones. How can you not?

Stern
(1991)

efore Howard Stern earned the title of "Shock Jock" (one I never really thought was fitting—he's just a funny, honest New Yorker), we used to listen to him spin records on WRNW in Briarcliff Manor, New York. He barely said a word. Then, all of a sudden, he was back in New York from D.C., after becoming "Howard Stern." There's never been a radio performer like Howard and I think he's great. (We did bust his balls once—at work in about 1985 at Ohlmeyer Advertising, we saw him being interviewed by Larry King back when King was on in the afternoon. They were taking calls so I dialed, got on the air and for the benefit of our lunchroom, said I was editor for a gay newspaper called *Tongue in Cheek*. Stern erupted—"You should keep your tongue *out of other people's cheeks*!"—while Larry King tried to maintain order—"Woah, hold on there, caller, what exactly are you saying?")

When Howard's show was going to start being broadcast on the West Coast, he came out to do an initial show from the original Spago restaurant. Given all the radio commercials I was writing back then, I was invited to the event by the station

(from left to right) **Me, Howard Stern and Jean.**

to have breakfast at Spago and watch the show. Wayne Gretzky was on, as was my friend, actress Edie McClurg, who got into an infamous dust up with another guest, Jessica Hahn (of televangelist Jim Bakker infamy). All in all, it was a wild, typically classic Stern show.

My wife and I were going to meet him after and I wasn't sure what to expect—you heard a million different things about what Howard was like. Well, we met him and I passed along some greetings from Pat McCormick and some other old-timer comics who liked Howard.

At that, Howard's eyes opened wide. "Really?"

He loved those guys and wanted to know all about them, and how he could get in touch with them. He was funny, gracious and very low-key, just a good, normal guy—the exact opposite of what you might think—and it reminded me that these are show people, playing characters. Even "real" people like Howard Stern.

Curt Gowdy
(1991)

I once wrote a radio show called *The Final Score*. It was sort of like the great series of Paul Harvey vignettes, *The Rest of the Story*, in that I'd write a two-to-three-minute story about some moment from sports and then reveal an ironic ending. You know, "So that kid who was fired as the Yankee bat boy grew up to be . . . William Bendix, who played the Babe in one of the worst sports films ever made." Stuff like that, sort of.

The host of the show was the famed broadcaster Curt Gowdy (he won the job after reading against Don Meredith and Steve Garvey). I'd research and write the scripts, then once a month I'd be on the phone with Mr. Gowdy, directing his reads from whatever recording studio around the country he'd happen to be in.

The show was fun for a few months but it ran daily, so soon it started to get tough to find enough material. Luckily, I'd stumbled into a series of books written by old-time sports scribe Bill Stern and then a couple written by another veteran, Mac Davis (not

With sportscaster Curt Gowdy in a recording session for "The Final Score."

the singer). They were crammed with hundreds of wild bits of sports irony, things I had no idea about (and I'm a huge sports history fan). When I'd go to double source the books, some of the stories seemed hard to verify, but Stern's in particular were so first person that he seemed to imply they were told to him first hand or, even better, that he'd witnessed many of these things as a fly on the wall. So maybe there were no other sources, maybe they were simply the Holy Grails of ironic sports stories, and besides, we needed material!

One time, I was going to be in San Francisco when Curt Gowdy was, so we met in person and did the recording together. This was exciting—finally, I'd get to meet the guy who read my words each month—the great Curt Gowdy! My wife Jean was with me, too, and he was very charming when we met him. We got into the recording and he stopped at one of the scripts—a story that dealt with his good pal, Ted Williams.

"Wait," he said. "That's not where his bats were made. And he never gave them to some sick kid. And that kid didn't grow up to be George Brett." (Or something like that.) Gowdy finished with, "This seems like some of the b——t a guy named Mac Davis used to write."

Gulp. Mac Davis?

"This guy simply made stuff up. But you wouldn't be using him as a source, right?"

In my head, I ran through the scripts. Davis only accounted for a couple and we could ditch those. The others were based on Bill Stern stories. *Whew*!

"No, sir, let's ditch this one though and move on to those."

Next he said, "Okay. . . . Man, the only guy worse than Davis was Bill Stern. How that guy stayed in business, I'll never know. That son-of-a-bitch made *everything*

One of the books Gowdy warned me about, *Sports Shorts: Astonishing Strange But True.*

up. You ever hear of Bill Stern?"

Was this the final straw on *The Final Score*? I went into the recording booth and explained to Curt Gowdy how I'd found the books. He was sort of mad at first, but he seemed to forgive me. I was young and still learning. On the spot, he

When he wrote his personal info down, I felt like such a big shot.

peeled off a bunch of personal stories of his to save the session. Then he took us to lunch and lectured me about writing stories. For the next year (as long as the show remained), I dug and dug and dug for material. I triple-sourced everything. And I keep those books on my shelf as reminders that short cuts are the enemy of good research.

Unleashing the Raider Within
(1994)

n January, my wife and I went to see the Los Angeles Raiders play the Denver Broncos in a wildcard game at the Los Angeles Memorial Coliseum. The teams were both at 9–6–0 going into this final game of the 1993 league season, and so a lot was on the line—a berth in the playoffs and home-field advantage, step one in the chase for the championship and the road to the Super Bowl. We had great seats, near the 40-yard line. In front of us for much of the game was O. J. Simpson—just a few months before he was acquitted of brutally slaughtering two innocent people with a machete.

There was also an earthquake during the game—a precursor to the massive Northridge quake that would hit us just about a week later. It was a weird day all around, made weirder by who was sitting just behind us.

During the first half, Denver, led by John Elway, was rolling. Behind me, I started hearing an ongoing analysis of what was wrong with the Raiders ("Hostetler's too tentative . . . too tentative! Where is the defensive pressure? Too tentative!"). Every play seemed to get a reaction from the deep-voiced guy, who was becoming a bit annoying with the never-ending patter.

"Elway's in a zone. A zone! You have to break the zone. You don't break the zone by being tentative!"

He was sucking up so much air, it's a wonder half of the Coliseum didn't pass out. On and on, over and over. "No! Yes!

No! Yes!" But the more I heard, the more familiar it sounded. I knew the voice, but from where? Who was it? Wait! Late-night TV! I turned around to confirm. Yes. The analytical voice was none other than famed infomercial motivator and self-help guru Tony Robbins, author of the mammoth bestseller *Awaken the Giant Within*.

He was surrounded a huddle of slighter, less impressive "yes men" who nodded feverishly after each of his assessments in full agreement. In fact, had Robbins said, "Guys, I think it'd be a good idea for all of you to strip naked, paint my 800 number on your butts and moon the crowd," my hunch is they would have kept nodding and agreeing while pulling their pants down and getting the paintbrushes out—they were that focused on his words. Problem was, we were also focused on his words, given that he wouldn't shut up.

At the half, Denver held a 27–13 lead. As the teams headed toward the tunnel, a Raiders assistant coach ran up into the stands near our seats, waving frantically at Robbins, who

Tony Robbins *(center)* analyzing the faltering Raiders offense before making his big move.

noticed the coach, got up quickly and followed him down into the tunnel. Huh?

Robbins made it back to his seat at the start of the second half looking relaxed—smug, even. He told the group with him, "I think we figured it out." Watching Robbins had become a game-within-a-game for my wife and me, and I was ready to watch him go bust. Come on. What could he have told them? The Broncos widened their lead to 17 points on a 27-yard field goal by Jason Elam. Uh-oh. Did the Raiders pay for this advice? Tony-baloney! I knew it was a scam!

Then something shifted. The Raiders started to rally. After the Denver field goal, Hostetler led a passing drive, not looking tentative at all, for a Raider touchdown. As the final quarter opened, the Broncos were up by 10 and in possession of the football.

The Raiders held, kicked a field goal and were down by just seven with 9:23 left on the clock. The Raiders blocked the Broncos' next punt, but were unable to capitalize. The Broncos regained the ball on their own 20, with 5:14 left and a seven-point lead. Linebacker Winston Moss, the Raiders' defensive captain, made one stop. Defensive tackle Chester McGlockton made the next. On third-and-six, safety Eddie Anderson dropped the Broncos' ball carrier for a loss of one. But a long punt of 54 yards pushed the Raiders back on their own 30.

Then Hostetler, perhaps channeling Robbins, exploded. They had to cover 70 yards with 2:59 on the clock, the two-minute warning timeout to come and three timeouts of their own. Several plays later, the Raiders were sitting at first and goal on the Broncos' four. The team's last timeout was used and two incompletions brought up a third-and-four from the four-yard line, with just eight seconds left.

Hostetler took the snap from Don Mosebar on what would be the final play. He spotted Alexander Wright open just inside the goal line and hit him. After the extra point, it was time for overtime. The Raiders had twice come back from 17-point deficits to earn the tie.

Even though Denver won the coin toss and chose to receive to open the "sudden death" period, they failed to score and Raider Jeff Jaeger kicked a 47-yard field goal to win the game. The Raiders triumphed, 33–30. We had witnessed a brilliant comeback.

Behind us, Tony Robbins—now more smug and self-satisfied than ever—was patted on the back and congratulated by his posse. But clearly he had done it. He had lit a fire. He forced them to walk the coals. The Raiders assistant coach signaled for him to come down once more and head to the tunnel, presumably to be part of the celebration. Robbins, clearly, had helped the Raiders "Unleash the Power Within." If I hadn't seen this myself, I might not have believed it. And all of a sudden, I had an urge to call that 800 number; all of a sudden, I was becoming a bit of a believer.

Nomo, Mr. Nice Guy
(1995)

My cousin David and I attended the 1995 Major League Baseball All-Star Game in Arlington, Texas. Through some business connections I had, we attended several All-Star games in the 1990s. We even had passes for all of the events, including the game, the Home Run Derby and the concerts, and in Texas, they closed down the Six Flags amusement park for a player party. This was the year after the baseball strike, and to try and win fans back, the league made players more accessible to fans, held more autograph sessions, etcetera. That's why I found it odd that on the invite to the player party, there was a warning to kids: "Do not approach players for autographs." The park would be essentially empty except for VIPs and some business people, a low-pressure event. The only kids who'd be in there would be those of big shots, so why state something so ridiculous on the ticket?

Soon after entering, we saw the rule get challenged. A pair of kids walked over to Barry Bonds and Bobby Bonilla, who were chatting alone at a makeshift bar. There was not another person around for about 50 yards. But before the kids could even get a pen out, Bonds shooed them away like bugs.

"Not tonight—read the rules!"

Then the two stars got back to laughing and talking. It made me think the whole fan-friendly push by MLB was just a con.

But not everyone got the memo that night. As we left, we noticed a crowd near the front gate—someone was being mobbed. We asked someone what was happening and they told us that Dodger pitcher Hideo Nomo was inside the mob signing autographs—as he'd been for some time and as he would continue doing into the night. (I read the next day that he never even made it inside, so pleased was he to be in such demand and so willing to oblige his young fans.) Nomo started the All-Star Game the next night, struck out three of the six batters he faced and won the Rookie of the Year Award that season. They should have given him the MVP Award for his performance at the player event, for reminding us that there still were a few players who understand that what they do is special, who understand the affect they have on kids and who understand that the little boy inside the man is an important thing to preserve.

My ticket from the 1995 All-Star Game.

Jerry Lewis
(1995)

My friends Jack Riley and Pat McCormick, who'd crafted a two-man comedy routine built around Pat's outrageous one-liners, were invited to appear on the Jerry Lewis telethon for muscular dystrophy. Jack asked if I felt like tagging along and I jumped. Say what you will about the telethon, but it's a classic chunk of pop culture. Okay, maybe it bends toward mawkish, over-the-top kitsch, but still . . . Jerry!

The show was being held at CBS in Los Angeles, and

My good friend, the legendary Pat McCormick.

as we saw from the limo when we pulled in, CBS had erected a massive circus tent complex for Mr. Lewis. As we entered the studio, the producer said that Jerry wanted to meet with Jack and Pat to say hi and catch up. We were led through the tent complex, a maze that seemed to go forever. There were various rooms off to the sides, but as we approached the main suite, we could hear Lewis—that high-pitched whine—and he was *pissed off.*

"Goddamn it! My little girl wants to watch *The Lion King*! Where is my goddamned

VCR? You promised me a goddamned VCR!"

Jack shot me a look as if to say, "This should be good."

We made it to the room and Lewis saw us, smiled, and slammed the phone down with a final, parting shot to whomever he was yelling at. "Get me that goddamned VCR you sons of bitches!" Then to us, cheerily, "Guys, how the hell are you, for crying out loud?"

Lewis's main tented area was a like a huge living room, a place for him to chill between breaks on the exhaustive telethon. He was thrilled to see the guys, but then finally said to me, "Who the hell are you?" I stammered and he said, "Ah, forget it, come over here." I followed him. On the counter was a new, state-of-the-art milkshake blender.

"You like milkshakes, you bastard? Help me figure out how to use this goddamned thing and we'll have a milkshake." We fiddled with it for a bit, I scooped the ice cream and soon, Lewis was pouring us frothy chocolate milkshakes. "Ah," he savored. "Goddamn, that is good."

This wasn't just Jerry Lewis; it was like Jerry Langford from Martin Scorsese's brilliant *The King of Comedy* (when Lewis played a self-absorbed talk show host and entertainer) had climbed down off the screen and into the tent for my benefit.

Soon, he was back on air, singing, joking, sweating— being Jerry Lewis. He eyed me at one point in the wings and winked, smiled and called me over during a short break.

"Wasn't that milkshake fantastic?"

I cannot have a chocolate milkshake today and not think of Jerry Lewis. How weird is that?

Be Like Mike

(1996)

I had never been much of a Michael Jordan fan. It was 1996, and up until that point, while I'd always appreciated what he did on the court, he had killed my teams too many times in the clutch. It was hard to enjoy his work due to the fact that, as a fan, it constantly came at my expense.

So when a friend called me in 1996 to ask for a Jordan-related favor, I sort of rolled my eyes. At that point in my advertising career, I was creating commercials for the Los Angeles Clippers. This friend thought it might be possible, through my affiliation with the Clips, to arrange a meeting for this kid he'd heard about who lived for Jordan.

As I was told, this little boy was very ill, so I made the call to the team. They explained that Jordan was too in demand, too impossibly over-committed. To Jordan's credit, he arranged several dinners and events a year to make sure he got to as many kids as possible, but on game days while on the road, he was off limits (totally understood).

Weeks went by, and a day before the Clippers-Bulls game, I got a call. The day before, the Bulls had come to L.A. early to catch a Lakers game. While there, someone who'd heard of this request mentioned to Jordan the kid I'd described.

My ticket from this memorable evening.

And he said, "Set it up before the game so we can meet." And all of a sudden, we were on.

I called the parents of the child. I was to escort them to the arena for the meeting, but first, they asked if I could come over a few hours early the day of the game to meet their son, Bijan. He was wary of strangers, and for me to be a part of the evening, he needed a comfort level. So I went.

This lovely child, who I believe was about 11, was stricken with a grave disorder that had left him severely physically handicapped. But his mind was spectacular. Creative, intuitive, funny, aware of the reality of his situation—and a Michael Jordan freak. The afternoon hours I spent that day with him and his mom were incredible.

But then it was time to go to the game.

Bijan's dad had hired a limo to take us all out to the Sports Arena for a designated meeting with our contact at five-thirty. Deliberately, we didn't tell Bijan about meeting Jordan—it was simply too unpredictable an event to risk breaking his heart. As far as Bijan knew, we simply had great seats for the game.

The Bulls at that time were as hot as it gets—a traveling NBA circus with Rodman, Pippen, Jordan and a few others—and the scene at the Sports Arena bore that out. In those days, the arena was a ghost town for many a game, let alone hours before tip-off. But at five o'clock when we got there, it was madness. Thousands of people outside waiting for the six-thirty door open-

We all pose with Jordan.

ing, vendors selling bootlegged Jordan shirts, Rodman wigs—you name it.

We entered a side door and went to the gate where we were to meet the Clippers PR person at five-thirty. Bijan, whom we pushed along in a stroller-type device, stared wide-eyed at the crazy scene taking place around him.

Five-thirty came, and no PR person. Five-forty. Five-fifty. Six. "Thank goodness we hadn't mentioned this to him," I thought. I placed a call on a walkie-talkie, but before I got an answer, she arrived—looking worried.

"Come on," she rushed us, "he's all set." (The team bus had been delayed, evidently.)

A few things now. We have to tell him, or we think the shock might be too much. (He had grown very tired, too, and needed to be woken up.) So as we walked, I whispered to him, "Bijan, something big is about to happen—the best thing in the world—just get ready, you are not going to believe this, buddy." And I, not even caring before about Jordan, was starting to get nervous.

We were led to a screened-off area near the locker room, a private "room" created for this event. We waited a few moments, then the door opened, and there he was: Michael Jordan. He was told I was the contact, so he came over to introduce himself and as he did so, he was looking at Bijan. I know he didn't expect a child this seriously ill because his expression changed—he shifted into some higher-level "hero" persona. He bent

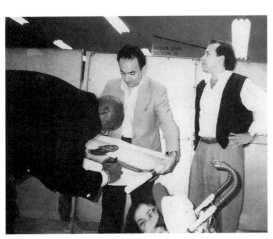
Michael Jordan signing items for Bijan.

down to Bijan's level, and for about 15 minutes, he controlled the flow of every molecule in the room. He held Bijan. Whispered to him how he wanted him to come visit in Chicago to meet his own little boy. Asked him questions and told him that, that evening, when he called his son at home in Chicago, he couldn't wait to tell him all about his new pal, Bijan. With all this, Bijan seemed to come alive. It was hard for him to speak, but he gave it his all.

Pictures were taken, then Jordan pulled me aside and said very seriously, "Look, you get these pictures developed—get two 8 × 10s and send them to this address."

Michael Jordan insisted on signing something for me—my son's birth announcement.

"Two?" I asked, to be sure.

"Two," he said, including Bijan now. "One that I can sign and send to Bijan. And one that I can keep in my office—where only the pictures of me and my best buddies are allowed to hang."

The 350-pound security guy nearby had tears streaming down his face. We were all choked up. We were witnessing a combination of greatness and compassion like we'd never seen before.

Jordan signed a ton of autographs for the kid, including the red "23" jersey Bijan wore. We all hugged Jordan goodbye, and I said, "Thank you." He got this surprised look on his face and said, "Hey, man, this is my job."

At our seats near the Bulls bench soon after, Jordan came over for one last high-five with Bijan. Now he was suited up. Clark Kent had become Superman. And he lit up the tough-fighting Clippers for 42 points.

Bijan died two weeks later. I went to the funeral because after just one night, his family felt like my family. (Those were some of the warmest, toughest people I've ever met.) Bijan's mom brought me back to see him before they closed the casket. And there he lay, peaceful in his signed Jordan "23" jersey. He is laid to rest a stone's throw from my dad at a cemetery in Southern California. Whenever I visit my dad, I always go visit Bijan. His plaque is engraved with a beautiful poem (that he wrote), and the corners are embossed with the Bulls logo.

I wrote Jordan a note about that, and while I'm not sure if he ever got it, it doesn't matter. He breathed life into this boy's soul on a night when he needed it most. He made everything better for a little while simply by being kind and using his gift in the best way possible. Michael Jordan made me and those I was with that wondrous night believe in magic.

Elgin Baylor
(1996)

n the 1990s, I helped create advertising for the Los Angeles Clippers basketball team. Sure, they're the butt of a lot of jokes (some deserved), but the Clips, for many an East Coast transplant, are a fun team to root for. The tickets were always affordable, from time to time they had young, exciting teams and if you're raised in the East, how could you ever root for the Lakers? Plus, they used to play at the old Sports Arena, a funky, intimate place with some of the best sight lines in pro sports (also where John F. Kennedy accepted the 1960 nomination for president of the United States).

We wanted to tape an hour-long infomercial for the team, basically a low-key walk around the arena with the legendary Clippers broadcaster Ralph Lawler guiding Clippers GM Elgin Baylor through why the upcoming season would be a good one. Baylor, the elegant, acrobatic hall of famer who starred for the Lakers for 13 seasons was enigmatic and aloof, and Mr. Lawler thought that since he knew him well, he'd be able to draw some stories, or at least some chitchat from Baylor just by ambling around the barn, forgetting a camera was following them. He was right. Baylor, whom I'd barely seen say more than a few terse sentences to people in meetings, was comfortable enough with Ralph to tell stories, reminisce and talk enthusiastically about the new Clippers squad. Once, I saw Baylor play when I was a kid in New York, when the Lakers came to town. Much as I hated them, in their purple satin road uniforms, that team was a regal, intimidating group that you never forgot once you saw

The 1990s . . . 201

them in person. Jerry West, Wilt Chamberlain, Gail Goodrich and, of course, Elgin Baylor, were icons of the game when they played, and as you may know, the NBA's logo is based on the silhouette of Jerry West. Baylor was my favorite of the bunch, though, so watching and listening to him in the empty arena was a treat.

When the taping ended, everyone but Elgin Baylor left. I saw him pry a basketball out that was wedged between two seats. Gazing around and seeing nobody but me, he said, "Hey, can you spot me?"

Huh? I must have looked like that kid in the classic "Mean Joe" Green Coca-Cola commercial.

With Elgin Baylor the day we got to shoot around.

"Can you spot me if I shoot around?"

I'm not sure if I ever actually said anything in response, but I did what he asked, chasing down the ball and feeding it back to him as he ripped one swish, then another, then another, and on and on. From just inside the three-point line, he worked his way around the arc, in street clothes and loafers, draining shot after shot.

"I like to see if I can hit about 20," he said.

I lost count, but I'm pretty sure he hit his goal. As my brain regained its ability to send signals to my mouth, I managed to ask a couple of questions.

"You played here, right?"

He nodded and said, "With the Lakers before the Forum was built. And in the 1963 All-Star Game." (Which meant that Bill Russell, Bob Cousy and Bob Pettit also played right there where we were shooting.)

This was one of the moments you wish you could slow down and stretch out for hours; a sports fantasy akin to Ted Williams asking you to shag flies for him at Fenway or Johnny Unitas telling you to go run a few patterns for him at an empty Memorial Stadium. But after he was satisfied, he nodded good-bye and started gliding away. Our cameraman came back to get the rest of his gear. My sense was that Elgin Baylor, once on his way, preferred to keep moving without interruption. Still, I asked him if we couldn't take just a second for a quick photo. He nodded again and stood for a moment, and even put his arm around me.

No matter how old I get, I think a great athlete (who's also a decent person) will always make me feel like an awestruck little kid. Elgin Baylor delivered me up to cloud nine that day at the old Sports Arena, and I'm not sure I ever completely came down. What I am sure of is that I miss the era of classy, team-oriented players that Baylor was part of. My old New York Knicks, featuring Willis Reed, Dave DeBusschere, Dick Barnett, Walt Frazier and, my favorite, Bill Bradley, still leave me in awe when I watch old clips of them and all the others from that golden age of basketball—so different than what we have today.

I know we sports fans tend to romanticize the teams we grew up with. But am I the only one who finds it hard to relate to this game today? Where are the graceful, stylish players like Elgin Baylor? Do they still exist?

(Crazy) Uncle Miltie
(1997)

Comedian (and friend) Pat McCormick, in his ever-accommodating mode of wanting to make sure I never missed an event he thought I'd enjoy, arranged for me to go to a Friar's Club roast of Mickey Rooney, held at the Beverly Hills Hotel. Pat and I went early together to have drinks in a private room where Milton Berle, George Carlin, Sid Caesar, David Carradine and many other old-timers shot the breeze and prepared for the evening's good-natured attack on Rooney. I liked going to these things with Pat because he was so revered among the attendees that just being with him meant you got the best treatment. It was "the Pat McCormick halo effect," and at events like these, I always had great conversations with comedic legends. This night, George Carlin talked my ear off about the Polo Grounds, which made the night special. Something else that made the night special happened after the roast.

As they do, the roast allowed the roastee to close the event with his own answer diatribe against everyone who spoke before him. But Rooney's wasn't funny. Rather, he was rambling, confused and downright weird—people started actually leaving in the middle of it, so tortuous

The Friars Club of California

A Hollywood Legend...
in honor of
Mickey Rooney

Wednesday, May 7th 1997
6:30 p.m. Cocktail Reception - 8:00 p.m. Dinner

The Beverly Hilton Hotel - International Ballroom
9876 Wilshire Blvd., Beverly Hills, CA

Ticket # № 1693   Casual Attire - $150.00 per person all inclusive

My ticket to the Mickey Rooney roast.

was the speech.

Once he finally finished, he received some awkward, half-baked applause and the ballroom started to clear. I hadn't had a chance to meet Milton Berle yet, so my friend Jack Riley introduced us. Uncle Miltie! Even in his eighties, he was friendly, funny and out-rageously tasteless—I loved him. As Mr. Berle walked away, I remarked to Jack that I'd wished I'd gotten my ticket signed. I never bugged any of these guys for that but this seemed different—a Friar's Club ticket, my first (and only) roast.

The autographed side—signed in rage!

"Why not?" Jack said. "You just had a good chat with him, I'm sure he won't mind."

So I tried and find him in the crowd. I caught up with him as he was shuffling away, handed my ticket over and said, "Mr. Berle? Can I have your auto—"

But something was wrong. Gone was the friendly old-timer, replaced by a snarling, seething, crazy old man, reading the riot act to a young hotel employee who was walking along-side him.

"You m——g c——r! I'll s——k your mother's t——s and make her s——k my c——k!"

The profanity was profound, colorful and downright vio-lent. As it turned out, he was mad because the hotel had allowed photographers in and Berle didn't want to be shot needing as-sistance walking out. In his rage though, Berle had grabbed my ticket after I asked for the autograph and was now using it to gesture in the guy's face.

"I'll have your b——s cut off and fed to my dog, you m——r!"

Walking alongside Berle, I didn't know what to do—would I get my ticket back? I could see the hotel guy wincing as Berle's spittle kept hitting him in the face. It was ugly and getting uglier.

But then, Berle pulled a pen out of his trench coat pocket, scrawled something on the ticket and slammed it back toward my face. "Now leave me the f——k alone you m——r!"

Jack and I watched Berle storm off, cursing all the way.

"You got an autograph, *and* a story," Jack mused. And he was right.

Jay Leno
(1998)

There was a point in the 1990s when my friends Fred Willard and Jack Riley appeared frequently in sketches on *The Tonight Show with Jay Leno* (Fred actually appeared for a few more years after Jack stopped). One day, while shooting a commercial, I was reading the *New York Times* during a break. There was an article about the original theater in New York where Abbott and Costello first did the classic "Who's on First" comedy routine. The theater was in the process of being moved by being placed on some sort of rollers. It gave me an idea for a sketch—what if the two foremen on the crew got into an argument about the process (i.e. "Whose idea was it to move this theater?" "No, who is the guy. . . ." You get it).

I called Fred at home and told him the idea. He liked it. A few minutes later he called me back to say he'd called *The Tonight Show*, they loved the idea, I should write it up and they'd be doing it on the show the next night.

Huh?

Fred told me that I could come spend the day there and watch them rehearse the sketch before the show was taped. A pass was waiting for me at NBC and when I entered the studio, I was stunned to see they'd

NBC BURBANK
VISITOR PASS

CLEARANCE DATE: 3/05/98   TIME: 14:17
GATE/LOCATION:
LAST NAME: EPTING   FIRST NAME: CHRIS
DESTINATION: TNT   ROOM/EXT: 2190 22222
PARKING LOCATION: BUS LIMO

WELCOME TO NBC

The pass from my *Tonight Show* writing debut.

built a fairly elaborate set for the sketch with a big, moveable brick wall, crane, etcetera. Fred and Jack were walking through the bit when I got there, and Jay was at his desk reviewing monologue jokes.

"Sit down," he invited, and so a few minutes later I found myself in the guest chair next to his desk. Jay was chatty. We talked a bit about Boston (we both attended Emerson College), and then went backstage to await the show's taping.

As it turned out, a massive car wreck on the 101 freeway created a traffic nightmare that prevented guest Kiefer Sutherland from getting there on time, so the taping was held up. Jay hung out in Fred's dressing room with us, talking over old times with Fred and jumping up from time to time to fetch drinks for people, check on the studio audience, ask a key grip how his sick kid was. . . . Leno was amazing in how little star ego he had. He was attentive to everyone within earshot; he was funny, down-to-earth and a "regular guy."

Finally, Sutherland arrived and it was showtime. Fred and Jack got ready, and the sketch—*my* sketch— was up just before the first guest. Would it kill? Would this open new career doors for me as a sketch writer? Would Jay pay me to give up writing commercials so I could write just for him? This was it!

I watched on the dressing room monitor as

The actual script of the sketch (Jack's copy).

the sketch started. Jay popped his head in to give me a thumbs up right after the two went on. Would the laughs be too big? Would they mask the witty banter I had crafted? Well, as it turned out, no worries there. The banter was plenty audible because the laughs were plenty few. Some how, some way, nobody seemed to get any of this who-what-why vaudevillian word-play.

Though it felt like about four hours, at the end of the four-minute sketch, the look on Jay's face said it all. He stared into the camera, made an expression like, "Well *that* was a helluva bomb, huh?" and went to commercial.

Yikes. Would Jay have me tossed off the studio lot? Have Emerson rescind my diploma? What would the King of Late Night do to me?

He came back after the show was done and said, "Hey, what are ya gonna do, huh? These audiences today, they don't get this classic stuff. Don't let their reaction throw ya. It was funny. These people don't get it."

A gentleman to the bitter end. Leaving the studio, I could still hear him making the rounds, chatting with stage-hands and makeup people. That's what I took away—his courtesy—because after the crash and burn of my first and only *Tonight Show* sketch, that was about all I had.

Chapter Four

RAZOR SCOOTERS

Napoleon Dynamite

reality TV

iPods

emo

hipsters

the Big Mouth Billy Bass

Mentos and Diet Coke

P2P FILE SHARING

robotic pets

The Da Vinci Code

poker

YouTube

Paris Hilton

MythBusters

Dance Dance Revolution

MySpace

camera phones

INDIE ROCK

The 2000s

High School Musical
Botox
DVD players
LOW-CARB DIETS
TiVo
Webkinz
Sudoku puzzles
fantasy
explosion experiments
sports
UGGS
American Idol
vintage fashion
geocaching
Hannah Montana
e-books
energy drinks
FACEBOOK
Oprah
speed dating
flash mobs
texting

And my personal favorites from the era:

TV Shows
I don't watch too much TV these days
except for news and sports.

Movies
Almost Famous (2000)
Best in Show (2000)
Shrek (2001)
Finding Nemo (2003)
Lost in Translation (2003)
Crash (2004)
Duma (2005)
*Borat: Cultural Learnings of America for
     Make Benefit Glorious Nation of
     Kazakhstan* (2006)
For Your Consideration (2006)
Avatar (2009)

Albums

Trouble in Shangri-La by Stevie Nicks (2001)

Say You Will by Fleetwood Mac (2003)

Liars by Todd Rundgren (2004)

Good Apollo, I'm Burning Star IV, Volume One: From Fear through the Eyes of Madness by Coheed and Cambria (2005)

A Bigger Bang by The Rolling Stones (2005)

Modern Times by Bob Dylan (2006)

Avenged Sevenfold by Avenged Sevenfold (2007)

Memory Almost Full by Paul McCartney (2007)

Gift of Screws by Lindsey Buckingham (2008)

Black Clouds & Silver Linings by Dream Theater (2009)

RFK
(2001)

O f all the thousands of places I visited for the pop culture and travel books I've written, this one truly stands out. In 1968, just after Sirhan Sirhan assassinated Robert Kennedy, my second grade teacher broke down crying in class as she told us about it. She'd been a campaign worker for RFK, and the sight of her becoming so emotional was a strange thing for us to witness—how often do teachers express such strong emotion? The vision of her sobbing before us has always stuck with me and it made me want to go to the site where RFK was shot. As an adult, when I started visiting historic sites and writing about them, the kitchen area at the Ambassador Hotel was always on my radar, but it was impossible to visit. The hotel had closed in the late 1980s, and existed as a fenced-off relic on Wilshire Boulevard in Los Angeles. While working on my book *James Dean Died Here* in 2001, I decided to head up there with my son Charlie (then about eight) early one Sunday morning. There was a story in the book about the event, and I thought the least I could do, in lieu of being able to get inside, was to shoot the hotel's exterior.

Entering the room where RFK was shot.

Where Sirhan Sirhan hid.

It was about six thirty as I shot the hotel from across the street, then moved in a bit closer to shoot the entranceway to the old Cocoanut Grove nightclub.

Noticing that one of the driveways had an open gate, I drove in to get some better shots. Charlie wondered what we were doing, and I told him we'd be out of there shortly. We hopped out of the car, and within about a minute a security guard came over to us. He told us we had to leave, so we made our way out. I asked if it was even worth asking to go inside. He said he'd get fired. We thanked him and walked away. Behind us, though, I heard him fire his walkie-talkie up.

"Weird," I said to Charlie. "We're leaving, yet he's calling someone."

A second later, he signaled us back.

"Hey," he said, now a bit more urgent. "My boss will be here in an hour, so there's not lots of time. But my partner, who patrols inside, can give you a tour. Maybe you can pay him something?"

Huge moment. I don't want to offend the guy by offering too little, but I don't want to blow needless cash either. And, like Albert Brooks in *Lost in America* when it's time to tip the Vegas hotel guy, I have no clue what is appropriate. But I do not want to botch this.

"Would 10 bucks offend him?" I ask.

"That's plenty," the guy said.

With that, I forced $20 into his hand so they both could have $10. Seconds later, a Hispanic male of perhaps 25 ran around the corner and motioned for us to follow him. He introduced himself, then without missing a beat, started his patter.

"Senator Kennedy's limo arrived at this spot on that night in June, 1968. He entered the building at this door," he continued, unlocking the door for us to enter. Was this really happening? Through the dank, abandoned hotel, moans and screams echoed in the

The door RFK walked through right before being shot.

dark. "Cats have taken over," the kid chuckled. Then the tour continued. Through the lobby, up a ramp, and then suddenly, "This the ballroom where Senator Kennedy last spoke." The kid turned on an auxiliary light, but it was still pretty dark. In the flash from my camera, for a second at a time, every detail was revealed: the stage, the podium and the old frayed curtains.

Next, our guide took us step by step through RFK's last moments before the shots. Through the door. Into the kitchen area. And toward the door.

"I heard someone scratched an 'X' into the floor where he fell. Is that a myth?" I ask.

"I'll show you the 'X,'" he said. "First though, I'll show you how it all happened."

He directed me to crouch behind a large console that looked like a water heater.

"You're Sirhan," he said. Charlie was shown where to stand in for RFK, and he played the part of Rosey Greer and others who tackled the shooter. On his cue, we walked through a choreographed, slow-motion version of the event. He stopped Charlie at one point, and motioned down to where the "X" was. We were on the spot where that famous photograph of RFK's head being held by the busboy was shot.

"X" marks the spot where RFK fell to the ground.

The time after this is a bit of a blur, so overwhelming was the experience. We went through the Cocoanut Grove nightclub and some more parts of the hotel, then back to where we started outside at the door.

"You know this event better than anyone," I said to our guide. "How? Why?"

"I'm here every day, by myself," he said. "I wanted to learn, I wanted to know, so I've studied it at the public library. It's now part of my life."

The first guard we'd met came over to say goodbye.

"I have to ask," I said. "Why did you arrange for us to go in? What changed after you told us to leave?"

He smiled. "You took 'no' for an answer," he said. "So many come here and demand to go in, threaten to have me fired, yell at me—you guys were just polite, and it looked like it meant something to you and so I thought I'd help."

At the site today, the hotel is gone. A school has been built, and there is no official designation at the exact site where this terrible event occurred (though there is a 3-D mural depicting the history of the Ambassador just opposite of the school).

North by Northwest
(2002)

In 1959, the Alfred Hitchcock classic *North by Northwest* garnered many exceptional reviews, and with good reason. A smart, tense, stylish movie featuring Cary Grant at his wittiest (and Eva Marie Saint at her prettiest), many people nod and smile when this title comes into conversation. What's not to like? It also contains several iconic scenes that I felt would be worth locating for inclusion in *James Dean Died Here*, which had a chapter featuring exact movie locations. The idea of standing in the spot where something famous was filmed has long been appealing to me, and after doing so, I can never see the film again without thinking, "I was right there, right where Rocky climbed the steps, or where Marilyn's dress billowed up or where Bogart bid farewell to Bergman." The scene I wanted to locate from *North by Northwest* was the one in the cornfield, where Cary Grant got chased by the crop-dusting plane. It's a marvelous scene, and though in the movie they're supposed to be in Indiana, I knew from research that Hitchcock had actually shot in the small city of Wasco, California, near

An aerial view of where the famed cornfield scene was shot. (Wasco, California.)

Bakersfield. (Wasco is known as "The Rose Capital of the Nation," and in fact, 55% of all roses grown in the United States are grown in or around here.)

I took a trip up there one day to do some research, searching for the exact cornfield where Cary Grant exited a bus and came face-to-face with another man before the plane emerged and tried to kill him. Driving into town, passing hundreds of acres of dusty, look-alike fields, I knew it would be tough. After speaking with some local experts in the library, it didn't seem like the exact location had ever been recorded by anyone. There was some vague knowledge that the movie had been shot there, but nothing specific. After a couple of hours, I packed it in to head about an hour west to the site where James Dean had been killed so I could photograph it for the book.

Driving out of town past the many anonymous acres, my cell phone rang. A woman I'd just been speaking to told me that someone overheard our conversation and remembered that the man who actually flew the plane in the film was in fact a local crop duster. What's more, he was still alive and she had his phone number. I called Bob Coe, then in his early eighties. He remembered exactly where the filming took place and, given that I was having trouble finding my way to the location he was describing, he took the time to meet me there—right at the exact site near Highway 46 and Corcoran Road. He told me how he never actually met Cary Grant, but that he liked Alfred Hitchcock, and that he remembered local high school students planting fake cornstalks to simulate the terrain of Indiana.

I told him that, had we not connected, that the exact site might never have been documented. He just shrugged and laughed.

"Well, whatever, got be getting back now."

Then off he rode, his vehicle kicking up clouds of dirt across the parched, barren fields. Mr. Coe passed away in 2007, but I'll never forget our brief meeting one sweltering day in a remote, dusty cornfield where, years earlier, he helped create cinematic magic—a chase scene for the ages.

Save-A-Landmark
(2003)

In the summer of 2003, I received an e-mail that changed my life, and my family's life. It was sent on behalf of Hampton hotels and asked if I had *any* interest in becoming the spokesman for a program they had, called "Save-A-Landmark." The role of spokesman would involve lots of interesting travel, lots of media exposure, the chance to help preserve landmarks and more. What had happened was that someone involved in the project saw a book of mine in an L.A. bookstore and thought it might be a good fit. Here we are now, almost six years in, and I can honestly say that being spokesman for Save-A-Landmark is the single most rewarding professional responsibility I have ever had. We've had the good fortune to visit and help restore landmarks all over the country: Alabama, Maryland, North Dakota, Louisiana, South Carolina, Kentucky, New Jersey, Wisconsin, Kansas, Oregon, Minnesota, Pennsylvania, North Carolina and more. My wife and kids have been along for many of the trips, getting messy as they help restore historic places,

Charlie and Claire helping to save the World's Largest Buffalo. (Jamestown, North Dakota.)

(from left to right) Judy Christa-Cathey, relatives of track star Jesse Owens and me at Owens's birthplace. (Oakville, Alabama.)

Charlie and Claire at their first landmark restoration, the Gingerbread Castle (where dinosaurs were also located). (Hamburg, New Jersey.)

and meeting people they may never have come in contact with. I've been on hundreds of TV and radio shows talking about the program. The folks at Hampton (and Hilton) have become like family to us and I could write a book (as I hope to do one day) simply about the Save-A-Landmark experience.

Where Martin Luther King Jr. was killed. (Memphis, Tennessee.)

My family with Tori Roberson from Hampton Inn at the birthplace of Amelia Earhart. (Atchison, Kansas.)

R E F L E C T I O N S
from Judy Christa-Cathey

Judy Christa-Cathey, Hampton's vice president of brand market-ing, and the woman who initiated the program (and today leads it), says this about it:

ampton wanted to connect with the communities where we have hotels, and the communities of business and leisure travelers across America. This inspired us to launch our Save-A-Landmark program, paying homage to both historic land-marks and the wonderful, quirky, iconic ones.

Save-A-Landmark has allowed me to meet the most wonderful people across America . . . from kids helping us paint the bells in California and garden in New York, to work-ing at the National Civil Rights Museum [in Tennessee]. We meet incredibly passionate hotel team members and members of each unique community where we do a restoration, and have an incredibly fun and productive time.

From a very personal level, it has been amazing to have my daughter join me on the Save-A-Landmarks trips, with her first one being in second grade at the world's largest Santa Claus.

Thanks, Judy. There are two moments I'd like to recount from my many amazing Save-A-Landmark experiences.

(from left to right) **Laura Bush, Hampton Inn vice president Scott Shrank, Judy and President George W. Bush, accepting the President's Award for Save-A-Landmark.**

The USS Laffey (2006)

The USS *Laffey* (DD-724) is the only preserved Allen M. Sumner-class destroyer, as well as the only surviving U.S. World War II destroyer that saw action in the Atlantic, where it acted as an escort for convoys to Great Britain. The destroyer helped bombard Utah Beach at Normandy in the D-Day landing on June 6, 1944. Sent into the Pacific, the *Laffey* was involved in one of the most famous destroyer-kamikaze duels in the war—the Battle of Iwo Jima. Hit several times, racked by explosions and fires, the *Laffey* remained afloat because of the valiant efforts of her crew. She earned five battle stars and a Presidential Unit Citation for her World War II service, and two battle stars for her Korean War service.

An American legend and larger-than-life relic of our nation's wartime history, the USS *Laffey* is known as "The Ship That Wouldn't Die." Today, the USS *Laffey* is recognized as a National Historic Landmark and remains honored at Patriots Point Naval & Maritime Museum in Charleston, South Carolina, one of the world's largest museums commemorating World War II.

With Charlie and crewman Sonny Walker aboard the ship he served on, the USS *Laffey*.

On November 7–8, 2006, more than 25 Hampton employee-volunteers from the Charleston area worked together to help clean, scrape, sand and paint the *Laffey*. The volunteers' commitment paid off—so much so that the museum was able to finish a new museum exhibit within the *Laffey* to showcase World War II-era artifacts. Hampton also contributed nearly $2,000 to help preserve the articles, ensuring that future generations can learn from the legacies and sacrifices of all American servicemen and women.

The night before the refurbishment, my son Charlie and I were asked by Sonny Walker and Fred Nardei, two men who served on the *Laffey*, to spend the night aboard the ship with them. Talk about an honor. We were shown our bunks, and around midnight, Sonny and Fred asked if we wanted a tour. In the heavy mist that shrouded the ship that night, we walked her. We saw where the planes hit, and the scarring that still existed on the deck. We saw the room where a group of young sailors died, almost instantly, after the first Kamikaze strike. And we saw the spot onboard where American soldiers fished a near-dead Japanese pilot from the water and nursed him through the battle. In the shadow of the USS *Yorktown*, Sonny and Fred solemnly recited the history, choking back a tear or two through the process. The next morning, about five o'clock in the morning, Fred was in the kitchen cooking us breakfast, as he'd done for many others years before. Sonny, today president of the USS *Laffey* Association, traded barbs with Fred over coffee; two of America's best at rest in the lair they loved—aboard their beloved USS *Laffey*. Thank you, men.

Mayberry (2009)

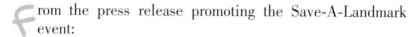From the press release promoting the Save-A-Landmark event:

> In 1960, the first episode of *The Andy Griffith Show* aired, and characters like Sheriff Andy Taylor and Deputy Barney Fife won over the hearts of viewers everywhere. The fictional town of Mayberry felt like home for many. Now, fans can visit familiar Mayberry landmarks, like the

Old City Jail, in Mount Airy, North Carolina, Andy Griffith's hometown. Today, volunteers from Hampton's Save-A-Landmark program will help restore this historic site. The jail is the 48th landmark refurbished in the 39th state through the Save-A-Landmark program.

The Andy Griffith Show is my favorite TV program of all time—at least the first five seasons (the black-and-white episodes). Blending morals, ethics, decency, humanity and of course, humor, into homespun parables, for me it remains unmatched. The show gave us Barney Fife, Otis, Andy, Opie, Aunt Bee, Floyd the barber, Gomer and Goober Pyle and Ernest T. Bass, among other loveable characters. But most of all, it gave us Mayberry, the town so many of us keep in our minds as the place we long to be (not unlike the town of Willoughby from a memorable *Twilight Zone* episode).

I'd been to the lake from the opening credits (Franklin Canyon, in Los Angeles), and the Culver City site where the exteriors were filmed. I had the pleasure of knowing Don Knotts (who played Barney) and Howard Morris (who played Ernest), but I'd never been to the place that inspired Mayberry—Mount

Airy, North Carolina. Neither had our 13-year-old daughter Claire, though it was a place she longed to visit after getting familiar with the show several years earlier. So off we went.

I was nervous that the town wouldn't live up to the Shangri-La image I'd created in my head over the years, but as Claire and I headed past

With Claire on Main Street in Mayberry.

Pilot Mountain ("Mount Pilot" in the show) toward the Blue Ridge Mountains, part of us felt like we were heading home. Walking Main Street in Mount Airy, you hear the famous theme song whistling out of storefronts. You see the diners, filling station and barber shop that inspired everything in the show (we even met the real-life Floyd). You see the real-life Snappy Lunch counter where, if you're lucky and they don't run out, you can savor the famous pork chop sandwich. You meet charming, helpful country folk who are warm and welcoming to a point that would melt any cynic's icy heart. There's even an Andy Griffith museum (right near the aforementioned Old City Jail). We worked on the refurbishment, but we also wandered the town to breathe in all of the nostalgic flavor and small-town simplicity. We sat outside Opie's Candy Store, ate chocolate and watched the Norman Rockwell-esque scenes before us. We did not want to leave, but did so knowing we'd be back. It may seem corny or overly sentimental and maybe it is, but we don't care. See, we like that. If you do too, and haven't been here before, I recommend a visit to this place, Andy Griffith's boyhood town and the real-life inspiration of Mayberry.

REFLECTIONS
from Mayor Jack Loftis

I asked the mayor of Mount Airy, Jack Loftis, what it is about Mount Airy that resonates with so many locals and visitors alike.

"I'm sure the Andy Griffith influence is a strong contributor but certainly not the whole picture. I think our friendly folks, our appearance as a clean and hospitable community, seasonal weather, a good place for a short vacation with reason-

With Sheryl Shelton and Christine Kelly from the Save-A-Landmark program and Claire.

able prices, a great retirement community, excellent health facilities, great recreation, etcetera.

"We have had writers that have spent some time here, written articles in *Reader's Digest*, the *Wall Street Journal* and a large number of tourist magazines, and they all admit some mystery over the total popularity of Mount Airy, North Carolina.

"Does all of this help our economy? Certainly, and we promote tourism all we can and recognize this is not the total answer to our economic difficulties. We continue to solicit new companies and industry to bring in new jobs and have an excellent infrastructure base to support our location with great highway access. A lot of great assets to sell and some great people that would like to have jobs and want to work.

"Chris, we are just who we are and understand this probably does not answer your question however your indication was you wanted to come back may say what it's all about. We will have your pork chop sandwich available anytime you can get in our vicinity."

Cooperstown and Friendship (2004)

n 2003, the *Sporting News* released a book I wrote called *Roadside Baseball*. It was exciting for me because it was an idea I had when I was a boy, this concept of traveling the country in search of historic baseball landmarks including former ballpark sites, markers, memorials, shrines—anything related to the history of the game. I could even tell you where I was when the thought popped into my head. It was at the Baseball Hall of Fame in Cooperstown, New York. My family had taken a summer vacation to the famed museum when I was 11.

The trip was only a few days, but it felt wonderfully long and drawn. We stayed in a classic roadside motel with a nice pool, ate at local comfort-food diners and, of course, we visited the Baseball Hall of Fame—Mecca for me at that age. I played baseball; I studied baseball; I ate, drank and slept baseball.

That's me and John, back row, far right (I'm on the left, he's on the right).

Standing before Babe Ruth's and Lou Gehrig's lockers, seeing all of the artifacts I'd read about, made me think—where did these guys come from? Where were they born? Where did they grow up, go to school or first play baseball? That's what *Roadside Baseball* would be—and that's what it became.

The *Sporting News* booked me to go speak at the Hall of Fame in Cooperstown about the book, so we took a nice, lazy train trip cross-country to New York City, then rented a car and headed north to the hamlet of Cooperstown, where the baseball ghosts reside. It was All-Star break, so we were invited to watch the game in the theater at the hall. We roamed the hall at night, privately, and I rediscovered all the magic that kept me awake in the motel when I was young. Ted Williams's bat. Jackie Robinson's jersey. And the Babe's locker.

We stayed right in town, there were heavy summer thunderstorms, and Lake Otsego was big and blue, the grass bright green from all the rain. I was getting nostalgic in a way that only baseball can make you feel. Especially the day I spoke. Had I known how the day would catch up with me, I would have better prepared myself. But I didn't.

Looking out at the crowd in the theater after being introduced, I first locked eyes with my son. He was 11, as old as I was when I first visited and when I had the idea for the book I was there to talk about. He looked as excited as I remembered being 30 years earlier. My wife and daughter were there, patient and smiling. There was also a young man named Kenny Foderaro sitting with his family. They were

The Mungos (John, D. J. and Matthew) and the Eptings (my wife, Jean, is at left).

visiting the museum from their home in Ohio, and I had met them the day before and we'd struck up a conversation about baseball, so Kenny insisted his folks bring him to my speech. Kenny is magnificently funny, knowledgeable and charming. He is also blind, but I felt like he could see me that day. Next to my family was John Mungo, my best grade school friend in the world, whom I had not seen for about 30 years. Recently back in touch, John made the drive up with his two sons to be there for my big day.

In that moment, all my cycles of life and boyhood dreams completed themselves right before my eyes. Watching my son smile, looking at John's sons and Kenny with his family by my family—well, if it's true your life passes before your eyes at the end, I'd like this moment to linger more than the others. What a day.

REFLECTIONS
from John Mungo

There is one friend in the life of each of us who seems not a separate person, however dear and beloved, but an expansion, an interpretation, of one's self, the very meaning of one's soul.
—Edith Wharton, *A Backward Glance*

Thankfully, my rekindled friendship with John Mungo has thrived since that time. We were so tight as kids; I'd always wondered what had happened to John. Through Little League, birthdays and all the other little moments of youth, we were as tight as friends could be—true pals. When I went off to another high school, we lost touch. John called me once for my birthday during college (our birthdays are just a day apart), but that was it. When I saw his name on an e-mail list promoting a school reunion, I had to write. That he answered so quickly was thrilling.

We met up soon after when he had a West Coast trip, went to a ball game and squeezed almost 30 years into three hours. I'll never forget that night, nor will I ever stop appreciating how fortunate I was to have reconnected with the best friend I ever had. John is a man of supreme poise and character. I grouse about technology taking over sometimes, but when connections like this are made instantly possible, I know I need to shut up.

For people like me who let too much time and space slip away between friendships, I'm here to tell you, it's never too late.

Friendships are important parts of all our lives. They have special places. Some are taken for granted, and some are just always there. Some are misplaced or lost over time . . . some return. I can honestly say from my age of 10–14, I had such a friend and we were best buds. But in a world without cell phones, text messaging, instant messaging, PCs or any other electrical gadgets, when we left middle school in June of 1975, we parted for different high schools and just lost touch. Fast forward 29 years. It was Memorial Day weekend of 2004, and an e-mail that I never expected to receive arrived at home and I read it once, read it twice, and was overcome with such excitement and joy that my old friend had found me before I found him.

I lived still fairly locally in New York, one hour from where we both grew up after traveling the world during a four-year tour in the U.S. navy.

Two pals at the Baseball Hall of Fame. (Cooperstown, New York.)

Chris relocated to Huntington Beach, California. I had a business trip previously planned to the West Coast and once Chris heard this, a get-together for dinner to meet his family and see his mom again was quickly arranged. The reunion was magical. The friendship as youngsters was rekindled 29 years later, both of us with miles of life experience between us, families of our own now, and sharing all of that between us became second nature. We really never had to get reacquainted. We were both convinced this was a blessing. A trip to New York by Chris and family with a stop in Cooperstown, New York, where Chris was speaking at the Baseball Hall of Fame was an opportunity to see Chris and his family again. I jumped at the opportunity, and brought my boys with me, Matthew, 10 at the time, and Dominick, 4. Walking the Hall of Fame and discussing baseball events that happened before and during our childhood brought me back to those years in the 1970s when baseball was played in a purer form.

That day in Cooperstown is something we still talk about today. It is ingrained in our minds. Listening to Chris with pride as he spoke at the Hall, and just sharing time with a long-lost friend in a baseball playground. Watching our boys play Wiffle Ball down by the lake in the rain. Some of my fondest memories as a kid were playing ball with Chris, and here we were reunited just a short time before and our boys were playing together. It's hard to understand why things happen the way they do sometimes. . . .

Stones Guitar Pick
(2005)

On November 4, 2005, I took Charlie to see the Rolling Stones for the first time. He was about the same age I was my first time, and I think he was just as excited as I was. Charlie had read that a fan at an earlier show had carried sign asking guitarist (and the guy I once hung out in a closet with) Ronnie Wood for a guitar pick—and that he obliged. So Charlie made his own small sign to hold up (our seats would become front row once the B-stage rolled out near the second base area, and so he thought he might be able to get Wood's eye). We got to the gate and the guard said, sorry, no signs allowed (why, I have no clue). So I had to run back to the car, ditch the sign and then head back to the gate. Charlie was really bummed. He had his heart set on if not getting a pick, then at least giving it a shot.

The show started though and he seemed to let it go, which was good because the show was fantastic. Mid-set, out the B-stage rolled, right toward us at mid-field—it stopped just

The Stones, as shot by Charlie.

several feet before us and there they were, within reach, the Rolling Stones. It was surreal watching them play from this distance, and Charlie took some cell phone pictures to document the moment.

The ticket to the show at Angel Stadium of Anaheim, November 4, 2005.

I knew this is where the pick sign would have been held up, and I was a little sad Charlie wouldn't get his shot. But then something happened. Ronnie Wood took a guitar pick and snapped it out to the crowd. My hand was on Charlie's shoulder as I was standing behind him. He never saw what happened, but it actu-

Mick Jagger, as shot by Charlie.

ally got wedged in between my right forefinger and middle finger. I didn't have to move a muscle. After "Get Off My Cloud," I showed Charlie the pick. He could not believe it. But I could. After all, these are the Rolling Stones, so anything is possible.

The cherished guitar pick, side one and two.

Oscar, Oscar, Oscar
(2005)

n Los Angeles each fall, the Southern California Independent Booksellers Association hosts an event in a hotel ballroom where authors table hop over the span of a three-course meal to talk about their upcoming release to booksellers from the area. I've done it a couple of times and it's both fun and productive—being able to get that sort of face-to-face time might otherwise be next to impossible. They feed the authors dinner before the booksellers are let in, which frees us up to move from table to table while the movers and shakers eat. It's hard to forget the first one of these functions I ever attended.

When I arrived, I saw one table almost full of about a dozen or so authors. I didn't know anyone there, so I instead looked over to a table where one older man sat, his back to me. Placing my hand on his shoulder, I asked if it

A thrill—with Jack Klugman.

might be okay if I joined him. He turned toward me and in a thin, raspy voice said with a big smile, "Sure, kid!"

It was Jack Klugman.

Like many other New Yorkers, I am an unfailing devotee of the TV series *The Odd Couple*. A freak, in fact. I can quote almost any line from any episode and Jack Klugman is one of my favorite actors on the planet, primarily for his portrayal of the gloriously sloven Oscar Madison. I warned him that I might not leave him alone, that he might not so much as enjoy one bite of food because of me. He ordered me to sit. I knew of his throat cancer and the fact a vocal chord of his had to be cut, and asked if it hurt to talk. Not at all, he said. It sounded bad, but he felt fine.

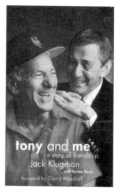

Tony and Me, the book Jack Klugman wrote about Tony Randall.

For more than an hour we gabbed, recreating dozens of bits of *Odd Couple* dialogue (he remembered everything better than I—and trust me, I know my stuff). He told me stories, talked about his life and showed me *Tony and Me*, the new book he'd written about his old pal, the late, great Tony Randall. I asked him about *12 Angry Men*, the *Twilight Zone* episodes he made and more. My favorite thing he said was what he felt what was wrong with entertainment today.

"Too lacking in sentimentality," he stressed. "Where is the sentimentality? People are afraid of real emotion, in movies and in society."

He had just one copy of his book to take from table to table that night. "But I want to give it to you before I leave," he said.

All night as I table hopped, I kept an eye on where he was. Would he remember the book? I wondered. As the evening came to a close, I saw him across the ballroom, as far as he could be from me. He was busy greeting people, but then he pulled away and started scanning the crowd. Could it be? Was he looking for me? We caught each other's eye and he motioned for me to stay put. My God. He was coming over to me. He handed me his book and then kissed me on the cheek.

"Thank you," he whispered in my ear, "for remembering."

Oscar, Oscar, Oscar.

A Winning Photo
(2006)

I n 2006, this photo I shot of our dog Marilyn and my daughter Claire won first prize in a national contest the Animal Planet television network had put together. Long story short, they sent a limo for the dog (and us), whisked us to Los Angeles where were stayed at the Beverly Hilton, wined and dined us and then Claire hit the runway with Marilyn in tow for a celebrity dog costume contest. Just thought you might enjoy seeing the photo.

My daughter Claire with our puppy, Marilyn. (Photo is signed by Animal Planet's Jeff Corwin.)

The Indian
(2007)

There's an Indian in our hallway. He stands about five-feet tall, his color has faded and you'd probably look at him and say, "Okay, a cigar store Indian." If you didn't say that you might say, "What is a cigar store Indian?" Well, simply described, cigar store Indians were originally created as ways to advertise places that sold tobacco. If you saw a life-sized, carved wooden Indian outside a store, it meant that establishment sold tobacco products. Over time, these statues started becoming collectibles, especially when many tobacco shops began closing in the face of the revelation that smoking was actually bad for you.

We live near Disneyland and go there frequently. Our family loves the history there, and to that end we have even collected some artifacts from the old park—tickets, a target from the old shooting gallery, even a leaf from the old *Swiss Family Robinson* tree house. But nothing prepared us for what we came face-to-face with at a small vintage toy store in Anaheim. It's like a museum, and we go there sometimes just to gawk at the old collectible toys and bits of pop culture.

One day, Charlie and I walk in and he stops cold. "Dad, look."

Cue the angelic choir as we find out selves face-to-face with one of the two original cigar store Indians from Disneyland. They marked the two places (on Main Street and in Frontierland) where tobacco could be purchased at the park. Once they stopped selling it there, the Indians remained, totems of a by-

The Disneyland Indian circa 1958.

gone era. In 2005, when the park turned 50, the original Indians were retired and replaced with exact replicas, boasting shiny new paint. And here stood one of the originals, the Frontierland statue.

Over the decades, people posed with this Indian, and his partner as well. Thousands of photos were taken of him. John Lennon even had a photo snapped as he hoisted a whiskey bottle up to the Indian's mouth. Both Indians became renowned as meeting places, stopping points and endless photo opportunities. And here before us, "Indian Joe" was for sale. He wasn't cheap. I called my wife and made my pitch. An early anniversary gift? Birthday gift? General family gift for having two such great kids? A "Hey, it's Tuesday" gift? Jean gulped and said, "Fine." After a bit of wrangling (think of the dad in the movie *A Christmas Story* as he wheels and deals for the tree), the Indian was in the back of my car en route to his new home—ours.

A matchbook featuring the Indian.

Today, he stands like a sentry in our hallway. As a tribute to his past glory, whenever someone comes to our house, the tradition is that they will pose with the Indian, sign the Indian photo album in the hallway and then receive a copy of themselves with the Indian. Remember that if you ever visit.

Actress Sally Struthers with the Indian.

Olympian Shirley Babashoff poses with the Indian. Note the Olympic gold medal around the Indian's neck.

Actress and artist Eve Plumb with the Indian.

Time for Kids
(2008)

Our daughter Claire, as of this writing, is in her second year as one of 12 national reporters for *Time for Kids* magazine. She earned the job by competing in *Time's* annual writing contest, after being an avid reader of the weekly magazine. Jean and I were very proud of Claire's accomplishment once she got the news, but it was sort of in the abstract— it's hard to imagine at that point what the experience will entail. That changed soon. Claire's third assignment was to sit down for one-on-one interviews with Vanessa Hudgens, Zac Efron and Ashley Tisdale before the movie *High School Musical 3* was released. This was heady stuff for a 12-year-old who was a big fan of this particular movie franchise.

Claire with singer Miley Cyrus.

As has become my enviable responsibility, I accompany Claire to many of her assignments and get to act as photographer. Approaching this day, I wondered how Claire would handle the tasks at hand— interviewing three of the biggest young stars on the planet while remaining composed and journalistic. After all, this was new to her. The day of the interviews, I followed Claire as she entered each private hotel room for her sit-downs. And one by one, I watched a calm, serious, professional young lady conduct tight, informative interviews while taking copious notes. My little girl. The stars all seemed taken aback that a 12-year-old in their presence didn't melt down.

Claire with actor Zac Efron.

Zac Efron started asking Claire about how she got the job and then said to me, "I can't imagine doing this at her age." I agreed. Since then, the *Time for Kids* job has become an ongoing adventure that's produced remarkable moments. I've watched Claire talk with big stars, famous athletes, writers and other serious movers and shakers. I've watched her fly the Goodyear Blimp, ride a 500-foot-high zip line and swim with Beluga whales. After writing dozens of pieces, lo and behold, she's developed a true voice. My little girl—my wonderful little girl.

Here's an excerpt from a piece Claire wrote for *Time for Kids* about her experience piloting the Goodyear Blimp (I saw it with my own eyes):

> Climbing into the blimp is a unique experience. The airship never stops moving. As you get on board, it feels like getting on a boat. There are no seat belts. Once you sit down, the ropes that hold down the craft are released. Then, you're off! Take-off happens fast, and it is very steep. Outside the window, the crew quickly become like toy figures that get smaller by the second. The engines roar loudly, and soon, the blimp is

Claire with the Jonas Brothers.

cruising smoothly at 1,000 to 1,500 feet in the air.

On this day, the aircraft headed toward the city of Long Beach, California, along the Pacific Ocean. It was amazing to watch the tiny cars below. The freeway looked like a huge asphalt snake, bending around and leading far into the distance. We were over Long Beach Harbor when I got a big surprise. Pilot Kristen Davis asked if *I* wanted to fly the blimp! I was stunned, but I still climbed into the pilot's seat. The controls were simple. Davis taught me how to move the blimp left and right by using the foot pedals. The big wooden wheel to my right moved it up and down. In no time, I was guiding us around the sky.

Claire takes the controls of the Goodyear Blimp over Long Beach, California.

The Dinosaur Hunter
(2008)

O ur son Charlie has been fascinated by dinosaurs since he was a little boy of about three years old. As he has become a young man, his interest has grown and grown. Charlie read dozens of books, papers and articles; we visited countless museums and started going on digs when he was about five. He volunteers at two museums and has had the honor of studying under the tutelage of Dr. Luis Chiappe, who, as of this writing is busy transforming the Natural History Museum of Los Angeles County into one of the country's premier dinosaur destinations.

Here is how I described Dr. Chiappe in a piece I wrote for *Westways* magazine:

Wherever you might discover Dr. Luis M. Chiappe—Mongolia, Argentina, Kazakhstan or Wyoming—his presence is always felt in Southern California. Chiappe is the Curator of the Department of Vertebrate Paleontology at the Natural History Museum of Los Angeles County, and his pas-

**Charlie and Dr. Luis Chiappe.
(Outside Blanding, Utah.)**

sion, expertise and visionary approach are helping the institution solidify its position as the best
place to enjoy dinosaurs in the western United
States. Perhaps most renowned for his discovery
of thousands of dinosaur eggs and babies in a
remote corner of Patagonia (along with his work
on the origin of birds as they relate to dinosaurs),
Chiappe is a giant in his field. And he has big
plans for Los Angeles.

And this is what I wrote in my newspaper column, "In
the Pipeline," for the *Huntington Beach Independent* about one
of our trips with Dr. Chiappe to Utah:

Last week, we headed off to a speck on the
map called Blanding, Utah. It's about 12 driving hours away, and so we split the journey into
two days, which left plenty of time for the important stuff: several national parks, a hike at
the Amboy Crater, and some slower travel along

Charlie at work in the lab at the
Natural History Museum of Los
Angeles County. Once, he was
on the other side of the glass.

Charlie near a bone he helped ex-
cavate. (Outside Blanding, Utah.)

as much of old Route 66 as we could find. We went on up through Arizona's Navajo Nation until we hit our spot about 15 miles outside the tiny town of Blanding. What brought us there was a chance to watch and work with some of the most impressive minds and bodies I've ever been around. They are members of the Dinosaur Institute, an organization within the Natural History Museum of Los Angeles County. They are the core of the museum's dinosaur program, and they are on a mission. In this specific case, the mission involves returning to work on several quarries, which have produced some spectacular dinosaur fossils. The higher goal? Make Los Angeles the preeminent dinosaur center of the western United States. If you were casting a movie and needed a colorful, eclectic group of adventurers and explorers, you could do no better than this bunch—think Indiana Jones meets the Dirty Dozen.

They are led by Luis M. Chiappe, curator of the museum's Department of Vertebrate Paleontology and director of the Dinosaur Institute. A world-renowned paleontologist and author, the famed Argentine's discovery of thousands of dinosaur eggs in Patagonia is one of the most significant paleontology developments in history. Curatorial assistant Aisling Farrell is a lithe, spunky woman of about 30, as pretty as her Irish accent. Armed

With Charlie in Utah.

with a master's in taxonomy and biodiversity, she plays a vital part in the expedition—made clear by her intense workload. Stephanie Abramowicz is an illustrator and fine artist who creates artwork of the dinosaurs while still managing to work in the field. Volunteer Susan Russak is there simply because she feels the calling. And lab supervisor Doug Goodreau blends brains and brawn into one strong physique, thus creating a fossil-collecting machine. There are others out here, too, including a hard-working team from the museum's educational division. For a solid month they'll be slaving. Some new members will shuttle in, but the core of the team is here the entire time.

In the field, the work is backbreaking. Carefully brushing, hammering, chiseling, digging, all the while being careful not to mar the precious, 150-million-year-old treasures. Then there's the excavation process, which first involves covering fossils in strips of burlap, creating a plaster "shell" to protect the bone (the only real way it's been done since the beginning). Then, somehow, these hundreds-of-pounds parcels are moved across mountains to waiting trucks for the ride home. Again, it is all backbreaking. As one bone is prepped—an impressive Sauropod humorous perhaps five-feet long—Chiappe pauses over it.

"Tonight he spends his last night under the stars," he offers in his rich Argentine accent.

There is also primordial poetry to all of this, it seems. Next, we're trudging across the soft red sand, off to examine some Stegosaurus tracks. Nearby, bits of Stegosaurus backplate lie strewn across the ground. They will be examined and cataloged later by another crew. Nights are spent under billions of stars, resting, eating good food and enjoying good wine.

At sun up, it all starts over. Tom Thornbury, chairman of the board of the Softub company, is here too, with his son, Cory. Thornbury underwrites trips like this (the team T-shirts read "The Thornbury Expedition"), and his passion for paleontology is evident. He gets right down in the dirt, digging and brushing. His effusive spirit is a wonderful force in the desert, and his generosity will be appreciated for ages. There are wonderful things happening at the Natural History Museum of Los Angeles County. But without what happens out in the desert, it wouldn't be possible.

As you watch the museum's dinosaur exhibits, like Thomas the T. Rex, take shape, keep in mind what brought those bones to Los Angeles: these amazing people—this crazy collection of geniuses, dreamers, artists and doers who perform the impossible in the middle of nowhere, just so we can enjoy the dinosaurs. As the museum evolves in the next year or two, it's going to leave a huge footprint in many lives. Paleontology plays a big part in our household because it's what our son has wanted to do since he was three. He's gotten me so interested that I plan on following the progress being made by the Dinosaur Institute. Their work is too important to ignore, and—after all—who doesn't love dinosaurs?

R E F L E C T I O N S
from paleontologist Dr. Luis Chiappe

For this book, I asked Luis Chiappe, one, why he believes it's important to nurture the next generation of dinosaur hunters and, two, where he would be this very second if he had his choice.

One, I truly believe that we ought to disseminate the science that we do as widely as possible. It is for that reason that I have always invested a good amount of my time doing outreach and education, writing popular articles and books, participating in TV documentaries, lecturing, etcetera. Being able to observe the public's fascination for what we do and being able to help students and dinosaur enthusiasts—especially kids—is incredibly rewarding.

Two, any desolate desert with extensive outcrops of Mesozoic rocks and an abundance of dinosaur remains always feels like a paradise. I feel completely at home. I love field work and what comes with it: the thrill of discovery, the vast landscapes, living surrounded by nature and being subjected to the same forces that shape the landscapes, magnificent sunsets and skies filled with stars and a good chat around a fire.

Wicked
(2008)

Claire wanted to go see the show *Wicked* when it was in Los Angeles, so we planned a day up in the city. We'd go have brunch at Grub, a wonderful little restaurant not far from the Pantages Theatre (where we were to see the matinee that day), then on to the show. Claire was excited because of all she'd heard about *Wicked* from friends who'd seen it. Me, I was happy that Claire was excited, but I went in with a bit of a cynic's view. I hadn't been to the theater that often and had grown tired of the (what I perceived as) mainstream, homogenized blockbusters tailor-made for tourists. I'd grown up going to see the classics on Broadway and I guess it turned me into a bit of a snob.

Settled in our seats as the theater darkened, I'll admit I was intrigued. The *Wicked* set was magnificent; the crowd was buzzing, and after reading some more about the musical in the *Playbill*, my interest was piqued.

As the show progressed, I began to understand the phenomenon. The story of Elphaba, the future Wicked Witch of the West and her relationship with Glinda, the Good Witch of the North, was compelling; simultaneously funny and tragic. As you may know, the story is based on the best-selling novel *Wicked: The Life and Times*

Claire's signed playbill from *Wicked*.

Claire meets Broadway actress Megan Hilty after the final performance of *Wicked* at the Pantages Theatre. (Los Angeles, California.)

of the Wicked Witch of the West by Gregory Maguire, a parallel novel of L. Frank Baum's classic story *The Wonderful Wizard of Oz* from the perspective of the witches of the Land of Oz. And while the story was richly layered and ingenious, it was the songs and lyrics of Stephen Schwartz that sucked me in. By the time the plaintive, confessional duet "For Good" was over, I was in tears. The lyrical themes and motifs Schwartz had interwoven with lush, smart melodies caught me completely off guard—by final bows I was a faithful believer.

Claire adored the show as well and it became something we now call "ours." We saw it two more times, including the final performance at the Pantages, and we listen to the soundtrack frequently—the show will always be something we share on a very deep level.

So many times it seems I enter these situations, ready to pounce on something and then, suddenly aware of my own obstinacy, I get blindsided by brilliance; schooled like some dopey kid who unwittingly challenges Michael Jordan to a game of one on one.

Wicked is a brilliant musical. Admittedly, part of the love I feel for the beautiful show stems from the love I feel for Claire, seeing that green sparkle in her eyes as she sits there, captivated and charmed by "Popular," "Defying Gravity" and "Dancing through Life."

And it makes me realize how vital artists like Stephen Schwartz are; they are essential creators who give the world pieces of art that will truly live forever.

REFLECTIONS
from composer and lyricist Stephen Schwartz

Schwartz rose to fame at age 23 with the release of Godspell *in 1971. It ran for more than 2,600 performances and earned Schwartz two Grammy Awards for its music, featuring the pop hit "Day by Day." He wrote the music for the shows* Pippin, The Magic Show *and a musical based on the Studs Terkel novel* Working. *He wrote the stage musical* Children of Eden *and collaborated on two animated Disney movies (*Pocahontas, *for which he won two Oscars, and* The Hunchback of Notre Dame*), as well as Dreamworks'* The Prince of Egypt *(winning an Oscar for best song). And he wrote the music and lyrics for* Wicked, *which began a multi-year run on Broadway in 2003.*

I was anxious to talk to him about the play for this book, and he graciously obliged.

As much as adults love the musical *Wicked*, did you ever envision that it would have such a powerful effect on young people? That it would become such an integral part of youth culture?

STEPHEN SCHWARTZ: The short answer is no. I knew, of course, that I felt a powerful sense of identification with the character of Elphaba and that her struggle to reconcile remaining true to herself with her longing to fit into society resonated deeply with me. And in seeking out [writer] Winnie Holzman to collaborate with me, I knew she was someone whose work had shown a great understanding of the inner life of young people, particularly young women, such as in *My So-Called Life*, the television show she created. But then both Winnie and I concentrated on trying to create the best show we could and tell the story that was most meaningful to us. We never thought about the

The talented composer, Stephen Schwartz.

impact it might have on an audience, or a segment of the audience such as young people. In retrospect, it's clear that because the leading characters are young, essentially school-aged girls and boys, and because the issues they're dealing with—popularity, trying to fit in, personal integrity, pleasing one's parents, etcetera—are ones that young people face daily, it speaks very directly to them. But it wasn't something we were conscious of when writing the show.

Do you hear from many fathers regarding what a special experience the show is to experience with a child, particularly a daughter?

I do, I'm happy to say. For instance, the following is an excerpt from an e-mail I received a few months ago:

> *I have a daughter who is 20 years old. Until recently, she's had a pretty challenging life. She was diagnosed with bipolar disorder when she was very young. That condition was accompanied by a host of ancillary issues including ADHD and oppositional defiant disorder. Her various mental illnesses presented a wide assortment of social and emotional problems both at home and as she battled her way through high school. I can sum up her first two decades by saying she was a very trying kid who could barely hold it together most of the time.*
>
> *Over the years, we had taken her to many psychologists and psychiatrists seeking help. About a year ago, we finally got her into a clinic to see*

254 ... Hello, It's Me

a prominent pediatric bipolar disorder specialist. He talked to her in direct terms, told her what she would have to do to get better and told her the decision of whether to improve or stay where she was rested completely with her. As chance would have it, within a few days of that meeting we went to see Wicked. *We were all blown away by the show, and particularly the music, but my daughter found something special in "Defying Gravity." She felt it was her call to action, to change the direction her life was taking. She told us that moment clarified her decision to seek help.*

Within weeks, she had seen a new psychiatrist and psychologist and embarked on a new course of medication. Six months later, for the first time in our lives, her mother and I met the daughter we knew had existed in her all along. She went from surly, defiant and non-caring to sweet, responsible and loving. She has continued to improve and, after barely passing her freshman year of college, made the dean's list last semester. It was truly a miracle.

Obviously, that's an extreme example. But I do hear frequently from fathers who have had a special experience with their daughters in attending the show. The fact that sharing *Wicked* together often proves such a powerful bonding experience for them is immensely gratifying to me, as you can imagine. Although I didn't set out to achieve that effect, it's one of the many things about *Wicked* that have made me very proud.

Reunion

(2009)

iven that I moved to California in the mid-1980s, I fell out of all-but-complete touch with just about everyone I knew in high school, which was unfortunate. For the most part, I loved high school. We had the benefit of spending our four years in a scenic country setting, surrounded by woods and right next to a big lake. Our graduating class was relatively small (maybe 180 kids or so) and comprised of some really amazing people—something that became extremely apparent to me on July 8, 2009. I'm sure many of you reading this have probably been to more than one of your reunions, so maybe this doesn't seem like too big a deal. But if

My high school graduation photo in 1979.

you haven't, and you do eventually go, be prepared. You may be caught off guard by the feelings that get unleashed. I certainly was.

And so we now interrupt this book for an open letter to some old friends:

Dear John F. Kennedy High School class of 1979 reunion attendees,
I admit, approaching our 30th high school re-

union this past summer had me concerned. Since I moved to California, I'd completely lost touch with all of you (except two people), I had never attended any of the previous reunions, and I had huge amounts of anxiety about what to expect. I shared this with nobody, in fact on the surface I acted like the reunion was no big deal at all, just a casual get-together 30 years later. My twin sister Margaret was excited and anxious and very expressive as to her anticipation of the event—the exact opposite of me. She was being honest, I was in denial. If I were to analyze it, I'd probably discover that my anxiety stemmed from the fact that I was so fond of many of you, so concerned with what you thought back then, so caught up in the intense emotion of high school life that few days go by without some adolescent memory from our four years together creeping into my brain.

We'd be seeing each other at our high school, not some hotel ballroom, which I thought was a good idea. In fact, I even had a hand in steering it that way, because a year or so earlier I was asked if I'd wanted to help with some of the planning— and I was so happy we'd all be back at the school. My wife and kids would be there, too, which I was thrilled about. After all, I've told them so much about so many of you over the years. That day, I was fumbling in the morning, deny- ing that I was anxious, but obviously feeling

My senior prom picture. I'm at far left, under the mop. Dave Howard is third from left.

pressure. I was relieved to see what a beautiful summer day it was—that seemed fitting. Driving up into the country near our beautiful school on the lake, tucked back off that winding country lane, images started flooding back. I could see all of you, 30 years ago—a scrapbook of yearbook images, basketball games, football games, tennis matches, parties, proms, hallway moments and crazy nights at carnivals and alongside a certain abandoned train bridge. And I could hear you laugh and sing over our soundtracks, "Running on Empty," "Freebird," "Wish You Were Here," "Like a Hurricane," "Truckin'," "Beast of Burden," "The Chain," and a thousand other songs.

Would I recognize you today? Would you know me? Would we have things to talk about? Would it be awkward? I never get nervous over any sort of meeting, presentation, or appearance. Today, I was a wreck.

We pulled into the school parking lot and I could see that a group had already started gathering. By now, my family sensed my intense nervousness, my insecurity, though I wouldn't admit it. Making our way to the clearing near the football field, we found the table that had had pins with our names and yearbook pictures on them. Then we saw you, Patty. And you, Carolyn. I hardly knew you in school, but here we were— you and Maggie and me—cobbling this event together over the last year. How did that happen? Lisa, Sally and Maura. John, Willy, Andrew, Sean, Tom, Gary, Joe (hey man, thanks for returning that library book I lent you 34 years earlier—amazing!) and you, Maureen! It's been so cool getting to "re-know" you in the pre-reunion buildup. Who would have predicted any of this?

We saw you, Donna, Rosie, Ken, Tim, Terri, Karen, Keith, Stephanie, Sue, Dawn, Vicki, Ann, Joanne, Barbara, Bill, Chris, Denise, Debbie, John, Mary, Mary Liz and my sister, Margaret. You were all sparkling, vibrant, funny, interesting and still a bit outrageous—truly a beautiful group, just as you were 30 years ago.

I loved how, one by one, as another person would arrive, we'd all fall over ourselves to greet them, hug them and laugh at the absurdity of 30 years gone by. And Sister Christopher and Sister Barbara were there, as well. At some point in the day, I looked up to see Dave, one of my absolute best friends in high school, making his entrance. We'd had some contact in college, but as it happened with so many of you, we just fell apart. I'd heard he might be there and I couldn't quite believe it. He and I picked up where we'd left off decades earlier, just like so many of you did with each other. Dave, as remarkable as the entire day was, you were a big highlight, old friend. Add to that the surreal sight of my wife and kids hanging out with all of you and, well, the joy is almost indescribable. (John L., I wish you could have been there.)

Our day together was so emotional and touching and weird and unforgettable and refreshing—it was one of the best days of my life. It was just over too fast. I know we headed out for drinks after, but still, as I watched some of you head to your cars at the end of the night, you all became like mirages—I didn't want you to leave, it was too good to be true. We had bent the wheel of time into our favor, but it all had to end, to disappear in some hazy, time-warped, 1970s black hole. In the warm summer evening air, after you all left, especially out on that football field, I could still hear your youthful laughter and feel all of those sweet memories along with the painful ones—a part of us will always remain in the air at that school.

I realized at our reunion just how intrinsically connected we are, whether we were close in high school or not, no matter what happens the rest of our lives. I realized that I cannot wait to see you all again, to stay in touch with you as much as possible and to be there for you if there's ever a need. I realized that the love I feel for you, my graduating class, is a deep, mysterious thing that is something I'll always cherish, and for all of my nerves, the day (and night) could not have been better—in fact they were like magic.

Thank you, old friends.

Until the next time,

Chris

Now back to our book.

(from left to right) **Tim Mertens, Carolyn Dei Delori, me, Tom Alfredo and Dave Howard. Seated, Sister Christopher and Sister Barbara.**

In Prog We Trust
(2009)

t seems the older I get, the more I bemoan the lack of bands today that still excite me the way music did when I was my son's age (as of this writing, 16)—bands that inspired you to doodle its logo on your spiral notebook during class, or write its lyrics out on paper, just because *seeing* the words made you feel connected to something bigger. Growing up, for me it was the Rolling Stones, David Bowie, Led Zeppelin, the Ramones, Todd Rundgren, the New York Dolls and others. I still listen to those bands, still see them play if possible, and it's frustrating to me at times that it seems like the bands that made my blood run hotter are no longer being created. That, of course, is a ludicrous point of view. There are always up-and-coming bands that are exciting and inspirational, you just have to forget your age, stop being stubborn and approach things with an open mind. Charlie has helped me a great deal with this, playing new music that, for me, creates sparks, and playing older music I never quite picked up and making me realize what I'd missed.

A couple of the newer bands include Avenged Sevenfold and Coheed and Cambria. There's one band, though, that after seeing recently, completely restored my faith in the power of performance, proficiency and, most importantly, the songs. Charlie loves heavy metal and prog

AC/DC, front row at The Forum, seats one and two—lucky! (Los Angeles, California.)

rock, things I was never that into. At Charlie's insistence, we went to see some bands *he* liked. We saw Ronnie James Dio (67 years old!) with the band Heaven & Hell. Great. We saw Judas Priest. Great as well. We saw AC/DC from the front row, center stage. Somehow through Ticketmaster, Charlie logged on and came away with those seats. That show was an eye-opener in that it was so loud, basic, ferocious and so much fun that I was sorry I hadn't been more into AC/DC in the past. Charlie was really getting me into things I hadn't discovered firsthand yet and I was loving it. How cool is it when your kids do that?

But then there is Dream Theater, made up of Mike Portnoy, John Myung, John Petrucci, James LaBrie and Jordan Rudess. I always admired the band, knew what exceptional players the guys were (some of the most skilled players on the planet), but that was it. Then our friend Bobby D'Ambrosio let it drop that he was friends with keyboard sensation Jordan Rudess from the band. I told Bobby that Charlie was a fan and so he contacted Jordan, who arranged for us to see an upcoming show in L.A.

Oh my God. We experienced a show with thunder, drama and a level of musicianship I'd never seen before. It was crazy.

With Dream Theater keyboardist Jordan Rudess and Charlie.

A ticket to paradise.

The redemptive power of Dream Theater, the long-dark-hallway energy and mystique of this prog-powerhouse band made me feel like I was 16 again. They reminded me what it felt like to see the Who, Pink Floyd and Led Zeppelin back in the 1970s. But it wasn't just the power of the music—it was the show they put on, too. In addition to being consummate players, these guys understand the need for some sparkle and magic onstage, and so they interweave awesome visuals and strange little set pieces to make it all even *more* interesting. And there were tons of fathers and sons there, like us—teenaged kids and late-40-ish dads. It was one of the greatest nights we've ever spent together, reveling in the power of music that is challenging and inspired.

R E F L E C T I O N S

from Dream Theater keyboardist Jordan Rudess

The show restored my faith in the power of the live show, and introduced me to the beauty, fury and complexity of true prog. So impressed was I by this magnificent band, that I asked keyboard player Jordan Rudess to answer a few questions about the fans, the music, the band and the show. He was more than generous.

When you meet fans, especially the ones a bit older, are there patterns to what you hear? Any consistent themes as to what they tell you about what Dream Theater's music means to them?

JORDAN RUDESS: Dream Theater's music seems to hold a very special place in the hearts of many! As someone whose life and musical path was greatly influenced by the whole progressive rock movement of the '70s, I can understand why our group has a special meaning to them. There was a real truth and power

Jordan Rudess of Dream Theater.

to the music that groups like Yes, Genesis and King Crimson brought to life in those days. They were forging new musical ground and combining stylistic elements of classical and jazz, fusing together harmonic and rhythmic ideas that shaped this movement we now call progressive rock. It's that spirit that people recognize in Dream Theater. It's the guys in their late 30s and up that are totally aware that DT is keeping those ideals alive while pushing forward into the future! I get a lot of people thanking me for the music, people grateful that, within the production line mentality that controls so much of the way we lead our lives, there are people like us that are true to our music and not caving in to commercialism and the automation of our humanity. Our fans like honesty and commitment. Our older fans are reminded of the amazing movement started in the '70s and it brings back the spark that lit so brightly for them back then!

How challenging is it to bring Dream Theater's studio work to life onstage and create a "show" versus merely a re-creation of the work?

When I started with the group back in 1999, we really began to think about our visual presentation, as well as our audio presentation. I was involved back then in some very interesting visual applications for the Mac that started the ball rolling. There was actually a time when I was controlling a lot of visual effects directly from my keyboard! That in general is still a cool idea, but our visual show has come a long way, and now we have a dedicated crew that takes care of making sure all that is in place.

Over the last couple of world tours, we have had the

264 ... Hello, It's Me

amazing Johnny DeKam operating a highly sophisticated video rig in which he runs all kinds of movies and custom special effects to our music. Another key element to our live presentation is an Australian named Robert Medina. He is our 3-D guy, and has brought many of our album covers to life on the screen. He also is the creator of the 3-D Wizard, which is a real-time 3-D animation on a screen behind me that reacts to every note that I play on the keyboard. It's all based on MIDI information and we go so far as to have a MIDI compass on my rotating stand.

This actually brings up another show element that I use that is not based on video. It is the rotating keyboard stand. Years ago, I decided that the days of being a static keyboard player sitting being a non-mobile keyboard stand had to end. To aid me in the movement towards a future of motion, I enlisted Dutch stand designer Patrick Slaats. Most every world tour, I introduce a new model rotating stand!

I'm conscious of my gear and the way it comes off in the presentation. I enjoy playing a custom keytar-type instrument that is called the Zen Riffer. It allows me to get even closer to the audience and rock out with the boys in the front of the stage. Although [we] are very serious musicians, it's still a show, and we like to have fun and make sure that besides the musical energy output, there are a lot of things to look at and your senses are complete!

What are the live shows you've seen throughout your life that have had a profound effect on you?
The very best show that I've seen in many years was Cirque de Soleil's *Love* show, based on the Beatles' music. That show just blew me away. Incredible sound and visuals, not to mention the talent of all the acrobats and actors on the stage.

Concert-wise, to this day the most memorable show was a Yes concert I had seen in the '70s that was outdoors. They had a spectacular laser light show and the music was glorious and uplifting. Genesis at [Madison Square] Garden in New York in those days was also tremendous.

Baseball in the Coliseum
(2009)

As I was finishing this book, I got a call. Would I be interested in heading up to the Los Angeles Coliseum the next day to shoot a TV pilot about the building's history with the host, Detroit Tiger all-star, Curtis Granderson? This is why I pinch myself sometimes.

The Coliseum is my favorite sports building on earth; it has fascinated me ever since I was a kid. In 2002, I wrote a book about it and have since become a sort of expert on the place, which blows me away. When I was writing the book, Charlie and I would take a football up there and play on the field when the place was empty—incredible memories. Now, I get asked to go show it off to a big-league ballplayer? Come on. I guess I'll always be like a kid around certain things, like stadiums and baseball players, and I'm totally comfortable with that. I raced up there and spent hours wandering the hallowed stadium with Curtis, and we had an absolute blast.

"Luck is the residue of design," famed baseball executive Branch Rickey once said, and that's an adage that defines a big part of my life.

Taping the TV show.

Have a plan, a design, and work hard to make it real. Believe in yourself. The more of that you do, the better luck has a chance of finding you.

I'm telling you.

With then-Detroit Tiger Curtis Granderson at the Los Angeles Memorial Coliseum.

More taping near the famed peristyle arches at the Coliseum.

The Rev
(2010)
(Dedicated to Avenged Sevenfold fans)

My son Charlie had started listening to a hard rock/ metalcore band called Avenged Sevenfold. A lot. An interesting footnote was that the band hailed from Huntington Beach, our longtime home. I thought at some point it might be fun to write about them. They were getting really big and I was interested in the local angle.

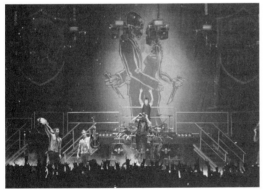

Avenged Sevenfold in concert.

Then one day, we found out an interesting piece of news. The band's drummer, Jimmy Sullivan, was the son of someone we knew through the Catholic Church. In fact, Jimmy's dad, Joe, was involved in some of the kids' sacrament preparation classes and so I got to talking with Joe about his son, nicknamed "The Rev." Hearing Joe talk about how proud he was of Jimmy got me thinking that an article about what it's like to be parents of a real-life rock star might be interesting, so I wrote this piece in 2008 for my newspaper column in the *Huntington Beach Independent*:

On the back window of a vehicle parked on a well-kept street in a neighborhood near Central Library, there is a sticker. It's for the band Avenged Sevenfold, and while you'd be right in assuming that the vehicle belongs to a big fan of the band, just which fan might surprise you. It's not one of the millions of high school or college kids who have helped make this innovative, intense metal band one of the hottest in the world right now. Rather, the vehicle belongs to Joe Sullivan, the drummer's dad.

Joe and Barbara Sullivan, who have lived in the same comfortable Huntington Beach house since 1977, may not look like rock-and-roll parents. Spend some time with them, though, and you'll realize how deceptive looks can be. Since their son Jim (a.k.a "The Rev") hit it big (literally and figuratively) with Avenged Sevenfold, they've become experts on the industry. They can just as easily discuss the importance of merchandise sales as they can the financial implications of headlining a gig versus being an opening act—and most importantly, they love the music. Raising their son (who is now 28) in this very house along with his two sisters, Kelly and Katie, they knew early on that Jim's life might eventually involve percussion. "He was desperately into music," Joe laughs. "In the bathtub, when he was tiny, he'd be banging away on things. Then, pots and pans—anything and everything." Barbara adds, "So finally we got him a little drum kit from Sears. And we knew—we just knew this was serious."

Neither of his folks are musicians, so Jim's mom went to a music store that used to be located at the corner of Warner and Springdale when

Jim was about six. There, they met a teacher named Jeanette Raitt who became very influential, teaching Jim for several years and helping to spark his passion for complex percussive challenges. Soon, the young drummer discovered the band Metallica, then Pantera. "Faster and faster stuff," Joe says. "And his teacher had him transcribing all the drum work so he could really understand what was happening."

At 10 years old, his folks got Jim a more serious drum kit—an old Ludwig set with lots of cymbals. "When his teacher found out he'd been figuring out the parts on a little toy set, she was amazed," says Barbara.

Jim played with several local bands, including Suburban Legends, before finding his way into Avenged Sevenfold, which has now been together for about 10 years. All five band members—M. Shadows (vocals), Zacky Vengeance (guitar), Synyster Gates (guitar), Johnny Christ (bass) and Jim "The Rev" Sullivan (drums)—hail from Huntington Beach. Supposedly, the band's name is a reference to the book of Genesis in the Bible and the story of Cain and Abel, where Cain is punished to live in exile, alone and miserable. Anyone who relieved Cain of his misery by killing him would be "avenged in sevenfold," or punished in a way that is seven times worse than Cain's punishment. However, M. Shadows, the frontman, driving force and de facto band leader, has stated in interviews that the band is "not really religious at all."

After forming in high school, they released the album *Sounding the Seventh Trumpet*. Their follow-up album was called *Waking the Fallen*. Their fan base grew quickly and critical acclaim

270… Hello, It's Me

was swift:

Rolling Stone magazine: "These guys excel at the complex, pummeling eighties-metal moves that first came into circulation when they were in diapers."

Spin magazine: "A Godzilla-size pileup of whiplash metalcore and Sunset Strip swagger, Avenged Sevenfold's 2005 major-label debut, *City of Evil*, won unexpected platinum status"

Blender: "Avenged Sevenfold transcended the headbanger heartland with 2005's "Bat Country." Its mixture of campy goth and '80s Sunset Strip debauchery was matched with a refreshing sound that fused florid guitar solos with frenzied nail-gun drumming, while M. Shadows shifted effortlessly between a snarl and a croon."

And 2007's self-titled album won the Kerrang! Awards Best Album award in 2008.

Joe and Barbara watched their son learn to live on his own as a member of an up-and-coming band that would soon be touring the world. "It wasn't that easy at first," Barbara explains. "Those first tours, like the first Warped Tour, they'd be in a van driving all night, not eating right. But they learned discipline fast, and the importance of hard work. These young guys work very hard."

Today, the families of the band know each other and it's a very close-knit bunch in the Avenged organization. Crew members went to grade school with the band, the musicians are all high school buddies—and it all happened here in Huntington Beach.

The Sullivans are amazed with their son's life and support every beat of it. "We love to hear how the music evolves when they're working on it," Joe smiles. "We love the shows, the feedback from fans and family members—it's an incredible experience." Barbara scrapbooks many of her son's musical moments and also collects much of the Avenged Sevenfold memorabilia, including lunchboxes, watches, coasters and more. She also remembers what it was like when all three kids were home. "While Jimmy played drums, his sister Kelly was playing classical music on French horn and his other sister Katie would be painting—there was always wonderful art being created around us."

Mom's favorite show to date? "A long time ago, right as they started catching on, up at the Ford Amphitheatre in Los Angeles. Jimmy still says that they weren't that good yet, but watching the kids in the crowd sing along to every song— you knew something special was happening." She pulls out the Moonman statue that the band won the as Best New Artist at the 2006 MTV Video Music Awards as proof of how right she was.

And what does Joe feel when he watches the band play live today before thousands of adoring fans? "I look at him up there under the lights, and I think back to the little kid in the tub, that little boy hitting those toys together. It's incredible to think about what he has done and where he's been. But you know, it doesn't just happen. He worked so hard—all these guys work so hard, and that's that thing I think people should realize. They're great because of the time they put in. How can you not be proud of that?"

Well, the piece came out, Jimmy liked it, the family liked it and the fans liked it. It didn't surprise me that A7X (the band's moniker) fans would like a peek inside Jimmy's world. But what did catch me off guard was the tone and amount of notes I received. And what sort of messages do intense, devoted, (and in many cases) young, tattooed-and-pierced A7X fans send? Thoughtful messages. Appreciative messages. Funny messages. I was impressed. I liked this bunch.

The Sullivan family.

Fast-forward more than a year and a half later. By now, Joe and I have become pretty good friends, Charlie and I are kept fully up to date on what the band is up to, from world tours to road stories to funny episodes at home with the Rev. For me at my son's age, this would have been the equivalent of getting the inside word on the Rolling Stones, so big a fan Charlie had become. Then, in late December 2009, I received an e-mail from a good friend. Had I heard? The Rev had been found dead at home. Charlie was at the store with my wife. I called them. He was numb. I contacted Joe to express the inexpressible. A day or so later, Charlie and I went to the Sullivan home. Jimmy's fiancée was there. His sisters were there. We all sat. And we all cried. He had simply been found in bed. No signs of anything afoul. Just like that.

My friend Jordan Rudess, from the band Dream Theater, got me in touch with Mike Portnoy, Dream Theater's legendary drummer. He was Jimmy's idol. Mike sent the family flowers, and a signed cymbal in Jimmy's honor. Within a few days, two services were planned at our parish for Jimmy, a Rosary and then, the next day, the funeral. The ceremonies were touching and beautiful and heart-wrenching—and profound. Jimmy's sisters supported their parents. Musicians poured in. Charlie found himself within inches of his favorite band sitting in the pew just behind him, where we always sit at Mass. What a strange sen-

The Rev, behind his drum kit.

sation. I cannot imagine how my son felt, but I know he was heartbroken. We went to the family home after to reflect, and celebrate the life of this big-hearted drummer who, based on the numerous remembrances, had changed many lives for the better. Remembering how strongly the A7X fans had reacted to my article on the Sullivans, I asked for permission to write a piece about the power of what we'd all witnessed the last several days—so that they could share in what had happened. Joe and Barbara said fine, and this is the piece I wrote in early January 2010:

I'm sitting here trying to make sense of and write this column about what I witnessed last week—the two services I attended for Jimmy "The Rev" Sullivan, the drummer (who wrote and sang) for the Huntington Beach-based band, Avenged Sevenfold. If you saw the column I wrote a few months back about Joe and Barbara Sullivan, Jimmy's parents, you'll remember that this tight-knit family knew early that the little boy banging on toys in the tub was destined for something percussive—but as the member of a spectacularly popular band? Well, maybe not that—but that's what happened. And as millions of fans remain in mourning, I wanted to write more about him—and his band. "The Rev" tragically passed away at just 28 years old the week before last, and while nobody is quite sure what happened, it really doesn't matter—what's important is that a family here misses their son (and brother). Joe and Barbara want to address the fans soon, and they will. For now, not as a columnist but as a friend, I asked their permission to convey the power of what I witnessed at the services and they said it was okay. But as I sit here, it's hard to know where to begin.

This lovely family (including Jimmy's sisters Kelly and Katie) was visible at the services not just gracefully tending to the assembled flock, but on the several scrapbook photo boards at the church featuring hundreds of family photos. Vacations, camping trips, birthdays, ball games, Jimmy playing one of his first sets of drums—they all grew up right before our eyes. So how do you begin to write of the vastness of this loss the family is feeling? I can tell you that as friends and family paid tribute to the Rev at the rosary service the night before the funeral, it was powerful, heartfelt and real—just like the Rev himself. The packed church was treated to stories from pals, relatives and his first drum teacher, who spoke of the young boy who understood and executed polyrhythmic theory in a matter of weeks—that was Jimmy. Grade school buddies recalled the happy-go-lucky athlete who became a real-life rock star—but who never forget where he came from. The four remaining members of Avenged Sevenfold entered together and then rose together to address the crowd. Tearfully, these young men, wives and girlfriends by their side, shared their love of their band mate. Finally, the Rev's dad, Joe Sullivan, spoke about his son, honoring him with an eloquent speech on how much he learned from his boy—and how it will affect his life going forward. There was pain in the room, but it was trumped by joy and love generated by the Rev, who many felt comfortable, justifiably, in calling him their best friend.

The funeral the next day was an equally dramatic, beautiful event. In addition to the hundreds of family and friends gathered (including Jimmy's fiancée, Leana), there were several bands in attendance, including members of Buckcherry and My Chemical Romance. Flowers, cymbals and drumheads signed by legendary bands were delivered—representing the love and respect among the band's brethren.

Avenged Sevenfold guitarist Brian Haner, a.k.a Synyster Gates, delivered a soaring eulogy with focus and class—you look at him and the other young men in the band, M. Shadows, Zacky Vengeance and Johnny Christ, and wonder what they must be feeling—but in their eyes you see the pain of their loss. I will tell you here that besides their music, what I love about Avenged Sevenfold is that they choose to remain part of Huntington Beach. They could easily have left after hitting it big—but they didn't. They bought homes here, they're known around town, they hire their buddies as crew—they're good guys. Rock stars? Whatever. They're hardworking, successful young men who got where they are because they're very good at what they do—and the city is better for having them here.

Back to the Sullivan family, as they clung together at the church and at the cemetery, surrounded by hundreds of mourners, it reminded one that the son they gave the world affected many lives—young lives. As I struggled trying to write this column, an e-mail arrived. It was from a young woman in Omaha, Nebraska, Rachel Lee. She's a 22-year-old librarian who loves

Avenged Sevenfold. Her note read in part:

> *I specifically wanted to thank you for hu-*
> *manizing the drummer and his family,*
> *giving a sense of what those of us who*
> *have looked up at their stage and sung*
> *their lyrics, begged for their autographs,*
> *have only sensed at a distance—that at*
> *the end of the night their loved ones back*
> *in Huntington Beach are truly their fam-*
> *ily and their home. While the fandom has*
> *suffered a great loss, we dearly wish to ex-*
> *press that they are not alone in their grief*
> *and there are a lot of us out there who wish*
> *we could do something to ease the pain of*
> *Jimmy's passing. Tonight, a candlelight*
> *vigil is being planned in a number of cit-*
> *ies in his memory, fans gathering together*
> *to talk and laugh and remember the Rev.*

She went on to tell me about a scrapbook project in honor of Jimmy being headed by a young
woman in Florida, Victoria Deroy, who also wrote
to express her sorrow over Jimmy's loss, and her
plan to help keep his memory alive.

> *Avenged Sevenfold saved my life and from*
> *the moment I heard of Jimmy's death, I*
> *felt as though my entire world had fallen*
> *apart,"* she expressed. *"I wanted to com-*
> *fort the men that I had grown to know*
> *and love through their music, DVDs and*
> *live performances. I sent out over 20 mes-*
> *sages to fan pages and tried to get several*
> *of my friends involved, and the end result*
> *was over 190 messages from fans all over*

the world. We received prayers, notes and stories even from people who had known Jimmy personally. I am currently in the process of handcrafting the scrapbook and will send it out as soon as I am finished.

Losses like this will never be easy for me to process, make sense of and write about—but the words of these fans brought some clarity. Jimmy's loss is being felt by millions all around the world—and especially by a family and a band of brothers here in Huntington Beach.

If you haven't listened to Avenged Sevenfold, I recommend you do. It's raw, passionate music played with skill, soul and unbridled fury. My 16-year-old son Charlie adores this band, so we have had the benefit of hearing them constantly—as I write this, their song "Critical Acclaim" plays loudly, and proudly, behind me. Listen to the music, listen to the magic and by all means, listen to the backbeat thunder. There's no better way to honor the Sullivan family—after all, that's their boy on the drums.

This piece ran. And then the messages started. Slowly at first, perhaps 10 e-mails a day. Then 20, 30, 50 and 100. And they kept arriving.

"I read your article in the *Huntington Beach Independent*. Thank you for sharing such a magical part of Jimmy Sullivan's life with us."

"I was truly touched by your article about Jimmy 'The Rev' Sullivan. As a fan with no personal connection to the band, it is difficult to find a way to express the immense amount of pain we feel."

"I want to thank you very sincerely for your article on Jimmy 'The Rev' Sullivan and your heartfelt message to the fans.

When the news of his passing first flashed before my eyes, I just couldn't believe it. I can't even put into words the pain I felt and still feel. It's like something irreplaceable has been torn right out of me. A vital organ. I can't imagine the pain that his close friends and family are going through as I am just gutted."

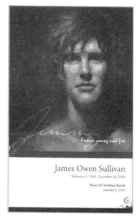

James Owen Sullivan
February 9, 1981 - December 28, 2009
Mass of Christian Burial
January 6, 2010

The program from the funeral.

They came from all over the United States, Japan, the UK and throughout Europe, Australia, New Zealand, Canada—from everywhere.

I had never experienced anything like this. I shared them with my son. I printed them all for the Sullivans. And I addressed the phenomenon in my column in February 2010:

Finally, a comment about the overwhelming amount of mail I received last week (and continue to receive) in regards to my piece on Avenged Sevenfold drummer Jimmy "The Rev" Sullivan. I've never experienced anything like this as a column writer. The majority of the messages were from young fans from all over the world. Collectively, they mourn, but individually, they expressed in vivid, heart-wrenching language the pain they feel from Jimmy's death. Their notes became like so much poetry—intense love letters and introspective reflections about a drummer and a band that are an integral part of their existence. This loss is a huge moment in their young lives, and judging from the writing I saw, this loss ties them all even closer together as a community. I wish all of you A7X fans, if you're reading this, peace and healing. And may the power of the music push you to do great things. Lastly, I'm in the process of answering each note received, and though it may take a while, I promise to do it.

And then I started staying up late into each night, carefully answering each letter. For anyone who thinks today's youth generation has forgotten how to write or express themselves in meaningful, deep and honest emotion, I have the letters—stacks of letters—to prove otherwise. The more I read, the more I learned about this amazing community of fans—a unified, supportive, faithful world nation. And I felt a bond develop.

One day in our church parking lot, I went to pick up Charlie, who'd been helping Joe there with a volunteer project. I found them both in Joe's car, listening to music—Jimmy's music. It was what he'd been working on at the time of his death. And it was incredible. Several nights later, in the Sullivan home, we listened to more of it. And our time together inspired the third article in my series.

"I hope you'll find your own way when I'm not with you."

The lyrics jump out to the listener. The sparse, haunting, discordant ballad, consisting only of Jimmy "The Rev" Sullivan on piano, drums and vocal, fills the room—the same room where, last May, my teenaged son and I visited with Joe and Barbara Sullivan, parents of the drummer from Avenged Sevenfold. We were there for a column I was writing about how proud the parents were of their son's success.

The song continues, and it is stunning; it's introspective and moody. There are no formal lyrics for the most part. Instead, what appears to be a "guide vocal"—random words serving as placeholders for what will be written later. But the line appears again, slightly revised, "I think you'll find your own way when I'm not with you."

Here in the same room where, in January, I watched the band members comfort the family after Jimmy's funeral; the same room where a little boy named Jimmy Sullivan grew into a big drummer.

The song ends with, "I know you'll find your own way when I'm not with you."

These are some of the last words recorded by the Rev, just weeks before his death.

Barbara Sullivan wipes tears away from her eyes. We listen to some more music that Jimmy had been working on up until the end, in preparation for the new Avenged Sevenfold album. When the songs end, Joe Sullivan breaks the silence. "He was really creating beautiful music and I think the fans would be comforted by that." The Sullivans are aware of the impact their late son had not just on people here in Huntington Beach, but around the world. That's why we're here—because they want to reach out to the fans, to comfort and clarify—to give them an update. (My son is with me this evening as well, because he not only loves the band, he loves the Sullivans, too.)

"I was planning on waiting until the coroner's results were in to talk about Jimmy—but realized that whatever the report has to say just really doesn't matter," Barbara tells me. "Now that a little time has passed, I am able to read some of the fan postings and want to share a few details that might bring them comfort. The last few months of Jimmy's life were good ones. Although Jimmy was never married (as is often erroneously reported), he had found his true best friend and soulmate, Leana. He had just had eye surgery that let him see without glasses. He called me one morning to

Jimmy Sullivan on Halloween with his fiancée, Leana, in 2009.

tell me the story of not being able to find his glasses, wanting to know what time it was, realizing he could see the clock and watching it for 10 minutes! Jimmy had just bought a condo and a new car, finally acknowledging that he was doing well as a musician. He had also spent a lot of time with his friends and family, especially over the holidays. Jimmy and Leana were Beauty and the Beast for Halloween, he sang Irish songs with the extended Sullivan family on Thanksgiving and he asked for (and received) a 'decorative chicken' (crazy Jimmy randomness) for Christmas!"

Barbara shares a photo from this past Halloween, taken just several feet from where we sit this evening in the living room. It is a beautiful image of a vibrant couple.

And she continues. "Most important to him, Jimmy had just finished writing songs for Avenged Sevenfold's new album—he even called one his 'masterpiece.' When he wrote songs, he would record tracks of his singing, playing the piano and drumming—then when he played them for me, he would sing the orchestra or guitar parts that would be added later. I am thankful that I got to tell him how much I liked and admired his music. Jimmy wrote some really good songs, I was so proud of him, and I know that even though it will be very hard for them, the band will do a great job getting them recorded soon. Needless to say, these 'all Jimmy' recordings are almost impossible for me to listen to yet, but what a blessing to have them."

Joe Sullivan adds, "We love what the fans have been saying. They're actually teaching us things about Jimmy with their words and stories. These young people, all over the world, are a real community and we appreciate all of their good thoughts. Also, we want fans to know how much we love the guys in the band. That brotherhood they have, they gave Jimmy a place to be himself, to create, to be the Rev. What an amazing group of young men—and women, and parents, too. The extended Avenged Sevenfold family is just incredible."

As tough as it is to recount, Barbara also wants fans to be aware of some other things. "I want to share with the people who cared about him that Jimmy died peacefully, in his sleep," she says. "No coroner's report yet, but she did tell me that his heart just quietly stopped. I am thankful that he was home instead of on the road, that he was not alone, that he was on top of the world, that I got to spend a lot of time with him in the last few months and that he will be remembered with a smile by so many."

This past Christmas Day, Jimmy told his mom he had a surprise for her. She asked what it was. He told her that the band's album *City of Evil* had gone platinum. But she already knew this. What was the surprise? She was puzzled.

He passed away just several days later. Days after that, the surprise arrived: Jimmy had ordered five customized copies of the platinum album, framed with the album cover art and inscribed to family members. One for Joe, one for Barbara, one for each of his two sisters and one for his brother-in-law. Looking at two of the framed pieces in the living room, it says a lot about the young man.

It was one final gesture that defined Joe and Barbara's big-hearted, life-of-the-party, over-the-top kid who, though he may have been a success-ful drummer in a wildly popular band, never took the thrill for granted—and never missed an opportunity to share his excitement with his family.

I ask Barbara if I can mention the story for this column. "Oh, I think his fans would like to know about this. He loved those fans so much. And this is just another one of those things that made Jimmy, well, Jimmy."

It made him Jimmy. And it made him "The Rev," a rock-and-roll hero from Huntington Beach who, for many, will live on forever. Or rather, in a spelling his fans have embraced, "FoREVer."

And once more, the letters poured in, and I stayed up late at night to answer them. As I will do my best to do whenever I have the honor of hearing from A7X fans.

Charlie still listens, of course, his ears paying closer attention to the Rev's drum hits. And it looks like the band goes on.

For the album they had just started working on at the time of Jimmy's death, Avenged Sevenfold managed to find a drummer—Dream Theater's Mike Portnoy—a legend stepping in to momentarily fill a void for a kid who worshipped him. What happens next? Who knows? But I am sure that the A7X family of fans will live strong for a long time and never let the memory of Jimmy Sullivan fade. As I've learned, that's just not how they are.

And to any Avenged fan that might be reading this right now, I'll tell you once more: Thank you for caring, for believing and for making a difference. You rock. (Thanks as well to Kortney Ehrhart for the amazing live photos.)

Chapter Five

Odds, Ends and Some Articles I've Written

Tennis

Tennis belongs to the individualistic past—a hero, or at most a pair of friends or lovers, against the world.
      —Jacques Barzun, *God's Country and Mine*

That quote exemplifies why I love tennis—playing or watching. I taught in high school and college. I've had the good fortune to meet all of my favorite players. Charlie has become a standout player at Mater Dei High School. We're a tennis family.

But I was given a new peak into the game when Charlie (and soon after, Claire) became ball kids. Watching them work on-court with the biggest names of the game is a surreal thing. I actually had the chance to try it, too. This is from a newspaper column I wrote for the *Huntington Beach Independent*:

As a tennis teacher in 1979.   **Me today—still a tennis bum.**

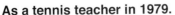

The 2008 East West Bank Classic in Carson will stay with me forever. At the invitation of Mark McGuire, who coordinates the ball kids at the tournament each year, I had the chance to work as a ball "kid" during the tournament's final, which featured Dinara Safina vs. Flavia Pennetta. My kids have both worked as ball kids for several years, and watching them has given me great respect for what these young people do at tournaments all over the world. Consider: What other sport puts kids on world stages, in the middle of play, to help maintain flow, order and action? It's kind of insane if you think about it, which is why I marvel at the poise and composure of ball kids. And so, when the opportunity came along, I could only accept.

I'm a huge fan of the game, I play a lot. Who would want to miss this? Sure, you play through your worst-case scenarios: You trip over your feet and it's an instant two million hits on YouTube. A 110-mile-per-hour serve finds your midsection

Charlie ballkidding for Tommy Haas.

Claire working as a ball kid.

before you can dodge. Or would there be merciless catcalls from the crowd? Thankfully, none of these nightmares played out. Rather, this was an exhilarating experience that amplified what I already knew to be true: The energy and pressure on the court is intense, and when Safina locks eye contact with you, it means you'd better hit her hand with that second serve ball. The whole experience was a bit of a blur; from the walk out of the long tunnel onto center court to racing over to shade the players with umbrellas during changeovers and keeping the balls moving to their appropriate places between points it's a lot of work and your mind cannot shut down for a second (lest you risk being admonished by the chair ump).

All I can tell you is, if you ever watch tennis, try watching the ball kids, even just for a few points. As the experts say, the perfect ball kid is an invisible ball kid—and so, with stealth efficiency, they keep the game moving, advancing balls, fetching towels, water and anything else the players want and shading them from

With Andre Agassi and Jean (c. 1991). (Los Angeles, California.)

With John McEnroe and my twin sister Margaret (c. 1991). (Los Angeles, California.)

sun—"serving the player" as they are taught to do. Safina looked at me as I entered the court for a moment with a slightly quizzical look, followed by a little shrug that seemed to suggest, "Hey, whatever—do the job and we won't have any problems." And I'm not sure I've ever taken any other job so seriously in my life.

R E F L E C T I O N S
from sportscaster Mary Carillo

After I started playing tennis, I heard about a third cousin I had who was a tennis player. I went to see her play Billy Jean King in 1977, and from the moment I met her, I adored her. She played on the circuit for a while, won the French Open, mixed with John McEnroe in 1977 and then entered the world of broadcasting where, today, she is one of the premier talents in the field—an honest, funny, brilliantly astute commentator: Mary Carillo.

With Mary in 1989.   **With Mary in 2009.**

Mary and I reconnected in California in the late 1980s and discovered a bond that was silly, emotional and substantial. Forgetting how charismatic Mary is (a lot), we just discovered a wonderful closeness. She has inspired me, whether she knows it or not, in myriad ways. In a world

With Jean and Mary at the U.S. Open (c. 1990).

of button-down, politically correct commentating, she shoots freely, honestly and openly. She says what she thinks, but more importantly, she knows what she knows. She does her homework and she has passion, and that combination allows her to do what few others do on TV—treat the audience with intelligence. I have all these wonderful notes from Mary, intense scrawls that look like her voice. When you are with Mary, she crackles with energy, never stops moving, talking, thinking, analyzing. You meet Mary once, you never forget her.

Recently at a family reunion, on a paddle tennis wall, Mary was playing and some teenagers, who didn't know how to play, watched. Then Mary did what she does, started showing them, getting them involved, mixing it up with them. They had no clue who she was. But you could see they loved her, because she was real. I've never met anyone remotely like Mary because I don't think there is anyone remotely like her. So you could all experience a bit of Mary, I asked her some questions for this book.

What are the biggest differences in the game today from when you played?

MARY CARILLO: The power and spin in today's game. I grew up with a wooden racket in my hand—the only way to derive the desired effect with that tool was proper grips, technique and body awareness. For more power, you needed to hit through the ball harder. For more control and safety, you slowed down the racket speed. Now, with incredible racket and string technology, lighter frames, etcetera, you need to speed up the racket head for more control—it will afford you more spin. Open stances are the norm. Hugging the baseline is a must, or you'll lose your court management skills and be banged off the playing field.

What was your most memorable match as a player?
Winning the French Open Mixed Doubles with John McEnroe in 1977. We were two kids from Queens, utterly unknown, on our first-ever trip to Europe. What could be more memorable than that?

As an announcer, it's still the Connors-Krickstein U.S. Open match from 1991. I called it with Tony Trabert and Pat Summerall, and I still smile at how little we said during the match—how little we *had* to say. These days that match would be ruined by constant chatter, unendurable stats, promos, nonsense. That match is how tennis should look and sound.

What is your approach as a broadcaster?
Trust the match. Trust the action. Give the viewer a lot of credit. Tell a good story if you've got one, but try as hard as possible to stay out of the way.

What would our perfect day together be?
A day together would be a Sunday in the West Village, where I have my New York apartment. It would start at the Pink Teacup for a leisurely breakfast with the Sunday *Times*, the *New York Post* and the *Daily News*. We'd hang on to the *New York Times Book Review*, and walk off the meal along the Hudson. Back to my apartment because it starts to rain, so we watch (yet again, and with just as much pleasure) *Broadway Danny Rose*.

The sun starts to shine outside again. We meet up with my brother and wander to the Strand with him, because that's where we always end up. Mosey through the stacks, find some out-of-print books, though I still can't find the damn W. C. Heinz anthology I loaned to a friend 23 years ago and never got back—the same bastid who never returned the A. J. Liebling collection of boxing stories. Hmmph. . . .

[We go to] Washington Square Park to watch the chess players. Some crazy bastard is playing a pretty good saxophone—we listen to him for a while; walk through the neighborhood, stop at an outdoor café on McDougal for a beer and decide we're hungry enough to eat again.

End up on the roof of my apartment, with the greatest view in the world, even though the rooftop slants a bit. Watch the sun go down, laugh a lot and try hard to stay up for *Mad Men*, and barely make it.

(Now you know why I love Mary so much.)

Acknowledging Two TV Classics: The Brady Bunch and The Partridge Family

If you grew up in the early 1970s, you might agree that Friday nights on ABC-TV represented one of the great one-two punches in pop culture history: *The Brady Bunch* at eight o'clock followed by *The Partridge Family* at eight thirty. Both shows were innovative in the then-conventional sitcom world. *The Brady Bunch* featured a mixed marriage of sorts—a widower with three boys and a widow with three girls. *The Partridge Family* boasted a recently widowed mom raising five kids alone (unless you count the assistance of band manager and comic foil, Rueben Kincaid). I think both of these shows were notable in that they celebrated the family, even though the families portrayed were unconventional for the time (there were other shows like this, too, including *Julia* and *The Courtship of Eddie's Father*), and these are the two I still watch today with my kids.

Some favorite lines from The Brady Bunch:

Bully (to Cindy Brady): "Baby talk, baby talk, it's a wonder you can walk!"

Carol Ann Brady: "Jan, I think you may need glasses."

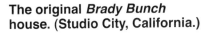

The original *Brady Bunch* house. (Studio City, California.)   **The Epting family at the *Partridge Family* house on the Warner Bros. lot. (Burbank, California.)**

Jan Brady: "Glasses! Oh, no, Mom! Not glasses! They'll make me look absolutely positively goofy!"

Marcia Brady: "It's so beneficial for me to be away from those children in junior high and to be with people of my own mature growth. I'm looking forward to the intellectual stimulation. Nice meeting you, boys. Bye."

Marcia Brady: "From now on, I'm beautiful and noble; I'm Juliet!"

Marcia Brady: "Ooh! My nose!"

And let's not forget: "Something suddenly came up," the Davey Jones episode, Peter's voice changing, Johnny Bravo (because he fits the suit!), the taboo Tiki statue, pork chops and applesauce and so many other moments.

What can you say? A near-perfect show that totally captured the times.

As I was finishing this book, I had an unexpected real-life Brady moment, if you want to call it that. As it turns out, Eve Plumb (who played Jan Brady) lives not too far from us here in Orange County, California. She's a local artist (mostly still-life; really nice stuff) and I ended up interviewing her for my newspaper column. The day she knocked on our door, for the first time in many a year, I was nervous about meeting someone. Just something about those people we grow up with I guess.

In my article for the *Huntington Beach Independent*, I wrote:

> On this day, here is Eve Plumb right here in Huntington Beach, talking about art, *The Brady Bunch*, acting—but mostly art—because that's what she does today and that's what is important to her. In a day and age when many TV icons spend so much time managing and dealing with their pasts, Eve has moved gracefully forward, letting the past be just that. Staring thoughtfully at her mug of coffee, she speaks with the philosophical weariness of someone who has lived it.
>
>
>
> "It's hard to get away from it sometimes," she says. "If you let your past define you, it can drive you crazy. My attitude is: find the good in it, work it into what you do now, and that's enough. I don't have a big interest in constantly living in the past."

Visiting with actress and artist Eve Plumb in my home after interviewing her for an article I was writing.

There she was at our dining room table, Eve Plumb, sharing stories over coffee. Another strangely wonderful, surreal pop culture moment for the scrapbook in my mind.

Oh, and if you want to visit the Brady house, you can. The abode used in exterior shots is located in Studio City. Built in 1959, the real house

Our children, Charlie and Claire, with actor Brian Forster (Chris Partridge #2) and actress Suzanne Crough (Tracy Partridge).

is a small, single-story ranch home. A false window was attached to the front's A-frame section to give the illusion it had two full stories during filming of the series' many establishing shots, all of which took place before the program debuted.

As for the Partridge family, they were a little hipper than the Bradys, but come on, they were a "touring band," so how could they not be?

From the Museum of Broadcast Communications:

> The Partridges were a fatherless family of six who decided, in the premiere episode, to form a rock band and tour the country in a psychedelically painted school bus. Most episodes began at the family home in California. Under the leadership of '70s super mom Shirley Partridge (Shirley Jones), the five Partridge kids survived various capers that almost always culminated in successful concerts.

My Partridge Family Top 10:

"I Think I Love You"
"I Woke Up in Love This Morning"
"She'd Rather Have the Rain "
"I'll Leave Myself a Little Time"
"I Can Feel Your Heartbeat"
"I'll Meet You Halfway "
"Doesn't Somebody Want to Be Wanted"
"Echo Valley 2-6809"
"Point Me in the Direction of Albuquerque"
"Morning Rider on the Road"

The Partridge Family house still stands, too, but visiting it is a bit trickier because it's on the Warner Bros. lot. But if you have a pal named E. J. Stevens, like I do, anything's possible. While working for Warner, E. J. kindly took us back to the lot. Located right nearby is the *Bewitched* house, *The Waltons* house and the fountain from the opening credits of *Friends*. To see my family in the Partridge family's house was weird, but cool. We've watched many episodes together; to be in the physical space of the show was a kick for all of us.

The kids with actress Shirley Jones.

The Brady Bunch and *The Partridge Family*—thank God it was Friday—in the early '70s, anyway.

"Back to the Bleachers"
(2006)

Arnold Hano is one of my favorite writers. Twenty years earlier, I'd written him a fan letter and received, from the jungles of Central America, a thoughtful reply (Mr. Hano and his wife had been working in the Peace Corps). A few years ago, my son and I were Christmas shopping in a local bookstore. I saw Mr. Hano's classic book, A Day in the Bleachers. *I bought it for my son and noticed that it was signed by the "local author." Arnold Hano, local? I looked his number up, called him to say in person how much I enjoyed the book and then, after a long conversation with him, had this idea for an article, which ran in the* Los Angeles Times Magazine.

In 1954, a writer named Arnold Hano went to an old bathtub-shaped stadium called the Polo Grounds to see his beloved New York Giants play the Cleveland Indians in Game 1 of the World Series. That game produced arguably baseball's most famous defensive play, Willie Mays's "the Catch" off Cleveland's Vic Wertz (though, as Hano pointed out soon after, it was "the Throw" after "the Catch" that was the real stunner). The game also produced what many consider to be one of the single best sports reporting works in history: a book Hano wrote called *A Day in the Bleachers*. Hano's writing career has included many articles and sports biographies, but *A Day in the Bleachers* is considered his masterwork. First published in 1955, a special edition was issued in 2004 to commemorate the 50th anniversary of "the Catch."

Hano didn't go to the Polo Grounds to write a book—he went to watch a baseball game. But from his outfield perch among the faithful, he became inspired and started scrawling observational notes in the margins of his program and his newspaper, filling up all available space (while still managing to keep score). More than just a brilliant account of the day, the book is a primer on how to watch a ball game in person. The notable baseball writer Roger Kahn called it "the first and, I believe, the best of all the baseball books written from the point of view of the man in the stands."

Today, the Polo Grounds in upper Manhattan is gone. But Arnold Hano is still in the game. Now 84 years old, he lives with his wife in Laguna Beach. When I learned recently that he lived nearby, it made me wonder: What might it be like to attend a game with him today? To go back to the bleachers with a man who so beautifully defined the fan experience? Is it still the game he loved?

Me? I adore baseball. But my faith has been shaken in these days of chemically bloated records and tape-measure salaries. Where does Hano stand? He, who saw Babe Rut and Lou Gehrig in Ebbets Field, the Polo Grounds and old Yankee Stadium.

Would he accompany me and my son to the bleachers of Dodger Stadium for a day of reflection and comparison? I called him and, thankfully, he was up for our journey. In preparing for our field trip, I also reviewed some of the things Hano wrote in a recent piece in the *Los Angeles Times Book Review*: "I have been watching major league games since I was four. I do not know whether this makes me dean of the school of fanhood, but surely I am an elder on the faculty. Most of the fires of my life have been banked. One passion remains hot and full. My passion is to attend ball games. It is an urge not to be denied. It sustains me. I am held by its elegance, its perfect calculus of 90-foot base paths and its pitching distance of 60 feet, 6 inches to home plate."

My son Charlie and author Arnold Hano in the Hano home. (Laguna Beach, California.)

I couldn't wait for game day.

On a late Sunday morning, I am driving Arnold Hano and my 12-year-old son, Charlie, to Dodger Stadium, where the boys in blue will play the Milwaukee Brewers. En route, my son and I learn that the white-haired Hano is sharp, informed and wonderfully funny in a tough, unsentimental New York way. Dressed comfortably in a checkered button-up shirt and blue jeans, he seems genuinely excited to be heading to a ballpark.

He remembers so much detail from the hundreds of games he's attended that it doesn't seem possible. But it is. We hear tales of Babe Ruth and Jackie Robinson (the two men he believes did the most for baseball), Lou Gehrig, Mel Ott, Rogers Hornsby and more; the days of going to the Polo Grounds with his older brother; and how he misses afternoon games and scheduled double-headers. Getting off at Stadium Way and heading up to the parking lot, he tells of his luck to have witnessed not just "the Catch," but also Don Larsen's perfect 1956 World Series game and Sandy Koufax's 1962 no-hitter, among other landmark baseball events. Would his luck rub off on us today?

As we walk to the left-field pavilion gate, Vin Scully's voice is being piped into the parking lot over the PA system, and Hano's ears perk up. "Don't you just love him? Listen to that beautiful voice. And the things he comes up with during a broadcast, the details he remembers." Of course, he's right. And the same thing could be said of Hano, who remembers not just pitchers from 60 years ago—but certain pitches. With Scully in the air, we enter the ballpark.

Our seats are in the left-field pavilion, Section 305, Row A, the first row right above the outfield wall. Hano thinks the view is splendid. "These seats are so close to the field," he says. "I almost feel like I'm back playing shortstop." (Hano was a standout player at Long Island University.) My son and I have developed our own simple pre-game rituals that mesh neatly with Hano's. Basically, we get to the ballpark as early as we can to soak up the environment and prepare for the game.

We watch the players warm up, study the out-of-town scoreboard and discuss starting pitchers. Hano notes that long ago, part of the experience was arriving early to watch full-blown fielding practice, to get a real sense of what kind of shape the players were in that day. These days, you're lucky to catch a little batting practice. On this afternoon it is Little League Day, so batting practice is replaced by dozens of teams marching by us on the warning track, a colorful parade of baseball's next generation. "What a thrill for a youngster to set foot on a major league field," says Hano. "When we were kids, we'd exit the Polo Grounds . . . through center field after a game. That was always exciting, walking on a major league field."

I fetch programs for him and my son, and they both fill out the lineup pages to keep score. When Charlie asks if he'd like a pencil to keep score with, Hano lets him know he's fine with his blue pen. Once those two are done, we all go for some lunch. Obviously, ballpark food has changed since 1954, but the hot dog remains a faithful connection to the past. At this stadium, they get no better. We agree that Dodger Dogs are the best ballpark food on the planet.

Back at our seats, we settle into baseball paradise. Dodger Stadium on a comfortable, breezy Sunday afternoon is magical. The old wooden bleachers are packed not with wiseguys and shady urban characters like those who must have been at the Polo Grounds, but with families and many 20-something Dodgers die-hards. The smell of suntan lotion, the occasional beach ball being pounded around—it's innocent and summery and I feel like it's 1976. I ask, "This environment is good, right?"

"Marvelous," says Hano. "Just wonderful."

Whew.

We talk more baseball while we wait for the first pitch. I ask if he feels that today's players are overpaid. "Everyone I know is overpaid," he says with a grin. "Except me." The steroid controversy? He looks away. "Terrible. Come on, it's cheating." He's a tough old guy. But you can see he's hurt by what certain players have done to his game. He waxes on about his current favorites, including Greg Maddux, Omar Vizquel and Vladimir Guerrero ("I love that he doesn't wear batting gloves—who wouldn't want to feel the wood on their hands?").

Then it's game time. From the opening pitch through the first couple of innings, it's apparent that, for Hano, being at a game today is not much different from attending one back in the '40s or '50s. He loves it, and he seems to be aware of what every player on the field is doing. He carefully keeps score, as does my son. The sight of the two of them carefully, quietly tracking each play is a nice snapshot. Charlie never got to attend a game with my grandfather or my father, and if he did, I imagine it would have looked something like this. Throughout our day, Charlie, a good student of the game, is awed by Hano's firsthand accounts of DiMaggio, Ruth and especially Gehrig. He keeps whispering to me, "Can you believe he actually saw those guys in person?"

Until now, talking with this baseball guru, it seems that very little has changed in his years of ballpark experience. That is, until Dodger Olmedo Saenz's two-run homer in the third. It is at that moment that I become aware of what Hano feels is the biggest difference in ballpark experiences, now versus then. The stomp-and-clap introduction of the song "We Will Rock You" thunders through the park. Also, the electronic scoreboard implores us to "MAKE NOISE." Hano winces. I ask what he's thinking. "There's the big difference," he says. "The entertainment factor. All this stuff is so unnecessary. They just feel we have to be entertained all the time. But it's a distraction. Why distract from the game?" The electronic histrionics found in most ballparks today eat away at what Hano believes is key to understanding and enjoying baseball: concentration. I offer that maybe it's the sign of the times, that more and more people are growing accustomed to near-constant sensory stimulation. He agrees. On TV, cellphones, computers—even in a ball-

Me and Mr. Hano.

park—we are barraged with messages and entertainment. But is it necessary? Sure, some of it is paid for by sponsors. But a lot of it is not. A lot of it is simply a way to force you to pay attention.

Hano argues that the game is enough stimulation for him, and I agree. Perhaps in a timed, highlight-driven sport such as basketball, hockey or football, the levels of intimacy are not as important. After all, bombast doesn't feel as out of place after a bone-crushing dunk, cross-check or tackle. But all of a sudden, hearing "These Boots Are Made for Walkin'" after a ball four seems totally unnecessary.

Listening to Hano throughout the day reminds me that before there were flashy scoreboards and noisy entertainment, the game still worked beautifully and entertained millions of people. Baseball rewards patience and concentration with sparkling moments of elegance, intelligence and grit. Blink, and you might miss the right fielder's early break to the ball, or the catcher hustling up the line to back up a throw. "We used to talk between innings," he recalls. "About the game. About who was up next. About strategy. What's wrong with a little time to reflect? People are afraid to be bored for one second. And as for cheering, if you have to be told to yell when your team is trailing by a run, or when there are two strikes and two outs—what kind of fan are you?"

A wave gains traction in the crowd. Hano rolls his eyes. "The wave . . . I thought it was dead . . . I'd *hoped* it was dead." Once again, the electronic message boards begin blinking in big, blue letters "Get louder!" The crowd responds. "Get Louder!" The crowd responds more. "GET LOUDER!" The crowd roars. The message disappears, and the crowd gets quiet. The three of us laugh—it is absurd. But being with Arnold Hano, it seems more ridiculous than ever. He is patient, he concentrates and he most definitely does not want to be told when to cheer. He clearly loves being here, but the environment no longer matches the character and simplicity of the game.

Apropos of nothing, Harry Belafonte's calypso chant "Day-O" is played to create a call and response. The crowd takes the bait. Animated auto races soon follow on the scoreboard, along with blooper highlights, movie commercials and more "entertainment." And while it never bothered me too much before at games, the fact that it bothers Hano bothers me. For the rest of the afternoon, my son and I focus on the game and talk more baseball with Hano. I think of some of the wisdom from his book as we watch.

At Dodger Stadium for the game I wrote the story about.

As Hano attributed to the legendary broadcaster Red Barber, when a ball is hit to the outfield, don't watch the ball—watch the runners and outfielders. A towering "routine" fly is hit to the Dodgers' outfield, and I'm reminded of another point in the book: how silly it is to term even the most basic fly ball as "routine." As Hano poses, "Have you ever tried to run 40 feet to catch a baseball that has traveled some 330 feet in length and has described an arc about 100-feet high?" I watch what sort of leads runners take, the shifts fielders employ and everything in between. Baseball is a strange game. There's no clock, and games usually last about three hours. During that time, the ball is rarely in play more than nine minutes. For Arnold Hano, just because the ball is not in play doesn't mean there isn't baseball to experience. Or talk about. As for the bleacher "fanhood" (what Hano calls "bleacher dwellers"), today they are smart and attentive, though a small, rowdy group of guys ride Brewers outfielder Carlos Lee mercilessly. When he hits a prodigious (though meaningless) homer in the ninth, Hano says, "That's the best way to shut them up." The Dodgers win the game, 10–2. I realize that all day, all we talked about was baseball. And all we thought about was baseball. We recount the game as we leave: Two double plays, four home runs (including Russell Martin's first-ever dinger) and a terrific job by Dodgers pitcher Aaron Sele, who is fighting to win a spot back in the bigs. Sele particularly impressed Hano, who had the benefit of growing up watching Carl Hubbell, Lefty Grove and Bob Feller.

Hano exhales as he gets into my car. "What fun that was," he says, smiling. "There's still nothing like going to a game. Even with the distractions. For all its faults, baseball may still be the most indestructible sport. And it's still our greatest, simplest game."

What might it be like going to a game 50 years from now? I wonder. "It will still be great. And I think, I hope, there's at least one woman playing in the league. Gosh I hope so. A pitcher, no, maybe a solid infielder." As we say goodbye, I think back to my favorite line of his: "A baseball game is a mystery, unfolding. Let the scoreboard tell me hits, runs and errors, and the scores of out-of-town games. I'll do the rest."

I have been to many games in my 44 years. But I cannot recall studying one this closely, or appreciating one as much as I did than when I was with Hano. That's because the old gentleman reminded me of how much silent magic there is between the lines.

All you have to do is tune out the distractions and let the mystery unfold. Lose yourself in the game. And never, ever let a scoreboard tell you when to cheer.

REFLECTIONS
from author Arnold Hano

A note from Arnold Hano about his memory of that day:

> Dear Chris,
> Despite the blare and glare of the scoreboard, and the overwhelming sound that enveloped me, I found a game still a game, and I enjoyed seeing young Charlie keeping score just as I would have kept score at his age. The lack of fielding practice bothered me; the sense that the game had become a spectator's sport and not a fan's. But you cannot beat the sense of beauty in the 90-foot base paths, the fluidity of the fielders as a play develops—all that is still what holds me to this most beautiful game.

A couple of years later, Mr. Hano graciously contributed the foreword to a book I wrote about the Polo Grounds. It's one of the best baseball essays I've ever read.

"A Weekend on Planet B"
(2007)

I wrote this piece for the Los Angeles Times Magazine. *The culture of the "autograph show" interested me as it seemed it was a way for many older actors and actresses to capitalize on careers that thrived before the big-money era.*

Marilyn Monroe once described Hollywood as "a place where they'll pay you $1,000 for a kiss and 50¢ for your soul," but what was one to make of the recent Friday morning scene at the Burbank Airport Marriott?

Everybody who was somebody in this town was schlepping Sharpie pens, 8 × 10 glossies and boxes of memorabilia into the ballroom for two days of low-grade celebrity adulation and commerce. It was the Hollywood Collectors and Celebrities Show, produced as it is four times a year by Florida-based promoters Ray and Sharon Courts, and it unfolded far from the recent A-list headlines, touting a bald Britney, a deceased Anna Nicole and the ever-dismissible Paris Hilton.

The scene was the flip side of L.A.'s celebrity phantasm—an event where the stars didn't burn as bright, but were eminently more approachable and accommodating. It was a place where Jose Jimenez, Gloria Stivic and Joanie Cunningham all seemed happy to see you, where recognizable faces from *All in the Family*, *The Partridge Family*, *Batman* and *Happy Days* still endured in this age of reality TV and 15-minute "stars."

The show, now in its 17th year, takes place in Southern

California for the simple reason that most of the event's main attractions still live here among us. Some exist in obscurity, many are still working, but they all like the idea of making some cold, hard cash for a weekend of easygoing meet-and-greets.

And why not? Many of them found fame without the fortune in those pre-syndication days, long before Charlie Sheen could command $350,000 per episode on a show as forgettable as *Two and a Half Men*. But just like retired baseball greats who sign autographs for cash while utility infielders today make millions, there's a price to pay for being a pioneer. Timing is everything, especially in Hollywood.

From the moment fans started filing in, this is clearly about making money. It is old school, cashbox-on-the-table, sure-we-can-break-a-hundred action. Most stars bring a helper to make change and take orders. Signs clearly spell out the deals, like specials on a deli blackboard: Pee Wee Herman (actor Paul Reubens) autographed photo: $30. Your item signed: $30. Your premium item (i.e. collectible figurine) signed: $40. Digital photo of you and Pee Wee: $40. The gathered stars pay the Courts nothing. Vendors pay for booth space, but for celebrities, the day is 100% profit (an attractive selling point for enticing bigger names).

Professional dealers come to collect autographs, but fans outnumber them by about four to one. It's easy to spot the difference. Fans gush and recount favorite memories, while dealers dourly instruct the celebrity on where and how they want the signature. ("Lower corner, black Sharpie, just your name, no other inscription.") Forget Kodak moments. These have eBay written all over them. Undaunted, Sally Struthers beams as she greets a legion of admirers. A woman nearly faints at the thrill of meeting Bill Dana. There's Kookie from *77 Sunset Strip* (Edd Byrnes). Chris—the second Chris—from *The Partridge Family* (Brian Forster)! Edie Adams! Julie Newmar! Several fringe players from the *Our Gang* series!

Fans pour in throughout the day, and everyone seems to be having fun. Familiar faces greet you every few steps—there's

Patty Duke's dad! And Karen Lynn Gorney, the tough-talking Stephanie Mangano from *Saturday Night Fever*! And is that the guy who played the pilot on that great episode of *The Twilight Zone* where they go back in time and find dinosaurs? The whole event has a certain *Twilight Zone* feel to it, with Tonya Harding next to Jane Russell next to Squiggy.

One recent twist in the memorabilia-hawking business: selling a deceased star's belongings. At the Burbank event, two tables are dedicated to that peculiar enterprise, one representing the recently departed Yvonne De Carlo (Lily from *The Munsters*) and the other hawking post-mortem memorabilia from Don Adams (Maxwell Smart from *Get Smart*). Both tables, maintained by associates of the two stars, seem like sad islands in the sea of revelry. Mr. Adams's golf shoes sit forlornly on a table along with a few of his other personal effects. (Had one of them been Maxwell Smart's famous shoe phone, perhaps there might have been more aggressive buyers.) De Carlo's belongings hark back to her days as a sultry star, along with the requisite *Munsters* pieces.

From the celebrity perspective, it's not an event for the faint of heart. As fans queue up around the tables of the bigger names, lesser-knowns sit hopefully, smiling politely, rearranging their stacks of photos, chatting among themselves. Some fans avert their eyes as they might to avoid eye contact with panhandlers. Others take advantage of the lack of interest, approaching the quieter tables so they can chat longer without feeling pressure to keep the line moving.

And what's this? Famed British musicians Denny Laine and Spencer Davis? They seem a tad out of place among the actors, but word spreads quickly and fans of the bands Wings, the Moody Blues and the Spencer Davis Group eventually seek them out. (Will someone will ever put together a rock-and-roll-style event on this scale? It seems like a natural.)

Save for a minor dust-up when Adam West's manager objects to a *Times* photographer snapping pictures, egos seem to play little part at this event. (West's manager, along with

Pee-wee's autograph from the show.

Burt Ward's, claims the former dynamic duo from the TV series *Batman* are "not doing any media" this particular day. The thought arises that if you're not doing media on a day like this, when are you doing it?)

Paul Reubens has the longest line of the day, proof that his resurrection from his much-publicized 1991 fall from grace is complete. The line pours out of the ballroom and spills into the lobby. Low-key and polite, Reubens is gracious to everyone he meets. And he's a strong cash generator too. Of the hundreds of people in his line, they all seem to be spending $70 to $100.

As the sun sets in this dim little corner of the celebrity universe, the stars pack up their pens, pictures and memorabilia after a long day. They'll be back at it again tomorrow, signing, smiling and listening as their fans confess and profess their love. One assumes that most of these familiar faces would rather not have to be here, trading celebrity for cash. But as they learned years ago, this is show business, and work is work.

R E F L E C T I O N S
from actor Paul Reubens

It would be hard to forget the throngs of adoring fans who lined up in the hundreds to meet Paul Reubens on this day. Despite the fact that he was long a national punchline after his much-

reported "movie theater incident," his fans remain loyal, faithful and loving toward the comedian, and he seemed genuinely taken aback by the the crowd that turned out for him. Here is a piece of my interview with him from that day:

With Charlie and actor Paul Reubens.

"I think this is unbelievable. Really fascinating. Like a whole subculture. I make a little list beforehand of who I'm gonna meet so I can catch up with old friends in between meeting fans. But at the one I did before in New Jersey, I was able to see the line. I like being able to see the line. It's more fun to scope it out. Partly why I'm doing [the event] is because I haven't done them before. If I did them all the time people might get tired, but once in a while seems like a lot of fun. It's like a huge ego booster, you sit here and all day long and people say really nice stuff. How great is that?"

"Against the Tide"
(2008)

This was an article I wrote in 2008 for Orange Coast *magazine, and I am very proud of this piece. (And thanks to my editor, Martin Smith, for his typically great work.) As you'll see in the piece, it was an extremely random event that brought Shirley and I together. Whenever that happens these days, I take it as a sign that a story is presenting itself. My family actually attended the 1976 Olympic Games in Montreal, which factor big in this article. Little did I know while watching the swimming back then that our paths would cross in this way.*

Olympic hero-turned-Orange County letter carrier Shirley Babashoff had the courage to speak out about East German sports doping in 1976. It's time for the International Olympic Committee to give the legendary swimmer what she deserves.

One evening in mid-August, a few friends and family gathered for an Olympics TV party in a wood-paneled Fountain Valley living room. Michael Phelps was about to swim a relay in Beijing, on his way to another gold medal and a legacy as the most honored Olympic athlete in history. Our hostess had added festive touches to her home for the occasion: paper lanterns, souvenir fans, a couple of colorful parasols and enough Chinese takeout to feed the Chinese army.

She disappeared shortly before the race started, and when she returned she was holding a blue canvas bag. She dropped it to the floor, and friends began pulling out eight 6-by-

6-inch boxes, some made of wood, a few of them in black slips. A moment later they were gently passing around their contents: eight Olympic medals, two gold and six silver. She explained to her guests that a poolside engraver etched her name into them as she emerged from the water after each race and that one of the chains broke as it was hung around her neck on the podium. Then, more serious, she added, "There should be six golds there—and then my life would have really been different."

With that comment the room went quiet. On the big screen, Phelps prepared to race toward destiny in China. But on that recent evening in Fountain Valley, there was an unmistakable sense that a long-ago destiny had been denied.

Realizing her melancholy comment had silenced the room, the hostess punctured the moment. "But I still love you guys, and I'm glad you're here!"

My mother, who lives just around the corner from us in Huntington Beach, had been telling me about her letter carrier, Shirley. They chatted all the time and Mom was impressed with how funny and thoughtful she was.

Then I received an e-mail from Shirley: "You don't know me, but I know your mom. I deliver her mail. I almost got to meet you yesterday, but I missed you. Anyway, I was talking to your mom and I had asked her if she was related to you, having seen your name on many of my son's books and also seeing it in various articles. She is so proud of you!"

And then the kicker.

"I have been trying to write a book for a while now, but really have no talent at it. My name is Shirley Babashoff. I swam in the 1972 and 1976 Olympic games. I have eight medals, two gold and six silvers. At the 1976 Olympics, the East Germans were taking performance-enhancing drugs and won nearly everything. Even though the East German doctors have acknowledged this, nothing has been done to have the medals returned to the rightful owners. Many women were affected by this blatant mishandling of sportsmanship. To this day, the Olympic Committee refuses to do anything. Anyway, I don't want to write about only this, but of all the training, devotion and sacrifices it takes to become an Olympic athlete. Thank you for your time."

She had me at "Babashoff."

I recognized her immediately as one of modern history's greatest swimmers, arguably one of the greatest athletes this country has ever produced. I also recalled how she stunned the world by publicly questioning the East German women's swim team in 1976. So Shirley Babashoff was my mom's letter carrier? It was like finding out that Michael Jordan reads your water meter. But that's how I found myself, months later at Babashoff's house, watching Phelps make sports history, and wondering how 32 years had passed without someone righting a long-ago wrong.

Open the paper, watch the news, or go online these days and count the number of times the word "doping" appears. Whether it's the ongoing debate about Barry Bonds's tainted home-run record, or Roger Clemens's testimony before Congress, or Olympian Marion Jones's conviction appeal, or a recap of cyclists booted from this year's Tour de France, or the tempered thrill of watching Jamaican sprinter Usain Bolt shatter the 100- and 200-meter records in Beijing, we live in a time when every great performance is suspect. Before all that, in 1976, there was Babashoff, standing with a lit match at ground zero of the explosion.

To the world's media, she had the courage to point out the obvious: East Germany's female swimmers had undergone a mysterious physical transformation. Her words carried the clear implication of cheating, and earned her the nickname "Surly Shirley." She was branded a sore loser and eventually retreated into the private life she leads today.

Still, she's as striking as she was during her time on the world stage—the blonde hair, pretty smile and mischievous eyes that captivated so many through two Olympics and other swimming championships are all intact. And yet, you rarely see Babashoff on TV or read about her in the papers. Though approached constantly, she avoids the media spotlight. For 20 years she has lived quietly in the company of her son, Adam, a close circle of friends, mostly from the local post office, and a feisty Brussels Griffon dog named Leroy.

SHIRLEY BABASHOFF

A Shirley Babashoff trading card.

But she remembers 1976 like it was yesterday, and she wishes others did, too. She's not afraid to talk about it, though I'm not sure Babashoff has ever been afraid to talk about anything. But her outspokenness in Montreal clearly took a toll. "Nobody wanted to be me," she says.

Telling her story seems particularly important now, at a time when the sports world needs to hear her most. Babashoff may have struck the match back in 1976, but the fire she sparked is still burning out of control.

By the time she arrived at the 1972 Olympic games in Munich, Babashoff already had squeezed a lot of life into her 15 years. Raised in a family of athletes in Norwalk, she'd grown up in a house that stressed fitness. Her dad, a former Army swimming instructor in Hawaii, gave Babashoff and her brothers a strict daily calisthenics regimen.

Mark Schubert, current head coach and general manager of USA Swimming's national team, coached Babashoff back then. "She was an extremely hard worker," he says. "She competed with the boys on the team, and many times won. The thing that set her apart was her competitiveness and pride at competitions. She just hated to lose."

Her hard work and dedication paid off. In the terror-marred Munich games, she won silver medals in the 100- and 200-meter freestyle events and competed on the gold-medal-winning team in the 4 × 100-meter freestyle relay.

A year after Munich, though, Jean Pierre LaCour

Swimming
Shirley Babashoff

Another Shirley trading card.

chronicled rumors about the East German athletes in the Paris newspaper *France-Soir*. His report, reprinted in the October 1973 issue of *Swimming World* magazine, referred to a "vaccine against fatigue" that improved performance and possibly contained male hormones.

Even then, skeptics were demanding justice. "The only way for the East Germans to answer these accusations is to open their training camps," LaCour wrote. "A simple denial will not be sufficient."

Babashoff had her suspicions, too. At the 1973 World Championships in Belgrade, Hungary, she says she and her American teammates experienced something altogether new and strange. "We get to the meet a few days early to get to know the water, get to know the pool. And then one day, we're told we can't go in because the East Germans were there—the pool was closed. That had never happened before. Nothing had ever been off-limits, and teams never practiced secretly."

During the championships, she recalls, "We got blown away by the East Germans—it was like swimming against aliens." The East German women won 10 of the 14 gold medals available, and set eight world records. "And we'd beaten them just a year before," Babashoff says. "Our team was in shock—how did we get killed like that?"

Two years later, at the 1975 World Championships in Cali, Colombia, rumors about the East German athletes were full-blown. "During the year, you'd get reports on the East German swimming times, which were very fast—so I started getting the sense that something was weird. But I think they scaled back their cheating in '75 because they didn't want to give away what they were planning for the Olympics."

Babashoff recalls how her frustration peaked the following year in the living room of the Fountain Valley house her family bought in 1971 and she now owns. Schubert, her coach, had come to visit.

"It was right there, right where you are sitting," she tells me. "I was like, 'I quit.' It was just before the Olympic trials in 1976, and the pressure sort of got to me. The press was saying that it would be me against the East Germans at the games, that I had the best chance of doing anything. I knew they were cheating, I was frustrated, so I quit."

Schubert made a plea, and a promise. "He told me something I thought was so corny then [but that] made sense to me: 'I don't want you to be known in history as the one who quit.' So I decided to swim. He decided then he would keep the press completely away from me."

Babashoff winces as she remembers the sense of impending doom among the American swimmers before the 1976 Montreal Olympics. She had tried to cheer up those who were lamenting the prospect of facing the powerhouse East Germans. "It was so odd to me—by then, everyone should have been happy—it's the Olympics! But they were in our heads."

The East Germans also were in their locker room. "We actually started screaming when we heard these deep voices," she recalls. "We thought they were guys and that we were in a unisex locker room. Then we turned the corner and there they were, the East German swimmers. Only now it's like they'd become guys. Really scary stuff. Very weird."

Diver Greg Louganis says he heard variations of Babashoff's account: "I do remember [1976 gold-medal diver] Jennifer Chandler being afraid to go into the women's locker room, thinking she heard men's voices in there. And it was the East German women's swim team."

Still just 19, Babashoff recalls being surrounded on that fateful day as she boarded a bus back to the Olympic Village. "All of the media thought it was going to be East Germany versus me, because they thought I actually had a chance to beat them.

Shirley on the cover of *Sports Illustrated* in 1976.

So there are tons of reporters there, everybody pushing microphones like it's Britney Spears today, and they're asking me, 'What do you think of the East German swimmers?' "

"Well," Babashoff said, "they're extremely hairy and have deep voices like men." That, she says, is when "the you-know-what hit the fan."

Babashoff's public criticism got the world talking about the biggest state-sponsored doping program ever known, as well as the transformations that were taking place among the East German athletes. Those troubling and ultimately tragic changes were chronicled in *Doping for Gold*, a documentary film aired last spring as part of the PBS series *Secrets of the Dead*.

After the Berlin Wall fell in 1989, many athletes—including Kornelia Ender, Barbara Krause and Carola Nitschke—came forward to describe their unwitting participation in the state doping program. Petra Thümer, who twice outswam Babashoff for gold in 1976, defiantly claims that unwitting participants in the program should not be considered cheaters. A German court later found East German officials responsible for what it cited as "systematic and overall doping in competitive sports." Suspended jail sentences and minimal fines were doled out. The East German government set up a $2.18 million fund for any affected athlete who wanted to file a claim to help cover their medical bills. By the March 2003 deadline, nearly 200 affected athletes had filed claims.

"Thank God that wall came down," Babashoff says. "That was the proof."

But it came far too late for Babashoff. Heavily favored to win multiple gold medals, she won just four silvers in her individual events. Even a decisive win in the 400-meter free-style relay with teammates Kim Peyton, Wendy Boglioli and Jill Sterkel invited derision among some.

In the September 1976 issue of *Swimming World*, Bob Ingram wrote: "The American women found themselves in the position of 'ugly Americans,' thanks to some comments from a few of the girls. . . . Rather than congratulating the winners, specifically the [East German] swimmers, as is customary in the true Olympic spirit of competition, a few of the American girls opted to cry sour grapes instead."

With or without the 1976 gold medals, Babashoff's career remains a thing of wonder. She was the 1974 Sports Woman of the Year, *Swimming World's* American Swimmer of the Year for 1976 and a 39-time American record holder. She won eight Olympic and 10 World Championship medals, set 11 world records and was inducted into the International Swimming Hall of Fame in 1982.

These days, it's clear that Babashoff has dismantled much of that chapter of her life. She coached swimming for a period after the Olympics, and eventually found herself a single parent to Adam, now 22. At the suggestion of her mom, she got a job with the U.S. Postal Service. For 20 years she's been living her happy, under-the-radar life. The phone rings all the time for interview requests, but she doesn't care. At 51, she doesn't even swim much anymore, preferring to get her exercise by biking, kayaking and delivering mail to about 600 homes a day.

Would she have preferred what life may have offered had she been awarded all those gold medals? Hard to say. Though some awards remain in her garage, much other evidence of her greatness in the pool has been given away—even thrown out. Offering a tour of her backyard garden, with its grapes, figs, tomatoes and eggplants, she seems as proud of her produce as she does her medals.

Still, what the East Germans did clouds what should be Babashoff's best memories. "I got this award, the Olympic Order, back in 2005," she says referring to the highest Olympic

**With Olympian Shirley Babashoff
—I'm glad we became friends.**

award, which is given to individuals for particularly distinguished contributions to the movement. "I was honored, but also angry at the ceremony. Why can't the Olympic Committee take our girls and just say, 'This is the award, the medal you should have gotten'? Or if not the medals, then just some acknowledgment that says, 'To us, you are the winners.' While everyone is here and alive—just honor them the right way."

In February 2002, the *New York Times* described how the International Olympic Committee had started righting some of the wrongs from past games. The newspaper documented that the U.S. Olympic Committee and USA Swimming asked the IOC to award gold medals to Babashoff and the other American swimmers involved in the 1976 games. The international body said it would consider requests on a case-by-case basis, but to date no additional gold medals have been awarded, nor have the East German swimmers been disqualified.

Back in her living room, Babashoff traces a finger around the lip of a wine glass and wonders if what she did had any impact at all. "We know more today, but more people than ever seem to be cheating. There will always be cheaters, I guess, which is sad. I just wish our team had some justice, you know? The girls deserve better. They were that good."

Vindicating "Surly Shirley"

"In hindsight, the coaches should have been the ones speaking out, but it was considered 'unsportsmanlike.' Shirley paid the price for having the courage to tell the truth. . . . She'll be remembered as the victim of cheating that never got the timely recognition that she deserved. I believe the records should be adjusted, as there is definitive proof of systematic East German cheating."

—Mark Schubert, former Babashoff coach and current head coach and general manager of USA Swimming's national team

"She's always been candid, and in exchange for speaking out she was accused of being surly. . . . In the ancient games, there was a 'hall of shame' for athletes who cheated. Today, I think it might be a good idea to create such a thing for our modern games. Let athletes know that if they're caught, there'll be some form of humiliation involved as punishment. After all, competing is not a right—it's a privilege."

—John Naber, U.S. swimmer who won four Olympic gold medals in 1976

"I totally applaud what Shirley Babashoff did. It was the right thing at the right time, and looking back, it had a tremendous effect."

—John Carlos, U.S. sprinter who, along with Tommie Smith, raised a black-power salute on the medal podium at the 1968 Olympics in Mexico City

"Shirley should have the gold medals—she's one of America's greatest athletes ever and she had a lot of guts. Even today, athletes won't speak up for fear of being called a sore loser, but that didn't stop Shirley."

—Jill Sterkel, part of the storied 1976 relay team that defeated the East Germans, now coordinator of athletics at the University of Texas

"Let's Spend the Night Together"
(2008)

This story won the Gold Award for Destination Story in Travelers' Tales Solas Awards for Best Travel Writing in 2009, so I thought I would include it. Originally, it ran at PerceptiveTravel.com. Thanks to editor Tim Leffel for the opportunity.

The author of Led Zeppelin Crashed Here *goes in search of rock star rooms with a grisly past, or "places to check out"—permanently.*

When booking a hotel room, what drives your decision? Price? Location? Size? Amenities? I'm drawn to rooms based less on the usual factors. For me, the most seductive quality in a room is if something notable happened there. Maybe it's a space where an artist worked (the La Quinta bungalow where Frank Capra wrote his classic scripts); or where an artist simply crashed (Jim Morrison's tiny space at the Alta Cienega Motel); maybe it's where John and Yoko staged their "Bed-In for Peace" in Montreal, or a Palm Springs suite where a frisky Marilyn Monroe lured the occasional lucky gentleman caller. I'm not sure why, but I think it's because I always get the sense that something from the past actions remain in these rooms—a mood, an echo or just some fleeting phantom sensation.

Sometimes an establishment will promote a room's notoriety, other times they'll deny a room's history altogether (going as far to even change room numbers as a means of discouraging the curious). Either way, if weaving some offbeat history into a trip is in your blood, there are some rooms waiting for you. In most cases, they're tucked away in odd little corners, away from tourists and traffic. What they might lack in glamour, they make up for with something else—an event, some random, bizarre brush with history that forever hangs in the air.

If you're a rock-and-roll fan, most times these compartments take on a darker edge. Death, after all, is forever intertwined with music and hotels. When I listen to the music of some of rock's fallen angels I get lost in trying to decipher what brought them to the last stop—and then I want to go stay in there. It's one part tribute, but another part adventure. What's it like where these young, talented, tortured souls expired? Is there anything to learn after spending the night where they bid farewell? Or is it just a way to feel closer to the legend, and supercharge the music I still wake up listening to? I don't know. All I'm sure of is that you will never forget the nights you spend in these rooms.

Kozmic Blues in Hollywood

Today, it's the Highland Gardens Hotel. Opened in the mid-1950s as the Landmark Hotel, it was designed as a place primarily for entertainers. It's a modest, low-key, rooms-built-around-the-pool sort of hangout where you can still find the occasional celebrity.

In October 1970, Janis Joplin was in Los Angeles laying down tracks for what would be her final album, *Pearl*. She left the studio on October 3 (after laying down the vocal for "Me and Bobby McGee," which would become her first number one record) and headed over to Barney's Beanery, a roadhouse-watering hole that hasn't changed much since then. With band member Ken Pearson, Janis knocked back a few screwdrivers before driving to the Landmark, where she was staying.

Once she got back inside room 105, she shot up her last batch of heroin before wandering into the hotel lobby to get some cigarette change. Janis chatted for a few moments with the clerk who was on duty that night (he didn't know who she was) and then returned to the room. Soon after, she collapsed near the bed from a heroin overdose, ending up wedged against a table with a smoke in her hand. When she failed to show up at the next day's recording session, a band member (John Cook) broke down her door and found the 27-year-old Joplin dead.

Room 105 has had some work done since 1970, but the layout in the modest room is essentially the same. I settled in one night with my wife, we sipped some good port and laid back to listen to copy of *Pearl*. The pain and ecstasy of Joplin's cries in the night are still stunning. It's raw, intense music, recorded hours before she died here in this very room. As it fills the room, you wonder what Joplin's last thoughts might have been. Did she have any awareness that this was the end? Was it fast? Did she suffer? I've brought with me some old interviews with Joplin. Reading them in bed, she almost comes to life in the room. Do I hear a distant drawl?

"Being an intellectual creates a lot of questions and no answers. You can fill your life up with ideas and still go home lonely. All you really have that really matters are feelings. That's what music is to me."

"On stage, I make love to 25,000 different people, then I go home alone."

On the stereo she sings, "Busted flat in Baton Rouge, waiting for a train . . . feeling nearly as faded as my jeans. . . ."

Some say Janis still wanders around, but for us it was quiet—even peaceful. We left with deeper appreciation for the whiskey-throated gal from Port Arthur, Texas. Though a chill did run through me as I cleaned our glasses out in the same sink that Janis used. Hey, what was that?

A Grievous Angel in the Desert

On a dark desert highway is perhaps my favorite little Hotel California. It's the Joshua Tree Inn, located just a few miles from the haunting, beautiful Joshua Tree National Park, where twisting, knotty Joshua Trees dramatically reach up toward the heavens in a permanent, natural pose. U2 found something special out here, but years before, so did Gram Parsons. The influential Byrd, Flying Burrito Brother and *Grievous Angel* used to escape here with his musical soul mate Keith Richards in the late 1960s. They'd stay in this circa-1950 inn, which features a horseshoe of 12 rooms facing a desert courtyard and huge swimming pool. They'd also climb the nearby craggy rocks at Joshua Tree, getting hypnotized by the black, star-splashed skies while dropping acid and keeping their eyes peeled for UFOs.

In 1973, Gram Parsons died in room 8 at the Joshua Tree Inn after consuming a lethal mix of tequila and morphine. It was a chaotic scene that ended with a pair of groupies trying to save him, but failing. The room is small, and only the mirror on the wall was there the night the deal went down, facing the bed as it did that night. Just before we stayed here, a film crew had become so freaked out, they up and left. Why? Because they say Parsons never really left the room. Reading the bedside journal where travelers record their thoughts, it's clear the soft-spoken musician touched many. As I leafed through the pages, the bedside light started to flicker. I checked the wires and bulb. Nothing was loose. Then it went off. And on. And off again. All by itself.

The Joshua Tree Inn, where Gram Parsons died. (Joshua Tree, California.)

A keytag to Room 8, where Gram Parsons died.

I settled into bed to read a book called *Road Mangler Deluxe* by Phil Kaufman, Parsons's manager back then. Have you ever read a detailed account of an event while sitting at the exact site where the event took place? It is so appealing to me, even when the event is this horrific. The room just comes to life. On the stereo, the haunting strains of Parsons's tunes including "Hearts on Fire," "Brass Buttons," "Return of the Grievous Angel" and "Love Hurts" filled the room. Parsons's songs feature mournful, ethereal melodies and they completely fit the mood within room 8. And then reading lamp went off again, though this time, it wouldn't come back on.

I rigged a different light so that I could finish reading the account of Parsons's death. Days after the death, Kaufman hijacked Gram's body and drove it to the nearby park where he set it afire, completing a pact the two men had (whoever died first, the other was to sacrifice, by fire, the other's body at a sacred site called Cap Rock). Reading this insane (though entertaining) account of Gram Parsons in Joshua Tree, I was distracted by something. A shadow slowly passed over the wall to my left. My wife was asleep, and there was no other movement in the room. I looked outside. Nothing. I am a bit of a cynic on these things, but the shadow is something I will never forget. It traveled the wall into the bathroom and disappeared near the shower. That's where the film crew say a shadow was as well, the one that made them leave. I didn't sleep much that night, and the next day we hiked up to where Gram's body was cremated, by Cap Rock. Nearby is a shrine, maintained by the faithful. The marker reads "Gram, Safe at Home."

Thunders Rolls On in New Orleans

The St. Peter's Guest House is in New Orleans. Though over the years there were always many rumors that the man had died, this was actually the last stand for the heroin-addled guitar slinger, Johnny Thunders. He died here on April 23, 1991. The former New York Doll legend had thought about moving to New Orleans, finding some new musicians and maybe starting a new band, but he never got the chance to complete his plan.

Thunders checked into room 37 in the late hours of April 23, and the following morning he was dead. Apparently, he had scored heroin upon arriving and dealt himself a lethal shot and died overnight. I remain a huge New York Dolls fan, I liked the Heartbreakers as well, and had the chance to see Thunders play many times (he actually fell over my shoulder one night in Boston back in the early 1980s and I carried him to a waiting taxi in front of the old club called Storyville).

The hotel room at St. Peter's Guest House where Johnny Thunders died. (New Orleans, Lousiana.)

Walking through the French Quarter on a muggy spring afternoon, 16 years to the day Thunders checked out, I felt sad. Johnny Thunders was a New York City wise guy who coulda been a contender. Jimmy Page knew it. Keith Richards knew it. Thousands of wannabe guitar heroes knew it. Instead, Thunders remained an underground legend for most of his life and one of rock and roll's most influential guitar players. When I checked into the tiny room, I felt sick to my stomach. The thought of how they found Johnny, fetal-positioned on the floor next to the bed, was depressing. But I had to be here. Listening to "You Can't Put Your Arms Around a Memory," I read Nina Antonia's excellent book, *Johnny Thunders: In Cold Blood*. When I got to the part about his death, the window actually rattled a bit. It was three in the morning, and I was thoroughly absorbed in the book. I actually said aloud, "That you, man?" And it rattled back.

Who knows? Maybe musical spirits are waiting for you to visit, to include them on your vacation itineraries. Maybe they still need an audience. Either way, there are rooms that act as shrines to some tragic, talented figures that left the stage too soon. They feel different than other rooms, because they are different. They hold history. And they hold magic.

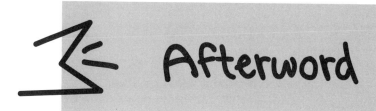

Afterword

End on a Good One
(October 31, 2009)

My dad had a rule when I was growing up: "End on a good one." Whatever you were doing, having a catch, shooting baskets—you ended on a good one so your last memory of it was positive. The adage exists in our house today and since we've arrived here at the end, I wanted to finish this book on a good moment.

It's Halloween night at Red Rock Canyon, near the Mojave Desert. For 10 years, Charlie and I have dug for fossils here with the Natural History Museum of Los Angeles County. Not dinosaurs, rather, it's 8–12-million-year-old giant camels, horses, oreodonts and other creatures that lay buried here (today we discovered a camel pelvis that was excavated and will be taken back to the museum).

Watching Charlie grow here from a five-year old boy scampering around the rocks into a 16-year-old young man interacting with these brilliant minds (Dr. Dave Whistler, Gary Takeuchi, Xiaoming Wang, Jack Tseng and Kamaron Sardar), searching, working and asking detailed questions about the scientific papers the paleontologists share with him—well, it gives a father great, proud pause, just like Claire does when I watch her do the things that she loves. It's wonderful to watch your children thrive, acting on the basics you've imparted to them and then running with them in their own directions.

At this moment my son, his belly full from toasted marshmallows, is sound asleep on this crisp autumn night. I'm here waiting for the fire to burn out, with yellow pad, orange pencil and black pickaxe. The logs come alive when nudged, glowing and pulsating in pearly neon pinks, oranges and purples. The maple crackles, hisses and wheezes. Flakes of wood, translucent from the heat, fall off the logs, tinkling like glass chimes. It's a hypnotic show, but as it often is in life, you must watch closely to appreciate it.

Time passes.

Coyotes wail plaintively to each other in the distance. A light wind transports the scents of desert sage and other fragrant plants, which blend nicely with the pungent campfire smell. Overhead, a full moon casts massive shadows as it rises beyond monolithic sandstone canyons that stand like ancient temples. A billion stars are splashed across a midnight-blue sky. The mood is exquisite, contemplative and spiritual. Staring up at the Milky Way, one gets lost in the galaxy. A satellite is visible, cruising through the constellations. A meteor streaks past Cassiopeia. The star cluster Pleiades twinkles. The universe, naturally and otherwise, is humming—perfect as always.

Time passes.

Indians lived at this site, as evidenced by their mor-

Charlie and his teachers—10 years apart, same spot.

tar holes in nearby rock. John Wayne made movies here, as did Gene Autry, Frank Sinatra and dozens of other stars. Aliens roamed Red Rock in science fiction films.

But tonight it's just a solitary spot to meditate. . . .

About that young man fast asleep, about my wife and daughter at home, about my mom, sisters, friends, family—and the memory of my dad who inspired this episode.

Charlie on the dig at Red Rock with the hip bone he helped discover (October 2009).

About those I have lost and those I have yet to meet.

About music, art and poetry.

About gods, angels and devils.

This remote desert outpost by a warm, fading fire is an ideal place for reflection. I could live here and I could die here. The mystical peace in these hills, the challenges of the weather and terrain, the powerful silence—it is sublime, supreme and strangely familiar.

Time passes.

White smoke curls heavenward, framed and morphing against the sky like a ghost dancing.

And the light from the fire is ebbing as the bright red embers start fading to black. It is almost completely dark so I can no longer see the paper I'm writing on—and that's the sign. Pencils down. Time to sleep, satisfied for now. Time to wake up, wander forth and discover whatever this road holds next. Time to start writing the next chapters.

This is the moment to end on, because it is a good one.

Thank you for being here to share it.

Chris

Acknowledgments

To Seth Swirsky for his eloquent foreword. Thank you, my talented friend.

To Bobby D'Ambrosio, for reading late into the night, and then taking time to talk about it.

Special thanks to John Losavio, Bryan Larkin, Tom Dooley, Rolando Feria and Terry Richens for their early, soulful support and solace. And a big thanks to the "Gang of 25."

Thanks and love as always to Jeffrey Goldman for his friendship, support and professionalism. To Amy Inouye for her wonderful design work (as always). And to Breanna Murphy for her patient, effective and truly stellar editorial work.

To those who shared stories, impressions and observations, thank you:

Shirley Babashoff
John Baron
Mary Carillo
Mary Cheever
Dr. Luis Chiappe
Judy Christa-Cathey
Lou Gramm
Ralph Grizzle
Arnold Hano
Richard Lloyd
Elliot Lurie
Benny Mardones
John Mungo
Jack Riley

Jordan Rudess
Richie Scarlet
Stephen Schwartz
Sally Struthers
Sylvain Sylvain
Mark Weiss
And the John F. Kennedy class of 1979

And thank you to the many others who have helped make these stories possible, including: Bill Smith, Bryant Lewis, Brian Carr, Fred Willard, David McAleer, the Gallos, the Catapanos, the DelGuidices, the Carillos, Uncle Frank, Martin Smith, Michael Miller, the Foderaros, Thom Sharp and Ronnie Schell.

Thanks also to my friends and associates with the Hampton Save-A-Landmark program, including Phil Cordell, Sheryl Shelton, Charmaine Easie-Samuels, Tori Roberson and Sharon Fells, plus the entire team at Cohn & Wolfe in Los Angeles, John F. Kennedy High School, Emerson College, Billy Steele, Mel Huntsinger, the crew of the USS *Laffey*, my teachers and my pets.

Follow Chris on Facebook at
www.facebook.com/authorchrisepting
and on his Web site at www.chrisepting.com

Permissions

The following articles by Chris Epting, either excerpted or in full, appeared previously and are reprinted here with permission, courtesy of their original publications.

"John Cheever" originally published (in part) March 2009. Reprinted with permission from LiteraryTraveler.com.

"Up, Up and Away," by Claire Epting, originally published March 2009. Reprinted with permission from *Time For Kids* magazine.

"Dr. Luis Chiappe," originally published in January/February 2008. Reprinted with permission from *Westways* magazine.

"In the Pipeline (featuring Luis Chiappe)," originally published June 23, 2008. Reprinted with permission from the *Huntington Beach Independent*.

"In the Pipeline (featuring the Sullivans)," originally published May 27, 2009. Reprinted with permission from the *Huntington Beach Independent*.

"In the Pipeline (featuring Jimmy Sullivan)," originally published January 14, 2010. Reprinted with permission from the *Huntington Beach Independent*.

"In the Pipeline (featuring Jimmy Sullivan)," originally published February 17, 2010. Reprinted with permission from the *Huntington Beach Independent*.

"In the Pipeline (featuring the 2008 East West Bank Classic)," originally published August 8, 2009. Reprinted with permission from the *Huntington Beach Independent*.

"In the Pipeline (featuring Eve Plumb)," originally published February 7, 2010. Reprinted with permission from the *Huntington Beach Independent*.

"Back to the Bleachers," originally published August 27, 2006. Reprinted with permission from the *Los Angeles Times Magazine*.

"A Weekend on Planet B," originally published May 6, 2007. Reprinted with permission from the *Los Angeles Times Magazine*.

"Against the Tide," originally published October 2008. Reprinted with permission from *Orange Coast* magazine.

"Let's Spend the Night Together," originally published September 2007. Reprinted with permission from PerceptiveTravel.com.

Photo Credits

The following photographs are reprinted here courtesy of their respective owners.

Photos on page 47 courtesy of Rolando Feria.

Photo on page 48 © Bettmann/CORBIS.

Photos on page 64 courtesy of Mark Weiss.

Photo on page 68 courtesy of the Behling family.

Photo on page 75 courtesy of Bryce W. Westover.

Photo on page 79 courtesy of Vic Rao.

Photos on pages 100, 103, 104 (top), 105–106, and 109 (bottom) courtesy of Syra Sable (J. Planet).

Photo on page 155 courtesy of Seth Swirsky.

Photo on page 239 (top) courtesy of http://davelandblog.blogspot.com

Photos on pages 267 and 273 courtesy of Kortney Ehrhart.

Also by Chris Epting

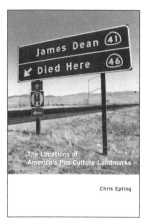

Takes you on a journey across North America to the exact locations where the most significant events in American popular culture took place. It's a road map for pop culture sites, from Patty Hearst's bank to the garage where Apple Computer was born.

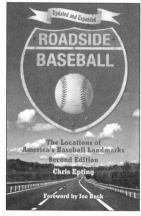

Capturing such quintessentially American pastimes as baseball and road trips in one fascinating work, this updated and expanded guide chronicles more than 500 important events in baseball history with detailed descriptions of the event and information on each location. From out-of-the-way spots to the most popular stadiums in the U.S. and Canada, no site is too small or insignificant to be included in this comprehensive directory.

An entertaining and rollicking road map through the entire history of rock and roll! From beginnings (the site where Elvis got his first guitar), to endings (the hotel where Janis Joplin died), and everything in between. Includes sidebars on musical greats like Bob Dylan, The Beatles, The Rolling Stones, and U2.

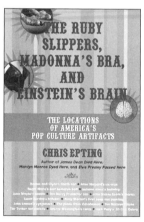

Anyone who has ever wondered where Dorothy's ruby slippers, George Washington's teeth, or the world's largest olive are located will be thrilled to take this journey to find hundreds of the most important items from America's popular culture.

Toll Free 1.800.784.9553 • www.santamonicapress.com